Return of the Junta

ASIAN ARGUMENTS

Asian Arguments is a series of books which explores life in Asia today. Written by experts from the fields of journalism, academia and politics, all of whom have considerable experience of living and working in Asia, the books reveal how citizens across the region – from China to Vietnam – are confronting problems such as environmental crisis, economic development and democracy.

Available now in the series:

The Trouble with Taiwan by Kerry Brown and Kally Wu Tzu Hui

China and the New Maoists by Kerry Brown and
Simone van Nieuwenhuizen

Leftover Women: The Resurgence of Gender Inequality in China
by Leta Hong Fincher

North Korea by Paul French

*A Kingdom in Crisis: Thailand's Struggle for Democracy in the
Twenty-First Century* by Andrew MacGregor Marshall

China's Urban Billion by Tom Miller

Ghost Cities of China by Wade Shepard

*Myanmar's Enemy Within: Buddhist Violence and the Making
of a Muslim 'Other'* by Francis Wade

Thailand: Shifting Ground between the US and a Rising China
by Benjamin Zawacki

Return of the Junta

*Why Myanmar's Military Must
Go Back to the Barracks*

Oliver Slow

BLOOMSBURY ACADEMIC
LONDON • NEW YORK • OXFORD • NEW DELHI • SYDNEY

BLOOMSBURY ACADEMIC
Bloomsbury Publishing Plc
50 Bedford Square, London, WC1B 3DP, UK
1385 Broadway, New York, NY 10018, USA
29 Earlsfort Terrace, Dublin 2, Ireland

BLOOMSBURY, BLOOMSBURY ACADEMIC and the Diana logo are trademarks of
Bloomsbury Publishing Plc

First published in Great Britain 2023

For legal purposes the Acknowledgements on p. x constitute an extension of this
copyright page.

Cover design by Charlotte James
Cover image: Myanmar army soldiers © Panos Pictures

Bloomsbury Publishing Plc does not have any control over, or responsibility for, any third-party
websites referred to or in this book. All internet addresses given in this book were correct
at the time of going to press. The author and publisher regret any inconvenience caused if
addresses have changed or sites have ceased to exist, but can accept no responsibility for
any such changes.

A catalogue record for this book is available from the British Library.

Library of Congress Cataloging-in-Publication Data
Names: Slow, Oliver, author.
Title: Return of the junta: why Myanmar's military must go back to the barracks/Oliver Slow.
Description: London; New York: Bloomsbury Academic, 2023. | Series: Asian arguments |
Includes bibliographical references and index.
Identifiers: LCCN 2022028364 (print) | LCCN 2022028365 (ebook) | ISBN 9781350289611
(hardback) | ISBN 9781350289659 (paperback) | ISBN 9781350289628 (epub) |
ISBN 9781350289635 (pdf) | ISBN 9781350289642
Subjects: LCSH: Burma. Tap' ma to'. | Burma. Tap' ma to'–Political activity. |
Military government–Burma. | Civil-military relations–Burma. | Burma–Armed Forces–
Political activity. | Burma–Politics and government–1988-
Classification: LCC DS530.65 .S598 2023 (print) | LCC DS530.65 (ebook) |
DDC 959.105/4–dc23/eng/20221011
LC record available at https://lccn.loc.gov/2022028364
LC ebook record available at https://lccn.loc.gov/2022028365

ISBN: HB: 978-1-3502-8961-1
PB: 978-1-3502-8965-9
ePDF: 978-1-3502-8963-5
eBook: 978-1-3502-8962-8

Series: Asian Arguments

Typeset by Deanta Global Publishing Services, Chennai, India

To find out more about our authors and books visit www.bloomsbury.com and sign up
for our newsletters.

For Dad, whose passion ignited my own.

Oliver Slow, who spent years living in and reporting on the country, has produced a gem of a book that describes and explains not only the background to the coup itself but how this hated institution's mindset and approach developed over time. He covers not only the headline stories of atrocities and violence but also critically important issues such as the military's approach to education and identity politics. *Return of the Junta* is essential reading for anyone who wants to understand the critical struggle now underway for Myanmar's future. **Scot Marciel, former US Ambassador to Myanmar**

Oliver Slow's narrative draws you in as he dives into the twisted psyche of the Tatmadaw, documenting the ruthless excesses and xenophobia of successive military juntas – culminating in the February 2021 coup. While this book laments how the outside world has failed the people of Myanmar, it also explores the reasons why the coup itself was a failure. **Jonathan Miller, former Asia Correspondent, Channel 4 News**

An urgent and necessary book – Oliver Slow's clear-eyed chronicle of how Myanmar reached this point of crisis is bolstered by illuminating first-hand accounts of pivotal events over the past decade, going beyond read-and-despair reportage to formulate a much-needed call to action. **Emma Larkin, author of** *Finding George Orwell in Burma*

Informed by almost a decade of reporting from Myanmar, Slow explains the toxic mix of paranoia, entitlement and sadism that makes up Myanmar's ruling military. Accessible but unsparing in its retelling of the country's tragic modern history, *Return of the Junta* also finds hope in the strength of its people. **Ben Dunant, Editor-in-Chief of** *Frontier Myanmar*

Return of the Junta is much more than a record of the military's disastrous impact on Myanmar and its people. Oliver Slow lived in Myanmar at a tumultuous time of both great hope and hair-raising events of unspeakable violence. He captures not only the horrific crimes of the ruthless military but also the realities of daily life and the aspirations of Myanmar's people. This book is a distinguished accomplishment that shows Slow's solid knowledge of his subject as well as his compassion and integrity. It should be read by all who want to understand how Myanmar's 2021 coup d'état came about and why popular resistance has never been stronger. **Laetitia van den Assum, a former member of the Advisory Commission on Rakhine State (Kofi Annan Commission)**

Incisive and penetrative reporting. *Return of the Junta* makes sense of a seemingly senseless crime: Myanmar's 2021 coup, a disaster for the country and even the military itself. **Patrick Winn, South East Asia correspondent for The World from PRX and author of *Hello, Shadowlands***

In deftly sketched prose, Slow describes how the military has woven itself into the very fabric of Myanmar's social and political life, and details the painful and ongoing efforts of political activists and ordinary people to cast it aside. Rich with on-the-ground anecdotes and historical analysis, it presents a vital examination of the country's tortured journey from independence to the troubled present. Anyone interested in what's happening in Myanmar today should read this book. **Sebastian Strangio, author of *In the Dragon's Shadow***

Carefully researched and well-told, this book illuminates Myanmar's complex history leading up to its recent coup. Oliver Slow travels across Myanmar to shed light on the diversity and tenacity of its people. **Celia Hatton, Asia Pacific Editor, BBC**

Contents

Acknowledgements

There are numerous people who have helped with the writing of this book, in many different forms. I'm grateful to Eli Meixler, Sean Gleeson, Thomas Kean, Nicola Williams, Kiira Gustafson, Susan Law and all my colleagues at Frontier, as well as countless others, for their feedback or comments, which helped to form the book's structure and content. Ronan Lee, Benjamin Zawacki and Francis Wade kindly offered advice on the publishing industry, a not insignificant aspect of this process, while I'm also grateful to Joe Freeman and Dan Quinlan for the many late-night conversations about the book and its content. Much of this book was also written during my time working with ASEAN Parliamentarians for Human Rights (APHR), and I'm grateful to the team there for their unending support, particularly Elise Tillet-Dagousset.

At Bloomsbury, David Avital, Olivia Dellow and Paul French displayed patience and offered useful advice throughout, while I'm eternally grateful for the love and support offered by Mum, Ben, Ed and the rest of the family. Debs in particular has provided laughs, support and gentle ribbing throughout, while also tolerating both my incessant talking about this project and many lost weekends and evenings of me being strapped to the laptop.

Finally, I owe a huge debt of gratitude to the Myanmar people, including interviewees, friends, colleagues and neighbours, whose kindness and humility I will never forget.

Note for readers

When the then-ruling military junta in Myanmar stood down in early 2011, initiating a series of reforms supposed to move the country away from decades of isolationist rule, it handed power to a quasi-civilian government filled with former generals.

This new government, headed by President Thein Sein, would rule according to a new Constitution, which had been passed in a sham referendum three years earlier, as part of the military's transition to "genuine, disciplined, multi-party democracy".

The new charter, replacing one from 1974, divided the country into seven regions and seven states "of equal status". The seven regions – comprising Ayeyarwady, Bago, Magwe, Mandalay, Sagaing, Tanintharyi and Yangon – are located in the country's centre and are typically dominated by the Bamar-majority population, while the seven states – Chin, Kachin, Kayah, Kayin, Mon, Shan and Rakhine – hug the country's periphery and are mainly home to ethnic minorities. The capital is in the very centre, Nay Pyi Taw.

Despite the military coup of February 2021, the country is still ruled according to this system.

Regarding the use of local names, for the large part I have used Myanmar over Burma, because this is the name most commonly used today by those inside the country. In 1989, the military junta changed the official name of the country, and those of several cities and regions, from the English to the Myanmar version. When describing events before this change, I have used the name that was in use at the time (Burma, Rangoon etc.). The country's majority ethnic group has variously been called 'Bamar', 'Burman' and 'Burmese'; I have opted for Bamar.

Due to the military's crackdown following the 2021 coup, the security situation in the country today is dismal. I have therefore taken care to change the names, and occasionally some small details, about interviewees who I felt could be at risk if identified.

Introduction

The last day of January 2021 was typically balmy for that time of year in Yangon, Myanmar's former colonial capital and still its largest city and economic powerhouse. An azure blue sky swept above the Shwedagon Pagoda, the golden, gleaming temple that looms proudly over the city, and the comfortable warmth of cold season was beginning to make way for the unrelenting torridness of hot season.

It was a Sunday, and twenty-year-old Khaing Lwin had a day off from his studies at Yangon University, the crumbling compound in the north of the city, although he had been studying remotely for most of the past year due to Covid-19. Pre-pandemic, Khaing Lwin had been actively involved in campus life, serving as a member in its Student Union, and after graduating hoped to find work in the country's growing tourism industry or the media.

That day, Khaing Lwin and a group of friends visited Yangon's Kandawgyi Lake, which was built as a reservoir to serve the city during the years of British rule. The colonists also established at the site a memorial park to Queen Victoria a few years after her death, and during Myanmar's partial opening that began in 2011, the area emerged as a popular hang-out for Yangon's youths, home to cafes, restaurants, arcades and well-manicured gardens.

The good weather helped the group's mood, and they were in high spirits. Sheltering from the sun beneath one of the park's large Htanaung trees, they played music and sang, shared food and posed for photos in front of the picturesque lake.

There was some tension, however. For the last few days, rumours had circulated that the country's powerful military, the Tatmadaw, was plotting a coup d'état against the civilian government that would put the brakes on the reforms the country had witnessed over the previous decade. Although flawed, the opening of political space and the economy had directly benefitted Khaing Lwin and his friends, who could freely offer their political opinions, find jobs in a range of sectors that were witnessing record growth and look ahead with optimism regarding their country's future. These options were not available to their parents' generation, who had lived under military rule since the 1960s.

'We'd heard the coup rumours for the last few weeks, but we didn't really believe them', said Khaing Lwin. 'We really hoped this wouldn't be the case, because we didn't want to return to military rule.'

But the next morning, the carefree existence of Khaing Lwin and his friends was drastically upended. In the early hours of 1 February, the military shut down the internet, deployed soldiers to towns and cities across the country and arrested figures from the political opposition. Particularly targeted were members of the National League for Democracy (NLD), led by Aung San Suu Kyi, which had resoundingly won its second successive general election a few months earlier, in November.

Almost immediately, the Myanmar people rose up with remarkable unity in the face of the power grab. Resistance came in the form of peaceful mass protests, particularly in the early days but also continuing even amid the army's violent response; a Civil Disobedience Movement (CDM) that aims to make the country ungovernable for the junta; a parallel government seeking recognition in the global corridors of power; and, as the months wore on, and international action demonstrated an inability to intercede in any meaningful way, armed revolution.

Khaing Lwin took the most radical option. In the weeks immediately after the coup, he helped organize the peaceful protests against it. Over the next few months, people from all walks of life in towns and cities up and down the country joined the protests, holding aloft signs and placards, chanting anti-military slogans and calling on the army to stand down.

Perhaps unsurprising for an institution that has ruled with astounding brutality and terror for decades, the military didn't listen, instead turning its guns on those demonstrating. With the international community offering little beyond statements calling for restraint, Khaing Lwin knew more extreme measures were needed to reverse the takeover and remove the military from power. With the help of friends, he secretly travelled from Yangon to a jungle area on the Thai-Myanmar border to join a newly established armed group that would soon begin active combat against junta forces.

Life is very different in the jungle, compared to his previous existence as a student in Yangon. The unit he's training with undergoes daily 'specialist' military training from one of the ethnic armed groups that has operated at the border area for decades. He wouldn't say which one.

'The training is very, very difficult, very intense', he told me over a crackly phone line on an encrypted app a few months after he arrived in the jungle. 'We have to make our minds and our bodies very strong. So, it's not only physical training, but also mental and morale training as well.'

His day begins at 4am, with the training continuing until late into the night, with few rests in between. He is adamant the sacrifice is worth it.

'We tried the other [peaceful] way before we came here, and it didn't work', he said. 'That is why we have taken this new way, to take up arms. The military is a very big, strong institution, so we will not win this battle in a short time. We have to continue working, to build up our training and our strength, and we can beat them eventually. That is my hope.'

'Before the coup, my experience was totally different from my life now, but I have to keep doing this', he said. 'I really wanted to attend university and focus on my education, but this changed because of the coup.'

His ultimate goal is to contribute to the widespread efforts to remove the military from power, then return to Yangon and help with the huge rebuilding efforts that will be necessary in any post-Tatmadaw environment in Myanmar.

'The political situation has been so bad for so long, and that is because of the military', he said. 'When we go back, we must deal with big issues in the country, improve the situation for the youth, enhance education, and provide jobs for the people. The whole political situation needs changing, and that can only be done without the military.'

Khaing Lwin is one of millions of Myanmar people whose life has been completely upended by the February 2021 coup.

Another is Win Ko Ko, a journalist in his late twenties. He grew up in military-run Myanmar in the early 2000s, but as press freedoms were lifted in line with the political and economic reforms that started after 2011, he began seeking opportunities to fulfil his dream of becoming a reporter.

Working for a local news outlet, he regularly travelled up and down the country, reporting on stories ranging from flooding in central Myanmar to conflict in the country's volatile north-east. He even found himself in Nay Pyi Taw, the military-built capital, when the coup d'état took place. He was there to cover the opening of parliament after the previous year's election but instead found himself writing about the military's power grab. He admitted to initially being exhilarated to document such an 'historic' moment.

But within months, the situation got drastically worse. As word of their atrocities spread, junta forces deliberately targeted journalists with beatings, arrests and torture. Speaking with Win Ko Ko in August 2021, he said he no longer felt safe enough to work.

'There are a lot of arrests in my neighbourhood at night, so I don't leave my room. I stay home, watch movies and cook, and only go outside once a week for groceries shopping', he said. 'I think I will leave Myanmar for my safety.'

A few months later, I got a message from Win Ko Ko, telling me he'd made it to neighbouring Thailand.

'I couldn't sleep for days before my flight, and the airport was terrifying with soldiers everywhere', he told me by text message. 'But now here at least I feel safe, and I can sleep. But I really miss my old life and my family.'

Away from Yangon, in mountainous Chin State in Myanmar's west, Stephen has spent the last several years documenting human rights violations against the mainly Christian Chin people at the hands of the Buddhist-majority Myanmar military.

Due to his work, immediately after the coup, he knew he needed to leave and fled across the nearby border into India.

'I am safe for now, but I don't know what will happen', Stephen told me in August 2021, six months after the coup. 'I am ok but my family are all separated. Some are in India, some in other villages, either in India or back in Myanmar. I don't know when we will see each other again.' I've not been able to reach him since.

The foregoing is a tiny snapshot into the lives of a handful of friends or former colleagues and how their lives have been affected by the coup. All have had their names changed, as well as other details about them, to protect them from potential repercussions at the hands of the military, which since the coup has dished out unspeakable violence against its critics, real or perceived. On top of arresting and torturing thousands, it has fired machine guns into crowds of peaceful protestors, deployed snipers to kill demonstrating teenagers, launched deadly airstrikes on defenceless villages and burned people alive on the streets, to name just a few of its cruel tactics.

Many other friends have had it even worse than those mentioned earlier. They've had family members or friends killed by junta forces or colleagues arrested and locked up in jails without trial. Those without the means to leave are still in hiding inside Myanmar, moving each night to different safe houses, while others have been forced to start new lives abroad, often away from their loved ones. All those I've spoken to feel a deep sense of hopelessness about the situation in their country.

Day of the coup

On the morning of the coup, a cheery online fitness instructor, live-streaming her routine in Nay Pyi Taw, unwittingly captured the moment army trucks descended on the nation's parliament, which was due to convene for the first time since the November election that morning. Elsewhere in the country, soldiers were deployed in major cities and strategic locations.

Amid the confusion in the early hours, state-run television had been down, citing 'technical difficulties', but at just after 8 am an announcement was made on an army-owned channel. It said that the military had been forced to trigger a clause in the 2008 Constitution – drafted by the Tatmadaw and passed in a sham referendum – to enact a state of emergency after the Union Election Commission (UEC), the government-appointed body that had overseen the November vote, had 'failed to properly perform their duties' by not investigating allegations of voter fraud.

A year-long state of emergency was declared and all powers handed to the head of the military, Min Aung Hlaing, who had been its commander-in-chief since 2011, replacing the retiring former dictator Than Shwe. The signs were already ominous. Even before the coup, Min Aung Hlaing was accused of being complicit in genocide and crimes against humanity, for his role in overseeing troops in a horrifying campaign of violence against the Rohingya in western Myanmar three years earlier. Those atrocities saw more than 9,000 Rohingya killed, homes and entire villages burned to the ground and about 750,000 refugees fleeing to Bangladesh, where most remain. In March 2022, more than a year after the coup, the United States officially declared that crackdown a genocide.

Min Aung Hlaing would rule under his newly established State Administration Council (SAC), comprised mainly of other senior Tatmadaw figures, including the vice senior general of the armed forces, the joint chief of staff as well as the heads of the navy and the air force.

Within days, this new body had sacked (and jailed) all union and state and regional ministers, replacing them with military-aligned figures, doing the same with almost the entirety of the country's local administrative apparatus. New military-friendly faces were also appointed as mayors of major cities or to head key institutions including the Supreme Court and the Central Bank.

One of the most notable SAC shake-ups, however, was a drastic re-organization of the election commission, which for months after the coup the junta blamed for not properly investigating what it said were more than 10 million fraudulent votes that had heavily contributed to the NLD's victory.

In a televised speech to the nation a week after his power grab, a nervous-looking Min Aung Hlaing, dressed in a mint-green military shirt, addressed the nation for the first time since his putsch, saying he believed that 'a free and fair election is the lifeblood of the multiparty democracy system', and that the UEC, parliament and the president had failed to 'settle the voting fraud issue'.[1]

'Until the last minute, the Tatmadaw upheld the negotiation process in line with the law', he said in a dull monologue. 'The situation was also reported to the people and the world through press conferences of the Tatmadaw. Authorities concerned failed to take their responsibility and accountability. Therefore, we announced the state of emergency and have taken the responsibility of the State in accordance with the 2008 Constitution', he said. He also laid out a five-point road map towards a 'free and fair election' once his concerns had been addressed.

Both his poll promise and his justification for the coup were nonsense, of course. Although the November 2020 election was not regarded as completely free or fair, in part because it had been held amid rising Covid-19 cases, and amid the cancellation of votes mainly in conflict-affected areas, international electoral observers concluded that its results were 'by and large representative of the will of the people'.[2] Beyond its ramblings in the state-run newspapers it controls the content of, the Tatmadaw has never provided any evidence of the widespread voter fraud it alleges.

With nearly all the NLD's leaders in jail on trumped-up charges, and the junta introducing increasingly repressive laws to target dissent and the press – as well as a UEC now filled with figures pliant to the regime – it's worth noting that no election taking place under the junta's watch could be considered even remotely close to being free or fair.

The 'voting fraud' issue was merely an excuse, and in fact the real reasons behind the coup were more closely linked to Min Aung Hlaing's long-held desire for the country's top job – the presidency – and perhaps more notably a concern among the military's top brass that the reforms initiated under a so-called 'transition to democracy' a decade earlier risked going too far and threatening both the Tatmadaw's grip on power and the deep-rooted economic and political control the generals had amassed for themselves.

Military's legacy and the 'transition'

Myanmar's military past is well known, with the dictator Ne Win taking power in a coup in 1962, putting the Tatmadaw at the apex of all political and economic power, while sending the country into decades of isolationism, authoritarianism and financial stagnation. The 1988 uprising against Ne Win's rule, a months-long protest ignited by students that reached almost all corners of the country, heavily spooked the regime. Despite it laying the groundwork for the nation's pro-democracy movement that emerged decades later, a new generation of military rulers who took power immediatcly after the mass protests – including the new leader Saw Maung, his successor Than Shwe and the notorious spy chief Khin Nyunt – continued the institution's isolationist policies from the rest of the world. They also heightened its distrust of the general population, and vice versa, while building up its military capabilities amid a perceived increased threat from foreign saboteurs.

Then, in the early twentieth century, a 'Seven-Step Roadmap to Democracy' got underway, pursued under a military-drafted Constitution designed to ensure that the Tatmadaw never gave up any real power, while improving its international standing by lifting political freedoms and opening what was billed as one of the world's 'last frontiers' to foreign investment.

Part of that road map included a general election, which took place in 2010. Yet few observers expected much to change in terms of the country's political direction, especially after the NLD boycotted the vote, and it was won by the military's proxy, the Union Solidarity and Development Party (USDP).

A few days after the vote, however, Aung San Suu Kyi was released from decades of house arrest, as were hundreds of other political prisoners over the next few months. Long-term dictator Than Shwe stood down as commander-in-chief of the armed forces, and a new 'quasi-civilian' government was installed, led by a former general, Thein Sein, who would initiate drastic reforms, including freeing of the press, amending restrictive laws and implementing economic policies that were friendly to foreign investment.

Than Shwe, who still wielded considerable power behind the scenes at the time, was widely expected to announce his direct replacement as Shwe Mann, his charismatic protégé. Instead, however, he handed the reins to Min Aung Hlaing, whose gravitas among the Tatmadaw's top brass had grown after he led the military's successful offensive in Kokang Region, near the border with China, two years earlier.

A year after the election, Aung San Suu Kyi's NLD (established after the 1988 protests to compete in an election two years later that it won but the results of which the military annulled) was permitted to enter a by-election held in 2012. It won overwhelmingly, sweeping up forty-three of the forty-four seats it contested, entering parliament for the first time.

This period coincided with my arrival in the country, as a wide-eyed English teacher interested in the country's politics and keen to learn the ropes for a potential career in journalism.

Myanmar had been on my radar since the 2007 uprising known as the Saffron Revolution – when at university I recall seeing grainy images of monks marching through Yangon's streets on the BBC – and I'd been monitoring political developments there at the time, notably the 2010 election and Aung San Suu Kyi's release. Completing a teaching contract in Jakarta, the Indonesian capital, I jumped at the opportunity when an offer came through to work at a newly opened school in Yangon's northern outskirts. As a mildly pretentious young twenty-something, I wanted to see Myanmar 'before it changed too much'.

And what a change I witnessed.

Just a few weeks after arriving, I was among the thousands of NLD supporters outside the party's Yangon headquarters as the 2012 by-election results were announced. Each time a new NLD victory was declared, a huge cheer went up, followed by chants of 'Dee-mocracy' that rippled through the masses of people present. Late into the night, Aung San Suu Kyi drove through the crowd, waving to the thousands who had lined the streets.

The good times kept rolling over the next few months. In the June, Aung San Suu Kyi was permitted to travel to Norway to collect the Nobel Peace Prize she had been awarded in 1991, for her peaceful protest against the military junta, and shortly after that Thein Sein visited the United States as a reward for the raft of reforms his government had initiated. The excitement reached fever pitch in November 2012, when I joined thousands lining the street outside Aung San Suu Kyi's Yangon home, where she had been held under house arrest for most of the last two decades, to catch a glimpse of US president Barrack Obama, the first sitting leader of the country to visit Myanmar.

Although there were setbacks over the next few years – most notably the outbreak of bouts of religious violence, particularly in Rakhine State – the upward trajectory of the apparent transition continued.

I was fortunate to get a front-row seat to witness these monumental changes, after my efforts to work in journalism bore fruit. In one of the strongest indications that the reforms taking place were set to continue, in 2012 the government abolished decades of prepublication censorship, leading to the explosion of outlets looking to capitalize on the new-found press freedoms. In this period of unbridled optimism, Yangon was also seeing previously exiled outlets such as *The Irrawaddy*, *DVB* and *Mizzima* open newsrooms in Yangon. Between 2012 and 2015, I worked for a number of these Yangon-based media outlets, either as staff or on a freelance basis, while also writing for regional and international media, covering stories such as the boom in the telecommunications market, which brought the general population online for the first time, as well as the NLD's early campaigns around the country to amend the 2008 Constitution. There were also gloomier assignments, however, including writing about the rising religious tensions and Buddhist nationalism that began to emerge around this time.

In early 2015, just months ahead of that year's election, which the NLD was expected to compete in and resoundingly win, I received a job offer from a former editor, who was helping set up a newly established weekly print magazine. Although not yet in circulation, the paper had considerable editorial pedigree as the brainchild of Sonny Swe, one of the co-founders of the *Myanmar Times* – at the time the paper of record – who had recently been released from almost a decade in prison as a political detainee.

I started work in the April, with a launch date set for early July. After much lively debate in our makeshift newsroom – a sweltering, dimly lit room on the top floor of a tired condo – a new name was decided for the magazine, *Frontier*, and over the next few months I travelled around the country, collecting stories that would fill the early editions. Those trips were often made with Thet, who acted as my translator and photographer and whose knowledge of local customs, traditions, history and dynamics was crucial in filling the gaps in my own understanding of such aspects of life in Myanmar.

The earliest idea for this book came around this time, although the initial premise was entirely different to the finished product. Having returned to Yangon from a trip in eastern Shan State, to report on life in the seedy semi-autonomous town of Mong La, renowned for drugs and wildlife trafficking, I began formulating the idea for a travel book. In the months before the Shan trip, I'd met with mahouts, politicians and leprosy sufferers in Mon State, in the country's south-east; priests and displaced farmers in Chin State in the west; and retired generals in the capital, Nay Pyi Taw, in the centre. I planned to use these interviews to write an upbeat travelogue documenting a range of voices throughout the transition from dictatorship to democracy that appeared to be taking place before us. Looking back on earlier drafts today, it was little more than a self-indulgent piece of nonsense (the opening scene was *quite literally* me nervously smoking a cigarette and drinking a beer in my hotel room the night before the 2015 election), but it did pave the way for what I hope is a much more useful book for the reader.

That cringe-inducing early draft of the book's introduction was set in Mandalay, from where I'd covered the 2015 election for *Frontier*. Keen to escape the global press pack that had descended upon Yangon to document Aung San Suu Kyi's every move, my editor had given me permission to travel north.

It had been an exhilarating day, which I had spent with a translator covering every corner of the royal city, speaking to voters. There were young women in their twenties, who had rolled out of bed in their pyjamas, and older ladies in their seventies decked out in their finest dresses, as well as rickshaw drivers in ripped vests and filthy *longyis*, the Myanmar sarong, stained with the grease of that morning's breakfast. All those I spoke to were voting for the first time, and all for the NLD.

By the time the late afternoon had rolled around, it was clear that the party was on course for a resounding victory. Throughout the day, however, there had been a feeling of anxiety in the air amid concern that the military, unhappy that its proxy, the USDP, was on course to suffer a humiliating defeat, would launch a coup, putting an end to its experiment with democracy.

But the coup never came, and instead there were words of congratulation by army figures, with Min Aung Hlaing saying within days that the military would 'do what is best in co-operation with the new government'.[3]

Perhaps the military's acceptance of the result was because it still held onto the main levers of power. Although the NLD had won more than 80 per cent of the available seats on election day, the military's constitution ensured that at least a quarter of those that actually existed in parliament would be automatically granted to their appointees.

Despite the NLD's resounding victory, which even with the military's quota granted the party a majority they could use to push through legal reforms, any amendments they wanted to make to the military's all-important constitution appeared off-limits.

Changes to the charter had been a key component of the party's campaigning ahead of the election. As well as the quarter of all seats granted to military appointees, it also gave the army control of three key ministries – Defence, Border Affairs and Home Affairs, the last of which oversaw everything from the police to local administration. During the year or so before the vote, the NLD, and Aung San Suu Kyi in particular, had toured the country, hosting rallies in almost every corner. I attended one of these events, in the dusty riverside town of Pakokku, where she promised that, if elected, her party would introduce a new constitution that worked for the people, not the military. In its election manifesto, the NLD promised to enact a new charter that 'ensures that all the people of our country can live together in tranquillity and security'.[4]

This appeared to be little more than wishful thinking, however. Afterall, it was almost impossible in the parliamentary system the military had created, and which the NLD was now a part of. According to the charter's own rules, any amendments to it would require 'the prior approval of more than seventy-five percent of all the representatives of the Pyidaungsu Hluttaw (the national parliament)'.[5] The military's guaranteed quota of a quarter of all parliamentary seats therefore granted them a veto on any changes.

'The military viewed this 2008 Constitution as the key document, the framework through which this so-called transition period would take place', a Myanmar security expert who has spent decades studying the Tatmadaw told me. 'This was the guidance through which they saw this period of rule taking place, and they weren't going to accept any changes to it.'

But then Aung San Suu Kyi blindsided the generals, demonstrating both a willingness and know how to work around their all-important charter. During its pre-election campaigns, the NLD had raised concerns about a number of apparently problematic clauses in the constitution, one of which was 59(f), which said that the country's president could not 'owe allegiance to a foreign power.'[6] Since Aung San Suu Kyi was widely popular across the country, and her late husband and her two sons were British, there can be no doubt this clause was introduced with her in mind.

After her party's resounding victory, the NLD leader had appeared to work around this issue by installing her close friend Htin Kyaw as a puppet president. However, within days of taking office, the NLD used its majority to create a brand-new position specifically designed for Aung San Suu Kyi. The state counsellor role, a clever workaround of the constitution found by legal expert Ko Ni, granted Aung San Suu Kyi powers comparable to prime minister.

The military was furious, with one of its representatives in parliament saying the move had amounted to 'democratic bullying'. Less than a year later Ko Ni was gunned down, while holding his grandson in his arms, in a brazen day-time assassination outside Yangon's bustling international airport. Because Ko Ni was Muslim, there was suspicion at the time that the killing may have been linked to the religious tensions the country was witnessing, but looking back now since the coup, it can be viewed as nothing other than vindication for his role in threatening the military's treasured charter. The three masterminds of the killing were all Tatmadaw members, including a former military intelligence captain, a retired lieutenant colonel and an ex-colonel who had served in Min Aung Hlaing's office until 2015.[7]

In the first few months of the NLD's term, Aung San Suu Kyi and Min Aung Hlaing, as the heads of the civilian and military factions, respectively, had made efforts to put on a united front. As time wore on, however, the men in green increasingly came to view her administration with deep suspicion. The NLD's efforts to amend the constitution quietened down over the next few years but never entirely disappeared. Although Aung San Suu Kyi's 2019 appearance at the International Court of Justice in the Gambia's genocide case against Myanmar was perceived globally as her supporting the Tatmadaw – indeed she defended its actions – she was there as a representative of the Myanmar state, and for her this was much more about protecting the country's external image than the military itself.

The Tatmadaw's distrust of the NLD was also heightened by the party's refusal during its term in office to convene the National Defence and Security Council (NDSC), even during times of crisis. The NDSC, an eleven-member committee formed of civilian and military figures, was established under the 2008 Constitution, and responsible for overseeing the country's security and defence affairs. Much to the annoyance of the military, however, it could only be summoned by the president, who had been hand-picked by Aung San Suu Kyi and did much of her bidding due to her constitutional banning from the top job.

'[The NLD's] refusal to call the NDSC was seen as yet another example of the party not respecting the military's all-important constitution', said the security expert.

In 2016 and 2017, the military conducted a terrifying campaign of violence against the Rohingya, during which more than 9,000 people were killed, including children being burned alive in locked homes and thrown into rivers, homes, mosques and villages torched by soldiers, and about 750,000 forced to flee into Bangladesh. In early 2022, the United States officially declared the atrocities a genocide. Aung San Suu Kyi's international reputation took a monumental hit due to her insistence on defending the military's activities and failure to stand up for the long-oppressed group. Here, the narrative went, was a Nobel Peace Prize laureate refusing to speak out against genocide.

Domestically, even though she remained widely popular (in fact, the international criticism had created a siege mentality that heightened support for her), there were questions about the effectiveness of the NLD's first term, notably a stagnation of the economy under their watch as well as continued restrictions on basic freedoms. As the 2020 election approached, military figures hoped that, through the USDP, it could convince most of the country's rural population that life was better under their rule.

The 2020 election

If the military didn't believe that the USDP could comfortably win the 2020 election, they certainly held out hope they could claw back many of the gains their rivals had made five years earlier.

But that didn't happen, and in fact the USDP performed worse in 2020 than it had in 2015, capturing just a few dozen seats nationwide, while the NLD increased its majority, taking more than 250 in total. There may have been questions about the party's performance during its first term, but the Myanmar people had once again said loud and clear what they wanted: democracy, not military rule.

The coup that took place three months later can in some ways be traced to the personal ambitions of Min Aung Hlaing, whose desire to be the country's leader has long been known inside the country. Officially due to retire when he reached sixty-five in the middle of 2021, there's certainly every chance that, having missed out on achieving his long-held desire at the ballot box, he crudely stepped in and took power purely for his own personal gain.

But the move, in fact, says much more about the Tatmadaw as an institution and how it views itself in the context of the Myanmar nation. As this book sets out to explore, ever since its inception as an anti-colonial fighting force during the Second World War, the Tatmadaw has viewed itself as the sole protector of the nation, responsible for keeping the Union intact immediately after independence and for repelling meddling outsiders and troublesome actors within ever since. The people, in the Tatmadaw's view, do not understand the sacrifices that have been made on their behalf.

When it began the process of initiating democratic reforms at the start of the twenty-first century, under its 'Seven Step Roadmap to Democracy', it did so on its own terms, which were to be strictly adhered to and respected according to the little green book: the 2008 Constitution. The NLD's obvious disdain for the charter, coupled with its successive electoral triumphs, risked spiralling those reforms well beyond the Tatmadaw's reach, threatening not only its role as the 'nation's protector' (and therefore everything the institution stands for) but also the huge economic powers the military's top brass had amassed for themselves over several decades.

When the NLD refused to take seriously the military's claims of electoral fraud, that was the final straw for the generals to step in, and take back what they believed was rightfully theirs, and in the only way they know how – not at the ballot box but down the barrel of a gun.

When the coup took place, it came as a shock to most of the world, including close Myanmar watchers (myself included – the day before I'd described its likelihood to a friend as 'unlikely although not impossible'). Look a little closer, however, and with the benefit of hindsight, and the warning signs were there.

In August 2020, leaders of the military-aligned USDP and other pro-military parties met with Min Aung Hlaing to complain that the UEC – the make-up of which was decided by the NLD – was unfairly running the election, and some urged him to push for a meeting of the NDSC.

Min Aung Hlaing told attendees that there was nothing he 'won't dare to do'.

'I am brave enough to do everything. Anything that could have a negative impact on the country, the people and the future of the military [is my concern]. I'm following everything', he said.[8]

A week before the vote he publicly criticized the UEC's handling of the election, expressing a need to be 'very cautious', in the kind of vague language that has long confounded Tatmadaw watchers, but any fears of a coup appeared to be assuaged on election day itself – although again with the benefit of hindsight, his remarks could be interpreted as a warning sign of what was to come. Door-stepped by a journalist shortly after submitting his vote in Nay Pyi Taw, he said he would 'accept an election result that reflects the people's will'.

Whatever he really meant, that was before the USDP's humiliating electoral defeat came to light, and over the next few months the Tatmadaw conducted a campaign to undermine the election results, and the integrity of the UEC in particular, claiming it had found millions of cases of 'voting malpractice', despite never offering any actual evidence for its claims.

In the mid-January, Min Aung Hlaing repeated his calls for the election commission to properly investigate the military's concerns, but the UEC remained resolute, saying it was investigating some voter list errors, but that these were not nearly enough to change the election result.

Widespread fears about a potential coup, however, did not begin to gain traction until 26 January, when military spokesman Zaw Min Tun refused to rule it out, saying the military would 'abide by existing laws including the Constitution' in dealing with the voter fraud issue.[9] The next day, Min Aung Hlaing poured fuel onto the fire, saying the Constitution should be revoked if it was not respected, and shortly after that armoured vehicles were deployed in major cities, including central Yangon.

Then the military appeared to walk back those comments, releasing a statement on 30 January saying that 'some organisations and media assumed what they want', and that the remarks by Min Aung Hlaing had been wilfully misinterpreted.

While all of this was playing out publicly, behind the scenes frantic negotiations were taking place between NLD representatives and their Tatmadaw counterparts. According to a *Reuters* investigation, army representatives made at least three demands: reschedule the 1 February opening of parliament, disband the UEC or review the votes under 'military supervision'.

During several days of meetings, Min Aung Hlaing's representatives reportedly called the civilian government 'rude and insolent', while Aung San Suu Kyi appeared 'resolute' and unwilling to accept the military's demands.[10] The talks went nowhere, and a few days later the coup took place.

Resistance to the coup

In justifying the takeover, Min Aung Hlaing and the military have repeatedly claimed that concerns about electoral fraud were widespread among Myanmar's population. It would be easy to dismiss this as yet another lie by an institution, and individual, that has the most tenuous relationship with the truth. It's worth remembering, however, that senior Tatmadaw figures in particular have almost no interaction with the general public and hold a heavily distorted view of the Tatmadaw's role in the national psyche. Put another way, they have no idea how much they're hated.

Perhaps when Min Aung Hlaing ordered his troops to arrest government officials, and deployed them around the country in the early hours of 1 February, he really believed that the people would accept such a drastic move, viewing it as a necessary measure to return 'stability' to the country. After all, went one way of thinking at the time, the Myanmar people had lived under military rule before, why wouldn't they accept it once more?

Within hours of the power grab, however, it quickly became apparent just how misguided this point of view was.

One of the first displays of defiance came on the night of the coup, and several nights thereafter, when Myanmar residents around the country took to the streets, or their apartment balconies, to loudly bang kitchen utensils, mainly pots and pans, to demonstrate their anger about the coup. The practice is traditionally associated with driving out evil spirits in Myanmar, where animistic beliefs remain strong.

'I've got nothing left to cook with, because I've ruined all of my [kitchen] equipment, but I don't care. I'll do anything to get rid of these motherfuckers', a friend living in Yangon told me at the time.

Other strands of peaceful protest also began to emerge within days of the coup. On 2 February, Kyaw Win, a doctor at a government hospital in Mandalay said he and his colleagues, including those working in hospitals elsewhere in the country, quickly bandied together and decided they would refuse to conduct their work under the military junta. That evening, doctors across the country began posing for photos outside their place of work, with some holding aloft the now ubiquitous three-finger salute, borrowed from the pro-democracy movement taking place next door in Thailand, itself taken from the movie 'The Hunger Games'.

This was the genesis of what would become the CDM, which, as well as health professionals, would quickly sweep up thousands of teachers, railway workers and staff from almost all government ministries, whose refusal to go to work aimed to make it impossible for the junta to govern. They were later joined by employees from the private sector, including banking and transportation, in industries considered crucial to the regime's ability to operate and survive.

'The aim of the CDM was to ensure the military junta cannot function. This is the concept of our revolution', Kyaw Win told me. 'By doing this CDM, the government cannot do anything, they cannot operate without us. This mechanism stops the functions of the administration of the coup, and we can see it is very successful.'

In an indication that the movement was rattling the junta, the military put considerable pressure on those taking part in the CDM to return to work. This involved including CDM participants on public 'arrest lists' as well as threatening, and even kidnapping, their family members as part of attempts to draw them out from the shadows, either to force them back to work or arrest them.

In part because they had been so influential in initiating the resistance, doctors were especially targeted by the junta's violence, and there were countless reports of security forces deliberately attacking healthcare workers who had voluntarily come to the assistance of those injured in the protests.

In one particularly ugly incident in northern Yangon in early March, captured on video and widely shared on social media, police officers could be seen kicking cowering health workers in the head and beating them in the face with the butt of their rifles. The health workers offer no resistance as the relentless blows rain down upon them. Security forces also destroyed ambulances and other medical equipment in what appeared to be little more than petty acts of fury.

When a fresh wave of Covid-19 ripped through Myanmar almost six months after the coup, the junta heavily weaponized the pandemic, including by confiscating already depleted oxygen supplies from the general public for their own use and attacking and arresting health workers. In some instances, doctors were called to addresses under the guise of treating Covid-19 positive patients but instead lured into a trap and arrested. Many healthcare workers remain in prison or in hiding.

Peaceful resistance didn't only come in the form of the CDM, however, and in the first few days afterwards a handful of smaller protests took place, including one outside the medical university in Mandalay. That demonstration quickly dispersed before authorities arrived on the scene.

In Yangon, the country's biggest city and where many of the anti-military campaigns of the past had been ignited, there had generally been an air of trepidation in the first few days after the coup. Then, almost a week later, the revolutionary spirit the city is well-known for ignited.

In its warren of densely packed streets in the heart of the city, one of the largest protests began on 6 February, led by two young women dressed in the traditional clothing of the country's Karen minority. Behind them dozens, perhaps hundreds, of young men and women, holding aloft flags, banners and the three-finger salute, marched through Yangon's streets, displaying their anger at the military regime.

Similar protests sprouted up elsewhere in the city, including in front of Sule Pagoda and City Hall, in the city centre and at Hledan Junction in the north. As an indication that this new generation of activists was standing on the shoulders of those who had gone before them, both sites had been important rallying points for anti-military demonstrations of the past, particularly 1988.

As the protests began to spread around the country, the junta ordered social media platforms such as Twitter and Instagram to be blocked, as part of a futile attempt to halt the movement's momentum.

It didn't work, and by the end of that weekend anti-military demonstrations had been documented in towns and cities across the country, from those located in Myanmar's far north, in the foothills of the Himalayas, to the southerly towns that hug the Andaman Sea, and countless more in between.

The protests continued for the next several weeks, and each day new towns and villages were added to the long list of those whose residents were willing to risk arrest or worse to display their displeasure about the coup. In those first few weeks, the demonstrations had been light-hearted, often led by the country's younger population, known as Generation Z, who capitalized on the power of social media and global meme culture, displaying images that mocked the height (or size of the appendage) of the coup leader, Min Aung Hlaing.

'My dick is longer than MAL's [Min Aung Hlaing's] height', said one placard that seemed to sum up much of the sentiment of those early protests.

The humour continued for a while longer. At one point, when the junta deployed higher numbers of security forces in city streets, people began parking their cars along main roads in Yangon, saying they had broken down. When asked by police, the owners said their cars appeared to be suffering from a bout of MAL-it is – Min Aung Hlaing's phonetic initials – a mysterious disease that had spread through the country since 1 February. During another protest at a major intersection just north of Yangon's downtown, as part of efforts to halt traffic, dozens of protestors stopped in the middle of the road to help pick up onion and grains of rice, often one by one, that had been 'dropped' there.

Those early protests also witnessed a remarkable unity between Myanmar's various ethnic groups that the country has not seen since independence. The violent and ruthless measures the Tatmadaw would shortly resort to in order to suppress the protests exposed many Bamar people, the country's dominant group typically dispersed in the centre, to the institution's vicious tactics for the first time. This created a new-found sympathy for the ethnic minorities mainly located in the country's border areas, who had suffered under those same methods for decades. There were even placards present at protests apologizing to the Rohingya for the support lent to the military's campaign of violence against them a few years earlier.

What's also been remarkable about the resistance movement since the coup is how quickly it moved away from focussing solely on Aung San Suu Kyi, for so long the face of Myanmar's pro-democracy movement. While there are still many calls for her release across the country, the movement's messaging quickly focussed on the need to remove the Tatmadaw from power, rather than highlighting the plight of one individual.

Crackdown begins

A few weeks after the coup, the light-hearted carnival-like theme of the protests began to give way to a much darker atmosphere, as the violent tactics many feared the junta would resort to came to life. The first known death of a protestor occurred in Nay Pyi Taw when Mya Thwate Thwate Khaing, who had turned twenty days before, died of injuries sustained after she was hit by what doctors said was a live bullet. A video shared widely on social media captured the moment she was killed, when a loud crack can be heard, and she crumples quickly to the ground.

From then, the situation drastically deteriorated, with just some of the junta's deadliest tactics being captured on camera phones and uploaded to social media. In one, filmed in Yangon's northern outskirts in the early March, police officers are seen dragging a man in a lightly coloured T-shirt towards a group of security officers standing nearby. He is offering no resistance. Then, an officer walks up to the man from behind and appears to shoot him at point-blank range, kicking him as he falls. The man's lifeless body is left on the ground for a few moments, before being dragged away.

On the same day in Mandalay, a nineteen-year-old girl peacefully protesting the coup was shot in the head and killed. Kyal Sin, known as Angel, was helping her fellow protestors, including by kicking open a water pipe so that they could wash tear gas from their eyes, when she was hit by a bullet. Images of her wearing a T-shirt with the slogan 'Everything will be OK' went viral, and aware of the dangers of taking part in the protests, she had written her blood type details on Facebook and requested that her organs be donated if she was killed.

Many Myanmar friends who attended the protests had done the same.

Some of the worst junta violence in the early weeks came on 27 March, which the Tatmadaw celebrates as Armed Forces Day, to mark the day when Burmese forces switched sides from the Japanese to the Allies during the Second World War. As protests against its rule were sweeping across the country, the military hosted an elaborate parade in Nay Pyi Taw, attended by a handful of foreign dignitaries, including those from Russia, China and India.

During the day, there was a quite pitiful moment from Min Aung Hlaing when, as the leader of an army that has tanks and fighter jets at its disposal, he displayed to Russia's deputy defence minister an assortment of goods used by protestors against his forces, which included motorbike helmets and a few empty beer bottles. At a gala dinner that evening, a bizarre drone image of a saluting Min Aung Hlaing was blasted into Nay Pyi Taw's starry night sky.

As these gratuitous events were taking place, Min Aung Hlaing's troops were committing violence on a mass scale against the people. On that day, forces killed more than 100 people nationwide, including a teenager in the southerly town of Dawei, who was shot when a soldier fired at random passers-by from the back of a pickup truck. The incident was captured on CCTV and was just one demonstration of how security forces had been given free rein to shoot, maim and kill whoever they wanted.

As the protests continued for many more months, so did the often sadistic violence meted out by Tatmadaw troops. In Mandalay, a man was burned alive in the street after being shot in the chest, while families often had the bodies of their loved ones returned to them with clear signs of torture. It took just six months for the number of people killed in the coup and subsequent crackdowns to pass the grisly 1,000 mark, a campaign of violence that the United Nations as well as various rights groups have said passes the threshold of crimes against humanity.

While their troops were committing this murderous campaign across the country, and the people grappled with a health emergency in the form of Covid-19, as well as a slide deeper into poverty amid the turmoil, holed up in their heavily fortified compounds in Nay Pyi Taw, the generals leading the SAC were interested in one thing only: legitimacy.

They threatened action against foreign news outlets that described the SAC as a military junta and regularly claimed that it did not commit a coup but is acting to protect democracy as part of a vain effort to claim some form of validity for its actions.[11] Shortly after the coup, it signed a US$2 million deal with an international lobbyist to 'assist in explaining the real situation in the country', although the deal fell through when the campaigner couldn't be paid due to restrictions brought about by US sanctions.[12]

Vying for legitimacy

Inside Myanmar, this much-craved legitimacy has been fully denied to the junta, in large part by the CDM and strikes that have continued for months after the coup, denying the military control of key areas of government and leading to some describing the power grab as a 'failed coup'. As legal experts have argued, the junta fails the 'effective control' test, which says that, to be recognized as a government, an entity must act as one, including by exercising territorial control, for example, of a country's administration and security.[13]

The junta's efforts for recognition have been made even more challenging by the emergence of a new 'parallel' government, in the form of the National Unity Government (NUG). The NUG was established in mid-April 2021 under the Committee Representing the Pyidaungsu Hluttaw (CRPH), the national parliament, which itself was founded shortly after the coup mainly by MPs-elect from the November 2020 election. Many are in exile, and meetings are typically conducted over Zoom.

The NUG, which has enjoyed huge support across the country since its emergence, aims to gain international recognition as the government of Myanmar, a battle that is playing out in the corridors of power in New York, as the NUG aims to convince the United Nations General Assembly of its credentials, above those of the junta.

Recognition of the NUG would be a huge boost for the democratic movement, and blow to the military's legitimacy efforts, and although at the time of writing the assembly had not made a decision, there can be no doubt that the NUG, which comprises democratically elected MPs, has infinitely more valid claims than its rivals.

It has developed a constitution of its own based on democratic and federal principles (the latter a hugely important point in Myanmar, which since independence has been ruled from the centre), developed policies related to tax and revenues and committed to the repatriation of Rohingya refugees from Bangladesh. The NUG certainly deserves scrutiny – one criticism is that its top echelons are heavily filled with NLD members and not enough ethnic minorities – but it has for the large part conducted itself in a manner you would expect of a government, in contrast to the junta.

'The international community must respect the will of the people of Myanmar, which was expressed on 8 November [the date of the election]', Dr Sa Sa, the NUG's minister for International Cooperation, told me by phone around the time the NUG was announced. 'The people of Myanmar elected more than 400 members of parliament to represent them. So, all the free world, the democratic world, should respect the will of the people of Myanmar.'

After months of peaceful resistance to the coup, as the military's brutal tactics escalated, and calls for international action to intervene went nowhere, the opposition to the military regime began to take on more drastic measures, with some hoping that an armed struggle would swing the balance towards the Tatmadaw's eventual demise.

As well as several ethnic armed groups, such as the Karen National Liberation Army (KNLA) and the Kachin Independence Army (KIA), that have been fighting the Tatmadaw for decades and seen increased conflicts since the coup, the military is also battling newly formed People's Defence Forces (PDFs), officially established as the NUG's armed wing, with the view to eventually creating a federal army. The NUG has established its own command structure, as well as rules of engagements for its troops, and aligned groups known as Local Defence Forces (LDFs), forbidding the torture and killing of prisoners of war as well as sexual harassment against civilian and military women. Soldiers are also urged to record any assets they have seized from civilians and submit reports to their superiors.

'Respective commanders must encourage and monitor their soldiers to ensure they adhere to these regulations', the directive says, part of a clear effort by the NUG to differentiate itself from the Tatmadaw, whose troops have enjoyed impunity for decades for the terror and violence they have meted out against the Myanmar people.[14]

Some PDFs are directly tied to the NUG's chain of command, while many others are looser affiliations of armed militias whose sole purpose is to remove the Tatmadaw from power, while operating under the PDF banner. While this creates challenges for the NUG in ensuring its troops, or those aligned with its mission, abide by their rules of war, it's also an insight into the level of chaos across the country, as well as just how widespread resistance is against the coup. Some groups referring to themselves as PDFs have committed targeted killings and other violent acts against junta members, or their apparent allies.

Local militias have mushroomed across the country, ranging from ad hoc groups comprised of a few individuals conducting guerrilla attacks with makeshift weapons to more sophisticated groups with their own uniforms and advanced weapons and training, often linking up with ethnic armed groups to launch deadly 'hybrid' attacks against Tatmadaw positions.

Although conflict has occurred in urban centres, including the major cities of Yangon and Mandalay, more than a year after the coup the bulk of the fighting was taking place in rural areas, particularly in mountainous Chin State in the west, the plains of Sagaing Region in the north-west and in Kayah State to the east. Kayin and Kachin states, home to some of the Tatmadaw's fiercest rivals traditionally, notably the KNLA and the KIA, have also seen a significant uptick in violence.

It's safe to say that since its inception in the 1940s, the Tatmadaw has never been tested like it is today. Morale among its rank and file is at its lowest ebb, with an estimated 90 per cent 'disliking the generals', according to Nyi Thuta, a former Tatmadaw captain who defected shortly after the coup and is now in hiding.[15]

'But disliking the generals is very different to them risking their lives and leaving the Tatmadaw', he told me.

Among the factors preventing wannabe defectors from leaving are fears for the safety of their family, financial worries as well as a concern that they have no other option but to remain.

Nyi Thuta is working to change that, aiming to encourage soldiers to switch allegiances to PDFs, many of which are located in relatively safe areas under the control of ethnic armed groups. Important to increasing the number of defections, Nyi Thuta says, is for the public not to vilify soldiers but to understand that they are not same as the generals at the top of the junta.

'We have to understand the lives of soldiers. They joined [the Tatmadaw] for their own reasons, often out of desperation or poverty. It's important for people to understand that they are people. If people do that, then I think we will see more defections in the future', he said.

A country in turmoil

Those fleeing, both Myanmar and the Tatmadaw, are leaving behind a country in complete turmoil.

'Bedlam. Total chaos. The [junta] has no control over anything. Economy in ruins. Countryside on fire. Bombings in the cities.'

That was the bleak assessment of a Yangon-based friend of what life was like in Myanmar almost a year after the coup.

For some people in Myanmar, notably the wealthier classes in places like Yangon and Mandalay, some semblance of normalcy has returned to their lives. As a form of survival mode, some have adapted as best they can to a 'new normal', reluctantly accepting life under the junta if it means they can provide for their families.

Many others have not and continue to do everything in their power, risking arrest, torture and death every day, to demonstrate their anger towards the military regime. That resistance shows little sign of letting up.

The CDM, where private and public sector employees have refused to work until democracy is restored, has contributed to an effective shutdown of most sectors, while the junta's power grab, and subsequent violence, has brought foreign investment almost to a complete standstill. While other countries in Southeast Asia were expected to make relative recoveries from the Covid-19 pandemic, the World Bank predicted Myanmar's economy would slump by 18 per cent in the months after the coup.[16] Millions across the country are now living under the poverty line.

Amid this utterly chaotic and tragic picture across the country, considerable criticism has been levied at the international community for failing to stand up and take steps to protect the Myanmar people from the military's unrelenting violence, to help remove the Tatmadaw from power and put the country back on the path to democracy.

Without doubt, much of this criticism has been deserved. As death after death has been recorded, as the economy has plunged into the ground leaving millions destitute, as basic rights have been stripped from the people every day, as people have been tortured to death, burned alive in the streets, teenagers shot in the head, as defenceless villages have been bombed by the Tatmadaw's air power, and a whole host of other horrendous acts committed against the people every single day since the coup, the promises of 'Never Again' after tragedies such as Bosnia and Rwanda have shown themselves to be utterly futile.

Many actors are to blame, including departments of the United Nations. The global body's secretary general Antonio Guterres has displayed a shocking lack of leadership on the issue, while the Security Council has achieved little beyond bland statements, raising the question of why it exists at all, if powerful countries can veto any action that doesn't fit their geopolitical interests.

Because of the level of access it has to the generals, in the early weeks and months after the coup the ten-member Association of Southeast Asian Nations (ASEAN), of which Myanmar is a member, deserved an opportunity to try and intervene, but has displayed the lack of moral backbone its critics expected of it, achieving little beyond a Five-Point Consensus agreed with Min Aung Hlaing that it has failed to implement.

Despite the global community's colossal failure to effectively intervene, it's also important to recognize that any resolution to the crisis in Myanmar will be decided, first and foremost, by the dynamics and developments taking place inside the country. Myanmar's future path will be charted by members of the CDM, those protesting in the streets, the NUG and its allies and increasingly those involved in the armed resistance against the junta. The outcome of what a future Myanmar might look like will also be decided by the Tatmadaw and whether or not it has the resources, resolve and loyalty from its members, to stand up against the relentless and unified campaign against it.

What those outside Myanmar can do is lend support to the people in their efforts to overthrow the regime, something they've made clear they want to happen since the day of the coup. As things currently stand in Myanmar, the Tatmadaw's eventual control over the country is far from a foregone conclusion. I hope this book can go some way in assisting the Myanmar people in their efforts, both by providing context and understanding how we have got to where we are today, as well as offering recommendations about how those not in Myanmar can support those inside the country striving for democracy. This book is not an everything-you-need-to-know about the Tatmadaw but an attempt to understand dynamics in the country, as well as the military's motivations and influence in Myanmar, and with that, what actions could be taken to help remove it from power, and for the country to be put back on the democratic path.

That few months' stay I was supposed to embark on in early 2012 turned into a seven-and-a-half-year stint in Myanmar, the bulk of which was spent as an editor at *Frontier*. I left in 2019, basing myself next door in the Thai capital, Bangkok, from where I would travel back to Myanmar every few months to conduct more research and interviews for this book. I wasn't to know it at the time, but the last of those trips came in March 2020, when a pretty obscure disease known as Covid-19 was trickling down from China into mainland Southeast Asia. I'd waited the pandemic out in Bangkok, planning to head back to Myanmar when the health crisis was over to complete my on-the-ground research. Those plans were brought to an end with the coup.

I mentioned elsewhere in this chapter that early drafts of this book were very different to the tome you are reading now. While it had started life as a relatively light-hearted travel book during the optimistic early days of the apparent transition, over the next few years Myanmar's story – and my own areas of coverage – became much more serious. This was most evident in 2016 and 2017, when the military's violent campaign against the Rohingya was at its peak. It was a story I covered extensively, including by twice visiting northern Rakhine State, the epicentre of the conflict, as well as to refugee camps in southern Bangladesh in 2017 in the midst of the Rohingya exodus from Myanmar.

It became clear to me that a different book was needed, particularly one about the military's sphere of influence, which was evident in almost every interview I conducted and story that I wrote.

The family who had no access to justice after their loved one had been killed in custody decades before? It was Tatmadaw members who had arrested him and come to the family home to inform them that the man had died 'resisting arrest'. The farmer in central Myanmar kicked off the land his family had owned for generations, with zero compensation? A Tatmadaw-linked project. The Rohingya refugees in Bangladesh, who told horrendous stories of their children being murdered, mothers raped and villages burned to the ground? They identified Tatmadaw soldiers.

It would be overly simplistic to say that all of Myanmar's woes today are the fault of the Tatmadaw alone; colonialism, geopolitics and a host of other factors have contributed. However, even before the coup took place, the military's influence was everywhere you looked, and its self-serving agenda and the arrogance among its top brass a major hindrance to any meaningful progress that was supposed to be taking place away from the decades of isolationism and authoritarianism its people had been forced to endure.

So, I set about reworking the book along these lines, particularly looking at what measures the Tatmadaw had taken over the decades to oppress the people and maintain its holds on power.

The clearest example of this is the unrelenting violence against the people, particularly during periods of strong anti-military sentiment, with heavy crackdowns taking place largely in the centre of the country. The aim of such brutal measures is not a complicated one: force the people to submit to the Tatmadaw's rule and not rise up against it. It was a strategy that worked for the large part until the February 2021 coup, after which the people collectively decided they would take great risks every day to try and remove the Tatmadaw from power.

Almost no soldiers, or generals, have ever been held accountable for these killings, and this freedom from consequences for their actions was perhaps the single biggest factor in why the coup took place. For Myanmar to eventually move into a world free from the Tatmadaw's tyrannic rule, this deep-rooted culture of impunity must be addressed.

A more subtle area of control has been the military's dismantling of the education system to one that suited its own needs, using it to try and train generations of subservient people and push a narrative about the country's past that justifies the Tatmadaw's existence. Education was an area that saw considerable progress during the reform years, a glimpse into the potential the country has when freed from the military's overbearing influence. The current situation, however, bodes poorly for the future of Myanmar's education sector.

Another way the Tatmadaw has maintained control over the country is through policies that promote Bamar and Buddhist culture and practices over those of other religious and ethnic groups – a process known as Burmanization. On top of creating a system that ultimately discriminates against those who are not Bamar Buddhist, and stoking almost perpetual war in minority areas to create deepened poverty and insecurity, the military has also formed part of a 'divide-and-conquer' strategy that has pitted different ethnic and religious groups against one another, often blaming each other for ills that are more likely to be the result of centralized policies.

Nowhere was this more evident than in the military's deadly campaign against the Rohingya in 2016 and 2017, which attracted large-scale support across much of the country. The roots of that crisis in fact go back decades and are linked in large part to the Tatmadaw's ultimate neglect of the area, contributing to tensions between different groups that bubbled over into devastating violence and suffering.

Finally, and one of the most important factors, is the economy. While the vast majority of Myanmar people have remained desperately poor, surviving on a few dollars a day, the Tatmadaw has used the country's vast natural resources to make itself devastatingly rich. To add insult to this, in particular under the leadership of coup leader Min Aung Hlaing, it has used these vast funds to acquire increasingly advanced weaponry, which it is now using against its people with deadly effect.

But before getting to that, and using that understanding to look at how the military could be removed from power, we first need to understand how the Tatmadaw views itself in the context of the Myanmar nation state.

To do that, there's no better place to travel than to Nay Pyi Taw, the vast, secretive and grandiose city in the centre of the country, which the generals have built in their own image.

The Abode of Kings

Myo Thint Thet's first impression of Nay Pyi Taw when she arrived as it was still under construction in late 2005 was 'the strangest place I'd ever seen'. 'We had never had anything like this before in my country. We were driving along huge, well-paved roads, and could see massive buildings in the distance', she said, comparing the grand structures she was seeing to the ramshackle buildings she was used to back in her hometown of Yangon.

At the time, Myo Thint Thet worked at the Myanmar military government's Foreign Ministry, out of its attractive but dilapidated red-brick headquarters in Yangon's west.

She didn't particularly enjoy the job, a mundane admin task filing documents in dusty cupboards on behalf of the ministry, nor was she a fan of the regime she worked for, but job opportunities were scarce in early 2000s Myanmar, and when she heard about a potential opening through a friend, she successfully applied.

'I felt very lucky to have a job, because many of my friends and family didn't', Myo Thint Thet told me in 2012, just after the country's partial opening began and at a time that economic prospects had improved enough for her to quit the ministry to work at a newly opened car tire shop in northern Yangon.

One day at work towards the end of 2005, she said the ministry staff were informed that in a few days' time the ministry – and all those working in it – would be moving several hundred miles north, close to Pyinmana, a small town in the centre of the country.

'I think we were all really surprised', Myo Thint Thet said, when asked how she and her colleagues had responded to the shock announcement. 'We thought, how could they move everything there in just a few days? I thought it was impossible.'

But it wasn't. A few days later, Myo Thint Thet left her family home in Yangon's sprawling northern outskirts and boarded a bus with her colleagues, making the bumpy 400-kilometre journey north towards Pyinmana, where they would live for the next few years.

'As well as the buildings and roads, there were also construction sites everywhere, and so much work going on that the air was filled with thick clouds of dust', she said.

A few days after Myo Thint Thet's arrival, the country's military rulers announced that her new home would immediately replace Yangon as the country's capital, and a few months later it was officially given a name: Nay Pyi Taw, or Abode of Kings.

The construction of this new capital – which has an official size of more than 7,000 square kilometres, bigger than entire countries – was shrouded in almost complete secrecy. Some of the only reporting on it came in early 2004, when a European diplomat travelling close to Pyinmana spoke of heavy machinery 'bulldozing the ground' in the area, while the International Labour Organization said it had received reports that thousands of villagers had been forced to construct military camps.[1]

'In addition to labour, each village had to provide roofing and construction materials and transport for the project', the March 2005 report said.

Nay Pyi Taw's grand coming out ceremony took place on 27 March 2006, Myanmar's Armed Forces Day, when Senior General Than Shwe, leader of the junta in charge of the country at the time and the brainchild behind the moving of the capital, presided over an elaborate parade of thousands of soldiers at Nay Pyi Taw's newly constructed parade ground.

'Our military should be worthy heirs to the traditions of the capable military established by noble kings Anawrahta, Bayint Naung and Alaung Phaya U Aung Zeya', he said in a speech in the shadow of three ten-foot-high statues of the aforementioned kings.[2]

Many theories abound as to why the capital was relocated to Nay Pyi Taw, but that opening speech by Than Shwe, and its location underneath those gargantuan statues, offers some insight. Anawrahta is regarded by many, particularly its Bamar majority, as the founder of what is today the Myanmar nation state, having established the Bagan Empire in the eleventh century. Five centuries later Bayint Naung oversaw the Toungoo Dynasty in central Myanmar, and in the eighteenth century Alaung Phaya U Aung Zeya established the Konbaung Dynasty, the last in a long line of empires in Myanmar that ended with the three-stage British annexation of the nineteenth century.

In the Tatmadaw's telling of the nation's history, where the apparent successes of Bamar historical figures are celebrated over those of the hundreds of other ethnic groups who call Myanmar home, the trio are billed as the nation's three 'great' warrior kings. They are lauded for having defeated meddling 'outsiders' and, according to the military and its supporters, doing more than any other figures in history to unify the country. Since its inception around independence, and particularly after Ne Win's 1962 coup, the Tatmadaw has viewed itself in the same way, as the sole institution responsible for holding the country together, having defeated various troublesome outsiders, and continuing the work of these Bamar warriors.

The decision by Than Shwe, therefore, to move his seat of power to the country's heartlands, and use numerous types of iconography to nod to the nation's warrior kings, strongly suggests a desire to use the move to portray himself as a reincarnation of these rulers.

Like everything in Myanmar, it's unlikely to be quite that simple, however, and there are countless other theories as to why the move took place, each likely holding a grain of truth of their own. One goes that the military wanted to be located physically closer to the country's border areas in order to tackle the various ethnic insurgencies dotted around the country (Shan, Kayin and Kayah states, home to various armed groups, are all located a few miles to the east of Nay Pyi Taw), while another says that they wanted to use the move to help boost economic development, and therefore their popularity, in the country's deprived rural heartlands.

Another says that the move was initiated by fears among the regime of a maritime invasion at Yangon, most likely by the United States. The Tatmadaw has long been suspicious of outside actors, linked to its foundation as an anti-colonial force as well as the incursion into northern Burma by Chinese nationalist forces in the 1950s, and these fears were heightened during the 1988 uprising, amid reports that a US aircraft carrier was located off the Bay of Bengal. Military paranoia increased in early 2005 when Condoleezza Rice, the US Secretary of State under George W. Bush, described Myanmar as an 'outpost of tyranny' alongside Cuba, North Korea, Iran, Belarus and Zimbabwe.[3] A move by Than Shwe from coastal Yangon to the landlocked centre would, the theory goes, make his regime less vulnerable to invasion by US naval forces.

A theory that also can't be discounted is the military's deep-seated distrust of Yangon and its population and a desire to move their headquarters to somewhere more fitting with what they view as the national character, in the country's central heartlands close to ancient capitals including Mandalay, Ava, Toungoo and Amarapura.

Yangon is essentially a colonial capital, established as Rangoon and the capital of British Burma in the middle of the nineteenth century. Previously a small fishing village in the shadow of the great Shwedagon Pagoda, it was built in a grid-like structure, with wide boulevards connecting the city with the Yangon River, for which the international trade of products including rice, teak and oil was essential. Such outward-looking characteristics stand in sharp contrast to an insular institution like the Tatmadaw.

The old capital is also closely associated with the country's historical revolutionary mindset. During colonial rule, Rangoon witnessed some of the largest demonstrations nationwide against the British, and this spirit of resistance continued after independence. Particularly since Ne Win's

1962 coup, many of the nationwide grievances against the military were ignited in the city, especially at the leafy Yangon University campus in the city's north, including the 1974 U Thant protests as well as the 8-8-88 uprising. With the 1988 movement in particular heavily spooking the men in green, there's little doubt that the generals felt that, should demonstrations flare up again, they would be safer in their sparsely populated and heavily fortified new capital.

Finally, there's the astrological argument. Myanmar people tend to be deeply superstitious, believing in astrology, fortune telling and the power of *nats* (spirits). Across most of the country it's common for people to seek the advice of soothsayers when making important decisions such as choosing the name of a newly born child or the date to move house. If a business opens a new office, for example, one of the first tasks is to invite Buddhist monks to perform ceremonies that ward off evil spirits.

Myanmar's rulers are no less spiritually minded than their countryfolk. The official time and date of independence from the British was decided by astrologers, while shortly before he was ousted by Ne Win in 1962, Prime Minister U Nu reportedly ordered the construction of tens of thousands of pagodas across the country in order to ensure peace. Ne Win's own superstitious beliefs have been well documented, notably his decision in 1987 to demonetize bank notes and replace them with those divisible by nine, his lucky number (I've found no evidence for the widespread rumours – repeated with glee by his many detractors – that he bathed in dolphin's blood to regain his youth).

Than Shwe is reported to be even more superstitious than his predecessors, and there is almost certainly some truth to the idea that the decision to move the capital was, at least in part, influenced by an astrologer's prediction that his government would be overthrown if it did not move its capital away from Yangon. This theory gained traction after Than Shwe opened eleven ministries in Nay Pyi Taw at 11 am on 11 November.[4]

Whatever the reasons are behind the move, Nay Pyi Taw is today Myanmar's capital, a sprawling, secretive and strange city carved into what had once been dense jungle in the country's very centre. From the government ministries and general's homes hidden behind grand iron gates to the excessive twenty-lane highway (rumoured to be able to land planes during emergencies) leading to the parliament building, the military's presence can be felt everywhere you look in Nay Pyi Taw. In fact, in many ways the city is the mirror through which the Tatmadaw views itself – majestic, proud and crucial to protecting the nation. The military's detractors see the same mirror on the wall, but the face looking back is very different – they view both as boastful, unnecessarily grandiose and largely redundant.

The latter is certainly true of the city's hotels. Nay Pyi Taw is home to a vast plethora of lodges, resorts and guesthouses, the most extravagant of which are owned by military-linked families or cronies, granted to them as concessions for their help in constructing the city. These are almost exclusively huge complexes set over dozens of acres that require golf buggies to get around, where workers spend the day watering the perfectly manicured lawns and cleaning the elaborate swimming pools and restaurants.

The only thing missing is the guests.

In fairness, the generals have made an effort to attract tourists to their vanity project, but even during the reform years there were few takers – largely expatriates living in Yangon hoping to escape the heat, hustle and bustle of the commercial capital. There's a zoo that is home to white tigers, crocodiles and kangaroos – although its aquarium was forced to close after regular power shortages reportedly killed the penguins living there. There is the opulent Gems Museum, which over several floors proudly showcase the country's precious, if problematic, gemstones, as well as the National Landmark Museum, a Myanmar-shaped park set over several acres that displays miniature replicas of the country's best-known landmarks (although non-Buddhist features are largely excluded, even those located in Christian-majority parts of the country including Chin and Kachin states). The Uppatasanti Pagoda, which looms proudly on a hill above the city, is a carbon copy of Yangon's famed Shwedagon, apart from being a few inches shorter.

Of all the curious sights aimed at visitors in Nay Pyi Taw, however, one of the most elaborate – and certainly the one offering the best insight into the military's mindset – is the Defence Services Museum, located on the north-eastern edge of town.

Opened in 2012, the museum aims to 'enable the youth and people to learn the independence struggles, historic battles and actions of the Armed Forces since its birth in 1945 till now, and to imbue the spirit to safeguard the independence'.[5]

Set over several hundred acres, the museum is divided into three separate areas, each dedicated to the army, navy and air force. Out front are dozens of fighter jets and helicopters meant to showcase the Tatmadaw's aerial prowess, while the entrance hall displays large portraits of perhaps the three most important figures in the Tatmadaw's history – independence hero General Aung San, whose image is hung just slightly above the other two; Than Shwe, brainchild of both the museum and the city in which it is located; and Ne Win, who died in 2002 under house arrest ordered by Than Shwe.

The museum also displays items belonging to the country's ancient kings and furniture used by the Tatmadaw's founders, while a large component of the exhibition is dedicated to the institution's 'achievements', including not only its apparent victories in important battles but also photos and other documents showing soldiers building roads, bridges, ferries and other infrastructure.

The intention of the museum is clear, to encourage visitors to view the Tatmadaw as it sees itself – an institution that has only ever worked for the good of the people and which has been the sole force since independence to fight off foreign interference and hold the Union of Myanmar together. Such language appears in a rare White Paper the Tatmadaw published in 2015, describing itself as 'an integral part of Myanmar history and safeguarding the independence and sovereignty of the Union up till now'.[6]

Clearly it wants future generations to view it this way too, and the museum's gift shop even sells My Little Tatmadaw figurines, replete with badges of one of its Light Infantry Divisions, the most notorious of its shock troops.

The Tatmadaw's self-perception

Anyone who has monitored developments in Myanmar in recent years will be aware of how far this perspective is from reality. In the early years after independence, the Tatmadaw's victories against myriad armed groups were crucial in keeping the young country intact, but much has changed since then. Since the 1960s, and increasingly since 1988, it has come to view the general population with deep suspicion, perceiving itself as something entirely separate from the rest of the country – manifesting in the shocking violence we have seen it mete out against its people, both before and after the February 2021 coup.

Since 1988 – one of a few crucial turning points in the Tatmadaw's history, as this chapter will discuss – the military has regularly touted its 'Three National Causes' – non-disintegration of the Union; non-disintegration of national solidarity; and perpetuation of national sovereignty – with the view of building 'a peaceful, modern and prosperous nation'.[7]

The Tatmadaw may believe it is the key to achieving this goal, but the truth is that it has done more than any other actor in the country to prevent it from happening. There is, of course, the devastating violence that has seen tens of thousands – perhaps more – killed, maimed and tortured by the Tatmadaw in the last few decades, which has left in its wake a deeply scarred population. But it goes deeper than that, with the military's legacy of self-protection and incompetence eking into almost every facet of life in Myanmar – education, administration, divided communities and the economy, to name a few.

As a Myanmar friend said to me: 'The military has fucked this country. There were always going to be problems, but our people are good, they want peace and they want safety for their families. But this Tatmadaw has ruined so many things in this country, and it's going to take a long time to recover.'

This conversation took place before the 2021 coup.

Of course, much of the Tatmadaw's bluster is fully fledged propaganda, meant to justify its own existence, but beneath that is also a deep-rooted belief, particularly among its senior members who have never known life outside the Tatmadaw, that it holds true.

In 2015, a few months before that year's election, I interviewed a retired Tatmadaw lieutenant general in Nay Pyi Taw, who had shorn his fatigues to become an MP for his home town in western Myanmar. In an interview in his government-provided accommodation, a small studio apartment where we were surrounded by dirty clothes and discarded snacks and bottles of whisky, I put it to the former lieutenant general that the Tatmadaw was unpopular among the general population.

'You cannot say that people do not like the army', he said, throwing his arms into the air in a swift performative moment of outrage that quickly dissipated. 'People in big towns, like Yangon and Mandalay, they do not know war and have never needed the army. But the people in villages, they know what war is and support the army.'

The lieutenant general was one of about half a dozen senior Tatmadaw figures I interviewed during my time in Myanmar, and none of the others – with the exception of one who was more contrite than the rest about the Tatmadaw's actions – were able to accept even the slightest criticism of an institution they had spent almost their entire lives a part of.

This dissonance largely comes from the fact that most Tatmadaw members have little to no interaction with the rest of the country. Since about the 1950s, it has built a state within a state, where Tatmadaw members live entirely separately from the general population, holed up in their heavily protected compounds that they barely leave, with their own schools, shops, hospitals and social lives.

As veteran Myanmar watcher Andrew Selth argues, the Tatmadaw is not only the most powerful political institution in the country but has become 'increasingly self-contained and self-reliant'.[8]

'They have their own mass media outlets, banks, educational institutions, hospitals, insurance companies, recreational facilities, social structures and support mechanisms', Selth writes, adding that military personnel, their families, close supporters as well as retired veterans amount to about 2.5 per cent of the population, constituting a 'privileged caste' within Myanmar society.

Lwin Ko Ko is not from a military family but spent three years living in an army compound in central Myanmar while in his teens. His father had established an ice-making business and agreed a deal with some friends in the military for his family to move there.

'The military compound was one of the few places in the area that had twenty-four-hour electricity, so he arranged for us to live there', Lwin Ko Ko said of his father.[9]

Lwin Ko Ko also spent his time in the compound attending its military school and said that because he was not from a Tatmadaw family, he was not allowed to interact with other children, adding that he was regularly threatened and bullied, both because he was not from the military and the fact he was Muslim.

'They [the military children] didn't have much contact with outsiders because they had their own schools, hospitals and markets inside the compound. They barely went outside', he said.

He also said that the children of more senior members of the military, such as officers, also received special privileges from the teachers.

'They could easily bully the others, and teachers pretended they didn't see if they did something wrong. Their scores were always better than the others, and only they were the ones allowed to be student leaders. The other children were scared of them', he said.

Thinzar Shunlei Yi's father was a captain in the Tatmadaw, and she grew up in a 'typical military family', much of it in army compounds dotted around the country.

'It was very rare for us to leave the military compound because we had everything we needed inside', she said, adding that interactions with members of the public were rare, but when they occurred, there was an uneven power dynamic.[10]

'Whenever we went anywhere [outside], people were submissive towards us, even me who was just a young girl', said Thinzar Shunlei Yi, who has since rejected this way of thinking and has become a vocal opponent to the coup and the Tatmadaw's role in politics.

'I didn't know anyone from the outside, and in fact I felt very powerful because I was the daughter of someone in the military', she said. 'We felt like we were there to protect everyone in the country, and had this mindset that we were superior to the other people.'

This feeling of dominance among Tatmadaw members is baked into the institution's history, first as an anti-colonial fighting force, then due to its efforts to suppress a series of insurgencies that sprang up immediately after independence, and came close to tearing the new nation apart. Also crucial to the military's self-perception is its success in eventually repelling an aggressive foreign force in the form of Chinese nationalists, the Kuomintang, around this time (although it's rarely mentioned in the Tatmadaw's version of history that this was achieved with the help of the KMT's fiercest rivals, China's People's Liberation Army).

In essence, the Tatmadaw feels it is not sufficiently appreciated by much of the population for the important role it played in helping the country survive the tumultuous first few years after independence. This may seem like a juvenile world view, coming from an institution portraying itself as the nation's omnipotent force, but it's crucial to understanding the Tatmadaw's mindset today, and to do so we'd need to look back through its history.

Burma Independence Army

Its first iteration, the Burma Independence Army (BIA), was a long way from the powerful institution we see today, formed as a resistance force with the help of the Imperial Japanese Army, aiming to end British occupation during the gruesome Burma Campaign of the Second World War.

The BIA had been formed off the back of widespread anti-British sentiment that had swept through the country in the early twentieth century, fuelled initially by the desire for the Burmese to have a greater say in matters that affected them but heightened by the often heavy-handed measures British forces used against those protesting against their rule. The most notorious of these was the farmer-led Saya San rebellion of the early 1930s, which saw thousands of rebels killed and its charismatic leader executed.

As Mary Callahan, a long-term scholar on Myanmar, has noted: 'The British state, which has long been characterized as laissez-faire in its organization of Burmese society for production, did not hesitate to employ coercion when there was any perception of a threat to British commerce and authority.'[11]

The soldiers and police dispatched to put down these series of protests were comprised almost exclusively either of Indians or those from ethnic minority groups in Burma, such as the Karen, Kachin and Chin. The British had ruled Burma as part of a two-tier administrative system, divided into 'Ministerial Burma' in the centre and home mainly to the Bamar and the 'Frontier Areas', closer to today's border areas and inhabited by ethnic minorities. The colonists typically felt a deep distrust of the Bamar, largely due to the vociferous nationalist movement, and as such they were actively discouraged from joining the armed forces.

After the First World War, Bamar battalions were some of the first to go when the British downsized their troop capacity as part of peacetime efforts, and by 1931 Karen, Kachin and Chin soldiers made up more than 80 per cent of the indigenous portion of Burma's armed forces, despite comprising just over 10 per cent of the population.[12]

Although the British lifted a ban against military enrollment of the Bamar in the mid-1930s, many refused to join a cause they viewed as collaboration with a foreign, oppressive power, and instead took up arms as part of small informal militias known as *tats*, typically formed by nationalist or religious groups working to oust the colonists.

Around this time, a select few of the Bamar intent on overthrowing the British found a new avenue for their mission, with a group known as the 'Thirty Comrades' linking up with the Japanese, who had long coveted British Burma, and India beyond, as part of their own expansion plans. In the build-up to the Second World War, Japanese intelligence officers had operated in Burma under covers that included dentists, masseurs and journalists to establish contacts with nationalist leaders.

One of these was Colonel Suzuki Keiji, a 'swashbuckling, eccentric character', who posed as a correspondent named Minami Masuyo in Rangoon[13] and in 1941 helped smuggle the Thirty Comrades to Hainan Island, then under Japanese control, to undergo military training in areas including traditional and guerrilla warfare as well as espionage.

Towards the end of that year, the cadets travelled to Bangkok where they established the BIA, joining the Japanese assault on British Burma shortly after. As they made their way through the countryside towards British-held Rangoon, they picked up recruits who wanted to join the first forces fighting for the national cause.

The Japanese ousted the British-Indian troops in a matter of months, initiating a desperate exodus towards the Indian border. In Rangoon, the British capital, institutions fell immediately, with prisons released of convicts, hospitals, government offices and universities evacuated, and even the animals of Rangoon Zoo shot dead in a 'bizarre and melancholy foray'.[14]

'The Japanese troops marched in, and the Burma Independence Army as well', wrote Maung Maung, a prominent Myanmar author who at the time was a teenager living in the country's centre.[15] 'It was thrilling to see Burmese soldiers and officers, wearing assorted uniforms, bearing assorted arms, tri-colour armband on the shirt sleeve, seriousness in the face. The BIA was on the march, a few months old but already a veteran of the war, and Burmans [Bamar] were responding to its call to arms.'

But there were also atrocities committed by the BIA, particularly against the Karen populations living in Lower Burma's Irrawaddy Delta. Hundreds of villages were destroyed and thousands of people killed, an example of the tensions between the Bamar and Karen, which were exacerbated by British policies and continue in Myanmar today. According to one account, Colonel

Suzuki ordered BIA soldiers to destroy two large Karen villages, killing all the men, women and children with swords, as an act of retribution after one of his officers was killed in an attack. The incident ignited a race war, with more massacres on both sides.[16]

The BIA would last only a matter of months in fact, with the Japanese quickly eliminating its 'unwieldy, disorganized, decentralized collection' of thugs, patriots and peasants, replacing it with the Burma Defence Army (BDA), a tighter-knit and more professional outfit with only a few thousand soldiers and a handful of battalions.[17]

Among the BDA's new recruits was the author Maung Maung, who had wanted to join the BIA when they marched through his village but needed to care for his ailing mother. After she died a few months later, he travelled to the BDA headquarters at Pyinmana – now the site of the nation's capital – before hitching a cargo train south to Rangoon where he enrolled in a military academy at Mingalardon in the city's north.

'All recruits had to have their heads shaven. I did that willingly', Maung Maung wrote. 'Then we were issued our uniforms . . . Suede boots that did not call for a mirror shine, but needed to be greased. Bayonet for side-arms which one wore proudly, working or walking out.'

Life was hard in the BDA training camp, Maung Maung said, with the troops living in barracks built of bamboo and thatch and sleeping on bamboo beds. Breakfast was typically rice, gruel and salt, although on some days it would be sweetened with brown sugar.

'We drilled and trained, crawled on our bellies pushing forward on elbows until they bled. I was always clumsy in doing the goose-step', he wrote.[18]

Maung Maung would eventually shed his fatigues and become a close confidante of Ne Win, even spending a brief period as the nation's president amid the turmoil of 1988.

He has written numerous books on Myanmar, including a more than complimentary tome on Ne Win's early policies, leading to accusations that he is little more than a propagandist. And yet, his skill with the pen is evident in his writings, which provide useful insight into the Tatmadaw's interpretation of this period. His description of the army around this time is an example of this, writing:

More than the size of the army, its spirit was inspiring. It was the first time after the British annexation that Burma had her own national army. Memories of Burmese days and the glory of Burmese arms and Burmese warriors such as Alaungpaya, Bayinnaung and [Maha] Bandoola revived. What was the most satisfying was that the [Burma Army] could organize, train, administer and fight; awareness that it could be done restored self-respect and confidence. That confidence was contagious, it spread to the people who gave their full support to the army in which they saw themselves, and placed their hopes.[19]

Within a few years the BDA, under the leadership of Aung San, would switch sides to the British, contributing to the Allied victory in Burma during the Second World War.

Post-Second World War

Although independence would finally be granted three years after the war ended, discussions around what this new country's armed forces would look like was anything but straightforward, with the British in particular pushing for a 'two-wing' solution that comprised Bamar and non-Bamar soldiers. However, this solution was 'in fact two armies with two different traditions, two separate destinies being charted, and two different maps of Burma in the minds of their leaders and soldiers',[20] and despite never materializing, discussions around it would add to the already tense relations between the Bamar majority and other ethnic groups, notably the Karen.

This tension between various groups all with different desires when independence came was further heightened by the presence of thousands of arms left over in the country, either from the war or the previous *tats* that had sprouted up before the conflict had reached Burma's shores. There were about 100,000 armed soldiers and guerrillas in Burma in the middle of 1945, according to Callahan.

There was also growing discontent about the country's precarious economic situation in the post-war period, with strikes by government workers demanding an increase in salaries leading to ports, railways and government offices being forced to close.

Crime was also on the rise, and tensions reached crisis point in July 1947, a few months before independence, when Aung San and members of his cabinet were gunned down in central Rangoon. Rumours immediately spread around the capital that British military officers may have played a role in the killing of the country's much-loved leader.

A month after the assassination, Hubert Rance, the governor of British Burma, wrote: 'A state of nerves exists in Rangoon from nightfall. Every night someone lets off his musket and this is taken up by all and sundry. . . . I consider that this state of affairs will continue for some time and may well get worse.'[21]

This was the general lay of the land when Britain made its exit on 4 January 1948, lowering the Union Jack for the final time and handing the reins to the government of the Union of Burma. Early military matters in this new country would be forged by the Let Ya-Freeman Defence Agreement, a controversial accord that granted the British a continued role in Burma's army affairs, notably through its British Services Mission. The heads of Burma's armed forces at independence were all British appointees, including its chief of staff, a hirsute Karen called Lieutenant General Smith Dun, whose short stature would grant him the nickname the 'Four-Foot Colonel'.

Smith Dun's forces were thrown immediately into turmoil when independence came, and the tensions that had existed in its build-up rose immediately to the surface. Within months, the Communist Party of Burma (CPB) launched an armed rebellion that would last the next forty years, and shortly after that Karen rebels, as part of efforts to carve out the homeland they believed they deserved at independence, took up arms, capturing Insein in the north of Rangoon. Both revolts would drastically reduce the Tatmadaw's already depleted number of soldiers.

Already suspicious of mainly Karen leaders in the military, within days of Insein being taken, Prime Minister U Nu placed Karen army, navy and air force leaders 'on leave' and replaced Smith Dun with Ne Win. The rest of the Karens in the army either joined the rebellion or were interned in military 'rest camps'.

By the time Ne Win had taken control of the armed forces in February 1949, he had fewer than 2,000 troops under his command, while about three-quarters of towns across the country were held by various insurgent groups.[22]

The Tatmadaw at this point could barely be differentiated from the dozens of other armed groups operating around the country, all with an array of different motivations and ideologies and all picking up arms almost at will from the surplus leftover from the war. It was hard to see how the Tatmadaw could remain in existence for much longer, let alone go onto become the country's most powerful institution over the next few decades.

Despite the Tatmadaw's internal woes, many of the insurgents' efforts of overthrowing the Rangoon regime began to dissipate by the middle of 1950, allowing the military to reorganize and gradually eke back control over large parts of the country, including the Karen stronghold of Toungoo and other bases previously held by the Communists. The government's offer of an amnesty to rebels at this time saw thousands surrender, while in August its troops killed the Karen leader Saw Ba U Gyi, striking a stunning blow to its rivals.

The situation improved enough for a general election to take place in 1951, and into 1952, which U Nu's Anti-Fascist People's Freedom League (AFPFL) won resoundingly. This new-found stability presented an opportunity for the Tatmadaw to rapidly expand, adding dozens of new battalions between 1948 and 1951, achieved through increased military spending in the government budget.

Other developments around this time would lead to the Tatmadaw taking measures to drastically improve its capabilities in the field, most notably the arrival into northern Burma of thousands of Kuomintang (KMT) troops that were fleeing China following their defeat in the civil war to Chairman Mao's Communists. Between 1950 and 1952, KMT troop build-up in Burma increased from a few hundred to 12,000, and although its primary motivation was to take back the homeland, aggressive expansion in Shan State – the funds of which were raised through the region's lucrative drugs trade – essentially made them an aggressive occupying force in the eyes of the Burmese government. As a result, their presence in the dense hills of northern Burma would be a significant factor in drastic reforms to the Tatmadaw, which at this point remained a poorly equipped guerrilla force.

As well as concerns about the KMT's presence in the Shan hills, the Rangoon government was also worried that the nationalist's presence could be used by the Chinese government to launch a potentially permanent mission into its weaker southerly neighbour.

Already spread thin by its battles against the Karen, Communists and other insurgent groups, U Nu's government first attempted diplomatic means to rid itself of the China problem, ordering the KMT to either surrender their arms or leave the country. When this demand was ignored, its military launched a series of attacks between 1951 and 1953 that made a limited dent in the nationalist's growing resources, supported both by the United States and Taiwan.

In February 1953, the Burmese military launched its first large-scale assault against the KMT, named Operation Naganaing (Victorious Naga), but was defeated within weeks. One Burmese air force pilot involved in the effort described it as 'a complete disaster'.[23]

These humiliating defeats against a powerful foreign force led to widespread recognition that drastic changes and increased resources were needed to transform the Tatmadaw from the scrappy guerrilla outfit it had been at independence to a more centralized force capable of defending the country against invasion.

Ne Win handed this reform task over to a new planning committee, which compared the Tatmadaw's capabilities and structure with armies such as those of the United Kingdom, United States, India, Australia and the Soviet Union. It settled on devising a new defensive strategy involving large infantry divisions, mass mobilizations and advanced weaponry, which would be able to contain external aggression for three months, the time estimated it would take for international assistance to arrive.

It achieved this through various means, including heavily reforming and then centralizing the command structure, sending its leaders on a series of 'shopping trips' abroad to learn about and acquire new arms and establishing new departments, including a powerful Directorate of Psychological Warfare, tasked with winning the hearts and minds of the public.

Some of the most drastic changes in this period, however, came in the restructuring of training and education, including the establishment of new institutions. Most notable among these was the Defence Services Academy (DSA), established at Bahtoo in Shan State in 1955, moving a few years later to the picturesque hill station town of Pyin Oo Lwin, where it remains, its heavily guarded compound located just south of town. Often billed as Myanmar's West Point, or Sandhurst, the DSA recruits high school leavers to take part in a multi-year training programme to prepare them for life in the military.

Before the February 2021 coup, in Pyin Oo Lwin itself (Maymyo under the British) there was little indication that the town was home to such a strong military presence, with a friend living there saying that pre-putsch soldiers were 'largely invisible'. That's changed in the current climate, however, with an increasing number of soldiers being seen around town, in tea shops and restaurants, as well as manning checkpoints, but the friend said that 'life continues here without major changes'. In fact, for most Myanmar people Pyin Oo Lwin, located on the Shan Plateau just north of Mandalay, is more closely associated with the quality of its produce (particularly its strawberries, although the strawberry wine is an acquired taste) as well as the welcome relief it offers from the often searing heat down on the plains.

Things are very different behind the gates of the DSA, however. Although the academy is modelled on its equivalents in the United States and United Kingdom, its social interaction is that of the Japanese 'Senphai-Kohai' (senior-junior) model[24] and as such has developed a notorious reputation for the bullying, beating and killing of younger recruits.

According to its official literature, the DSA 'nurtures and produces a hard-core of young leaders'. Its motto is: 'We are the victorious warriors of the future.'

Writing in an article for *The Irrawaddy* in 2011, a DSA graduate said that in his first week at the academy, after passing a series of medical exams, he and his fellow new recruits were ordered to go to a hall to attend a 'fresher welcoming party'.

'The first thing I noticed when I entered was how dark it was. We could hardly see each other, but after several minutes of waiting, we saw more people enter the hall – a lot of them. Then, before we could even guess what was going on, the punching started', he wrote.[25]

In an attack that lasted about thirty minutes, the new recruits were punched in the stomach, chest and back, although not the face.

'As hard as we tried to protect ourselves from the savage blows that our unknown assailants were raining down on us, there was nothing we could do to stop the barrage. We couldn't even think of helping each other: we were all completely on our own.'

The following day the attackers, who were second- and third-year students, explained to the new arrivals that the attacks were part of 'brainwashing' efforts, and a necessary step before the formal training began, to establish a respect for hierarchy that would form an integral part of their life in the Tatmadaw.

The beatings and torture didn't end after the recruits' first day but continued throughout much of their time at the DSA, including being forced to perform countless frog jumps, push-ups, handstands and somersaults. If pressed for time to perform the exercises, cadets had the option of being punched by their superiors.

The DSA rules have since reportedly changed and physical assault has been deemed an 'illegal punishment', but the abuse almost certainly remains an integral component of the academy's culture. In late 2016, a second-year student at the academy died after being punched and kicked by a senior student as punishment for not cleaning his dormitory.[26]

These drastic steps the Tatmadaw took to improve its capabilities didn't bring an end to the series of conflicts it was facing, however, with new insurgencies popping up around the country almost at will throughout the 1950s and 1960s, including among the Kachin, Shan, Pa-O, Mon and Karenni (separate to the Karen and mainly located in Kayah State). The economy had also heavily stagnated since independence, contributing to tensions within the civilian government that led to a formal split in 1958, into U Nu's 'Clean AFPFL' and the 'Stable AFPFL'.

Tensions also existed within the military, notably with field officers resentful of the more comfortable existence of their central commanders in Rangoon, as well as concerns about U Nu's efforts to lessen the military's influence and capacity. In 1958, worried that the powerful field commanders would launch their own takeover of the government, Ne Win and his advisors stepped in and convinced the prime minister to hand power to a 'caretaker' government headed by Ne Win.

Although the general would hand back power to U Nu's government two years later, following an election that the 'Clean AFPFL' resoundingly won, this custodian period would see Ne Win and his fellow generals first hint at a disdain for parliamentary democracy that would rationalize both the decisive 1962 coup d'état and the increasingly autocratic Tatmadaw that would emerge over the next few decades.

It came in the form of a paper published within weeks of the 1958 coup, entitled 'Some Reflections on Our Constitution', which displayed deep contempt for democracy and the electorate, as well as freedoms enshrined in the constitution enacted at independence. The study, published by the military's new psychological warfare department, said that the population's 'general apathy' had left them susceptible to the 'skilful propaganda' of rebel groups.[27]

'What we dread most is that unscrupulous politicians and deceitful Communist rebels and their allies may take advantage of these flaws, weaknesses, contradictions and inadequacies in the Constitution and bring about in the country gangster political movements, syndicalism, anarchism and a totalitarian regime', it read.

As Callahan points out: 'The Tatmadaw's reading of Burma's first decade of postcolonial rule was that elected political leaders could not be trusted with holding the Union together, and citizens were potential enemies because the Constitution allowed subversives to brainwash them into destabilizing the country.'

The impacts of this document, and the ensuing mindset it has helped create among the Tatmadaw's top brass, are still being keenly felt in Myanmar today. Over the next several decades, this reluctance to grant the people a say in the country's future direction was witnessed in many of the policies and actions taken under Ne Win's watch and that of his successors.

The 1988 protests, and the election that followed when the people overwhelmingly displayed their aversion to the military ruling them, deepened this mindset further. Even when the military introduced a quasi-parliamentary system after the 2010 election, it implemented a model that ensured no meaningful changes could be made without the military's say-so, through strict rules related to amending the 2008 Constitution. When, in the 2020 election, for the second vote in a row (third if you include the 2012 by-election and fourth if discussing the 2017 by-election), the people overwhelmingly chose the NLD over the military's proxy party, the army decided enough was enough and stepped in to take back power in the only way they know how.

1962 coup

When Ne Win conducted his 1962 coup, he left no space for opposition or pluralism, arresting leaders of the civilian government, shuttering free press and establishing a one-party state headed by his Burma Socialist Programme Party (BSPP). Measures were also taken to put an end to outside influence, with foreign institutions banned, international correspondents banished and the country effectively closed off for decades.

This isolation occurred within the military as well. Throughout the 1950s, the Tatmadaw had sent officers and other ranks abroad to places like the United Kingdom and United States for military training, as part of efforts to build up its capabilities and know how. These trips ended almost entirely after 1962.

Although Ne Win's coup had brought the military into power, his takeover didn't necessarily lead to material improvements for the army as a fighting force. Government spending on the Ministry of Defence increased in 1962, but it wouldn't start to drastically climb, in line with overall increased budgetary spending, until the late 1970s.[28]

'Our state is in the midst of building a socialist economy and is a developing state. Therefore, we cannot afford to appropriate the national budget preferentially for only defence spending', a senior figure in Ne Win's regime said in 1969.[29]

Instead, in the year before the coup, the military had undergone a drastic restructuring that gave the commanders in Rangoon more control. The number of regional commands was increased from two to five – partly to reduce the influence of the powerful northern and southern commanders – and brigades were dissolved and reorganized.[30]

Although the number of battalions and soldiers would drastically increase during Ne Win's rule – the latter from 120,000 to 180,000 – the conditions these forces were fighting under barely improved, and they lacked the necessary training or equipment to conduct often brutal wars in the country's dense jungles. Between the mid-1950s and mid-1960s there were reported to have been between 2,000 and 5,000 deserters from the Tatmadaw per year.[31]

'It was very much a light infantry force [at this time] – very little mechanisation, no air support, no casualty evacuations, except in rare cases', said Anthony Davis, a security expert who has spent decades covering Tatmadaw operations. 'If you were a "grunt" [foot soldier] in the Tatmadaw in the 1960s and 1970s, and you were fighting in the Kachin jungle, or the mountains of Karen State, and took a serious bullet wound, the chances were you'd die. This lack of mechanisation and logistical support honed an army and a military mindset in exceptionally tough operational circumstances.'

As well as undergoing harsh conditions of their own, these ground troops were also tasked with implementing increasingly brutal tactics against their enemies, or anyone who might be perceived as one. Since about the 1960s, there have been countless reports of Tatmadaw soldiers using local villagers, often men, women and children from ethnic minorities, to act as human shields or as porters during their operations in rural areas. These tactics are still in use by the Tatmadaw today.

The 1960s also saw the introduction of the Tatmadaw's notorious 'Four Cuts' strategy, another tactic still in use, that aims to cut off enemies' sources of food, funds, intelligence and recruits. The theory was first introduced in the 1960s by Western military advisors – in particular Australian defence expert Ted Serong, an advisor to the Burmese military during this period – and also has parallels with the Japanese army's 'Three Alls Policy' ('kill all, burn all, loot all'), a scorched earth approach it used in China during the Second World War. The strategy was a key component of the Tatmadaw's military successes in central Myanmar in the 1960s and 1970s.

The impunity that Tatmadaw soldiers enjoy today can in many ways be traced to the 'Four Cuts' strategy, when troops operating in border areas and elsewhere were often given free rein by their commanding officers to murder, loot, rape and steal, practically at will.

This brutal tactic has been deployed right across the country, including in Rakhine State as part of the military's horrendous crackdown against the Rohingya there in 2016 and 2017, which saw women and children raped and burned alive in homes, thousands killed and hundreds of thousands fleeing into Bangladesh. The military claimed it was conducting 'clearance operations' against terrorists, but the United States has officially declared that operation a genocide.

Scorched earth techniques have also been used elsewhere in the country, including in central and southern Shan State in 1996, when Tatmadaw troops were sent to the area to try and crush the newly formed Shan State Army-South. Soldiers displaced hundreds of thousands of villagers, killed more than 1,000, burned entire villages to the ground and committed torture and mass rape.[32]

'They [soldiers] told us that there must not be anyone, not even a dog, left in the villages', said one resident. 'They would shoot anyone dead in the deserted village – three of our villagers were shot dead . . . and their corpses were burned with dry rice plants.'

Among those who committed these atrocities in Shan State, and many more over the country in the last few decades, were soldiers from the 77th Light Infantry Division (LID). The LIDs are often billed as the Tatmadaw's 'specialist' shock troops and in contrast to other units are centrally rather than regionally commanded. LIDs are another problematic legacy leftover from the policies introduced as part of Ne Win's efforts to tackle the growing insurgent problem. The first LID, the 77th, was established in 1966 at Bago, tasked with tackling the CPB insurgency operating in central Myanmar, and the latest, 101st, was established in 1991 at Pakokku, in the country's dry zone. There are ten LIDs in the Tatmadaw and they are recognizable by the dual numbered names of their units – 66th, 77th, 88th – with the exception of the 101st.

The LIDs are the most notorious of the Tatmadaw's units, with many inspired by a 'sadistic esprit de corps',[33] and they have been complicit in some of the Tatmadaw's worst atrocities in recent years, notably in the 2016 and 2017 campaign of violence against the Rohingya. Although established as a force to conduct battles in the country's dense jungles, they have also been deployed to urban areas during major disturbances, including in 1988 and the 2007 uprising known as the Saffron Revolution. LID troops, including those from the 33rd, 77th and 101st units, have also been involved in the brutal crackdowns that took place following the February 2021 coup.

Anthony Davis, the security expert, described the LIDs as the Tatmadaw's 'lean, mean go-to guys' during major flare-ups.

'That translates directly into brutality, because they are pushed continuously into frontline combat situations, where frequently they will take very high casualties – sometimes up to 20 percent', Davis told me. 'And the rotations can be long – three months, six months in a frontline position – which, in any Western or NATO context, would be totally unacceptable. But this is what they do.'

The LIDs are often described as the Tatmadaw's 'elite' units, but Davis argues that the description is not entirely accurate.

'They are not an elite force in the sense typically associated with highly trained special forces in modern armies such as the British SAS or Russian Spetsnaz. Their "elite" status stems rather from their role as the reliable and invariably ruthless sharp end of the Tatmadaw spear and the esprit de corps that goes with that', he said.

In 1974, Ne Win began making changes to his administration, introducing a new constitution and creating a legislature called the 'People's Parliament', which he billed as having completed Burma's 'transition to civilian rule'. In reality, it was nothing of the sort, and the changes brought about in 1974 were largely cosmetic, including the new parliament, which was nothing more than a rubber stamp for government policy. For Ne Win, it had been a symbol of a government that ruled according to the 'wishes of the people', despite doing nothing of the sort in practice.[34]

In fact, the make-up of the People's Parliament – and other institutions overseen by Ne Win – would demonstrate one of the most problematic legacies of his rule, a mindset that would be fortified by his successors and heavily dominant among the Tatmadaw's top generals today: Burmanization. Throughout his rule, the vast majority of the People's Parliament members were from the Bamar majority, with just a few seats granted to those from other ethnic groups such as the Rakhine, Shan and Karen.[35]

Having been established off the back of the Bamar-led nationalist movement of the early twentieth century, the BIA, the Tatmadaw's first iteration, was an army representing the country's largest group, which makes up roughly two-thirds of its population, largely in the centre. However, the Tatmadaw that emerged at independence was supposed to represent the entirety of this new country, which – despite issues with what appeared at times to be ad hoc demarcation by the British – includes more than 100 ethnic groups.

Ask many of these groups today, and few would have any interest in being part of what they view as a violent, occupying force, but things may have been different if more inclusive policies had been introduced around independence and members from an array of ethnic groups invited into top jobs in both the military and the government.

The Tatmadaw's founding father, Aung San, may have been open to this. He may have been one of the most fervent pro-Bamar nationalists during British rule, but there are indications that as independence approached, he was at least sympathetic to some of the demands of Burma's other ethnic groups. This was evident at the 1947 Panglong Conference, where an agreement was reached by various ethnic groups although never fulfilled, when he told the ethnic minorities present: 'If Burma receives one kyat, you will also get one kyat.'[36] This may have just been words to appease those present at the ceremony, but his assassination a few months later means we will never know how inclusive a country Burma would have been under his leadership.

Ne Win was never open to such ideas. When launching his 1962 coup he declared that 'Federalism is impossible. It will destroy the Union',[37] putting an end to any hopes minority groups had held since independence that they would have a say in their own futures. His distrust of Burma's ethnic minorities was evident in his speech and his policies, including the 'Four Cuts' strategy, which heavily targeted ethnic minorities. It is one of the strongest factors in the distrust these groups feel towards those ruling at the centre today, while the make-up of the various institutions Ne Win oversaw – including, among others, the Revolutionary Council and the BSPP – had almost no one except Bamar figures at its top levels.

SLORC rule

This policy of Burmanization would be taken to new levels by Ne Win's successors, when he was forced to stand down amid the turmoil of the

1988 uprising. Although the general was believed to still be wielding significant power behind the scenes, his BSPP, which had been the country's sole legal party since 1962, was dissolved and replaced by a new generation of generals forming the ominously named State Law and Order Restoration Council (SLORC).

The leader of this new cohort was Saw Maung, who had burnished his fighting credentials in a series of battles against Communist rebels and ethnic minority insurgencies throughout the 1970s. By 1985, he had earned the trust of Ne Win enough to be promoted to deputy defence minister, and when the SLORC administration – allegedly at the behest of Ne Win – launched a coup d'état in 1988 to quell that year's huge anti-government uprisings, Saw Maung was announced as its new chairman.

Close behind him was Than Shwe, a postal clerk in central Burma shortly after independence, but whose tenacity in a series of battles throughout the country saw him reach the rank of brigadier general, and then vice chief of staff, by the mid-1980s. He was announced as vice chairman of the new SLORC administration, and when Saw Maung stood down in April 1992 citing 'ill health' – reports from the time indicate he was mentally unstable – Than Shwe took the top job, ruling until 2011.

The 8-8-88 uprising would shake the political foundations in Myanmar, and it was the first time the people had displayed their displeasure at the regime on such a monumental scale, with anti-military protests taking place across the country. Although the demonstrations would ultimately be quelled, they were crucial in creating a fresh generation of politically minded citizens who were willing to push back against the military's totalitarian rule.

Instead of listening to these voices, however, after 1988 the generals closed ranks and took drastic steps to strengthen their hold on power. When the newly formed NLD resoundingly won the 1990 general election, sweeping up about 60 per cent of the popular vote, the military leaders annulled the result and arrested NLD leaders. It was a move that would once against demonstrate the Tatmadaw's distrust of the people, notably their apparent apathy and inability to see through the 'brainwashing' of meddling outsiders, thirty years after Ne Win had first communicated this mindset. In fact, much of the regime's messaging at the time would blame the turmoil around the country on 'destructive' elements including communist and Karen rebels.

Rattled by the 1988 uprising, and anxious about a potential invasion from abroad – notably the United States, concerned they would link up with the thousands of pro-democracy activists congregating at the Thai border planning an assault on Rangoon – the new SLORC administration made it a priority to build up the Tatmadaw's capabilities, weaponry, expertise and manpower.

This included an overhaul of the country's intelligence apparatus, so much so that by 1998 a Thai military intelligence officer described it as the 'fourth most efficient in the world', borrowing techniques from Israel's Mossad, the UK's Secret Intelligence Service (known as MI-6), the US Central Intelligence Agency (CIA) and Federal Bureau of Investigations (FBI) as well as the Soviet Union's KGB.[38]

Although it escalated after 1988, the intelligence revamp in fact started five years earlier, when a relatively unknown colonel called Khin Nyunt was recalled from a posting in the field to Rangoon, to become the regime's new chief of intelligence. The catalyst for that promotion came a few months earlier, when North Korean agents snuck into the country and staged a catastrophic bomb attack in central Rangoon, targeting the visiting South Korean president Chun Doo-hwan. Chun survived, but dozens perished, including seventeen South Korean officials and four Burmese nationals. Ne Win was furious at the embarrassing intelligence failure and ordered a complete restructuring.

Over the next two and a half decades, with Khin Nyunt at the helm, the country's military intelligence apparatus drastically expanded, focussing on areas including counter-intelligence, combat intelligence, foreign intelligence and counter-narcotics. Khin Nyunt's chief agency, the Directorate of Defence Services Intelligence (DDSI), better known as the Military Intelligence Service (MIS), had an estimated 2,000 men attached to twelve regional commands across the country.[39]

The DDSI's main focus was surveillance of members of the NLD after the party's emergence, but it also closely monitored the rest of the population through a mixture of professional intelligence officers, and a large network of informers, both paid and unpaid. Spies infiltrated universities, with an estimated one in every twenty students working on behalf of the government. They were also placed into the armed forces themselves, tasked with rooting out potential dissenters.

Agents working on behalf of Khin Nyunt intercepted radio traffic, listened in on domestic and overseas phone calls, recorded private conversations and opened mail. As computer and internet use began to increase in the 1990s and beyond, they monitored emails and social media accounts. A string of networks was also kept abroad, mainly in neighbouring countries to keep an eye on dissenters there. For example, military intelligence sent spies to Thailand as 'beggars, laborers, and even Buddhist monks'.[40]

While Khin Nyunt's DDSI was the dominant agency within the intelligence network, the military relied on a host of other groups and methods. This included the police's Special Intelligence Department (SID), otherwise known as Special Branch, as well as the Criminal Investigation Department (CID), and the Bureau of Special Investigation (BSI), sometimes known as 'Burma's FBI'.

There was also the ubiquitous government apparatus, most notably the General Administration Department (GAD), with its presence in all of the country's wards, villages and townships and whose members were encouraged to report on any unusual activity. The government also used members of the mass Union Solidarity and Development Association, known as 'White Shirts', who were encouraged to report signs of 'social deviance' and 'disloyalty', as well as violent vigilante groups such as *Shwann Ar Shinn*, heavies usually taken from the country's rural poor, sent into intimidate those involved in anti-government protests.

At one point it appeared that intelligence may become a fourth service of the Tatmadaw, alongside the army, navy and air force, and Khin Nyunt became so effective at capturing dissenters that he earned the nickname 'the Prince of Darkness'.

Then it all came crashing down. By late 2004, Khin Nyunt was the third most powerful member of the ruling junta, now renamed the State Peace and Development Council (SPDC), behind only Senior General Than Shwe and Vice Senior General Maung Aye. There were known to be tensions between Khin Nyunt and the other rulers, however, not least because of the powerful intelligence apparatus he controlled. Khin Nyunt was also widely celebrated in international media as a 'moderate' more willing to engage the international community, in contrast to Than Shwe's favoured isolationist approach.

'I think that the future of Burma will be decided by two people – Khin Nyunt and Aung San Suu Kyi,' US Congressman Bill Richardson said in 1994, while Singaporean leader Lee Kuan Yew once lamented the country's generals as 'dense', 'stupid' and 'obtuse', describing Khin Nyunt as 'the most intelligent of the lot'.[41]

However, in October 2004, a one-sentence notice appeared on the front page of the state-run *New Light of Myanmar*, signed by junta leader Than Shwe, saying that Khin Nyunt had been 'permitted to retire' on health grounds, junta speak for sudden dismissals. Khin Nyunt was immediately removed from his positions, and months later sentenced to forty-four years in prison on corruption charges, later commuted to house arrest, while many of his allies were also sentenced to lengthy jail terms.

Ostensibly his demise was related to corrupt practices by military intelligence officers at the Myanmar-China border that Khin Nyunt was accused of turning a blind eye to. In reality, veteran Myanmar watcher Andrew Selth argued his downfall was related to 'policy, power, personal, pillage and preservation theories'.[42]

Reporting at the time said that Khin Nyunt's arrest dealt a blow to those hoping for democratic reform in Myanmar, with the 'moderate' losing out in a power struggle. However, a US Embassy cable at the time disagreed, describing Khin Nyunt as 'a hardliner, albeit a more polished and approachable one'. 'He was a pragmatist who cultivated foreign countries and a purported dialogue with the opposition simply as a means to mollify the international community and perpetuate the regime's absolute control.'

The ousting of Khin Nyunt and the purge of his vast network of spies and other intelligence apparatus that followed created a major void within the regime. Although information-gathering on the population continued after Khin Nyunt's removal, including 'black lists' of junta critics abroad and the following of foreign journalists in country, intelligence failures occurred, including several bomb attacks in Yangon, the culprits of which were never identified.

Amid rising concerns about potential enemies abroad and at home, the SLORC regime also spent heavily on new weapons, including from countries such as Pakistan and Singapore.[43] By far its largest supplier in this period, however, was China, which was eager to increase its foothold in its southerly neighbour. In October 1989, a high-level Tatmadaw delegation travelled to Beijing to meet with Premier Li Peng. Despite initial reluctance to get involved in what it said was Burma's 'civil war', China eventually agreed to sell large supplies of weapons across the border, and over the next few years the Tatmadaw would go on to spend a reported billion dollars on procuring new military equipment from the Chinese, including fighter jets, armoured vehicles and gunboats.[44]

This expansion would also pave the way for plans to drastically increase the number of troops the Tatmadaw had at its disposal. Shortly after the coup, SLORC drew up plans to increase forces from about 200,000 in 1988 to 270,000 by 1992, and an ultimate goal of 500,000. It fell short of this target, having an estimated 400,000 soldiers by 2007.[45]

The Tatmadaw's opaque nature has always made it difficult to get an accurate read on its true number of troops, but the 1990s certainly saw a concerted effort across the country to get more soldiers join its ranks, both through official means and otherwise.

Although successive military governments have long considered the idea of mandatory military service, it has never been formally introduced. Officially, the Tatmadaw is a volunteer army, and many of those who sign up do so out of choice, whether it's for the glamour and prestige of the uniform, a desire for adventure, the opportunity to earn an income amid a dearth of job opportunities or to protect their families from harassment by government officials or troops. Others also join to escape troubles at home, or punishment for breaking the law, or because they are orphans who have no support net and want to feel a sense of camaraderie.

But forced conscription, including of children, has also formed a large component of the Tatmadaw's recruitment process for decades. Since 1988, one common tactic has been for village heads to be forced to fulfil 'recruitment' quotas.

'We can't refuse to send the recruits', said a village head in Bago Region, central Myanmar, of the military's threats in the 1990s. 'If the township authorities can't get as many people as the SLORC demands, then they have to go themselves, or else be put in jail. So, if they don't have enough people for one month, they [local authorities] go and grab anyone, just so they won't end up in jail. All they want is just to get 300 people, no matter who.'[46]

Another youth forced into conscription in the Tatmadaw, speaking in 1995, said he had just finished classes for the day in Bago Region, north of Yangon, when SLORC soldiers surrounded his school.

'We'd just finished one or two subjects that afternoon. There were 40 or 50 of us all leaving together, and we were all arrested. We were all 15, 16, 17 years old, and we were all afraid of the soldiers', he said.[47]

The boy said they were sent to Aung San Stadium, a crumbling arena in central Yangon, where they stayed for a night before being transferred to a military camp at Mingalardon, in the city's north.

'Our parents had no idea what happened to us. They weren't told anything and neither were we. Some people had money to pay off the SLORC officers, but most couldn't. I didn't know what was going on, and they didn't explain anything to us', he said.

During the 1990s and early 2000s, there were also reports of Tatmadaw officers abducting roving youths in train stations and other public places, and transferring them to military camps, either to fulfil quotas of their own or accept bribes from other recruiters that supplemented their meagre wages.

Treatment hardly improves once these new cadets enter the Tatmadaw. As mentioned earlier in this chapter, those sent to the DSA are subjected to almost daily beatings and humiliations, while those dispatched to the front lines face dismal conditions.

'For the rank-and-file soldiers, their lives are miserable. The soldiers are not happy, and they feel undervalued', said Nyi Thuta, a former captain in the Tatmadaw who defected shortly after the 2021 coup.

'Many soldiers have to spend years on the frontline, and life there is so difficult. On the frontline, food and shelter is not arranged for them, so they have to arrange it themselves. If a soldier lives in a hut, for example, they have to search for bamboo in the forest, or go into nearby towns to buy it. Often this costs money, which many soldiers do not have.'

Nyi Thuta added that rank-and-file soldiers are also treated poorly by their superiors.

'Beatings by officers to the soldiers are very common. In the military, if you are scolded, you are beaten. It has become almost like a tradition.'

Human wave tactics by the Tatmadaw have also been documented, demonstrating the callous way officers often view the soldiers under their command.

During some of the most intense periods of fighting between the Tatmadaw and Karen forces in the 1990s 'waves of troops were sent up a steep open slope against heavily fortified positions', Human Rights Watch said in a 2002 report.[48]

Between 1991 and 1995 'thousands of soldiers were forced to run across an open killing ground full of barbed wire and landmines straight into Karen machine-gun emplacements'. These gunners reportedly admitted that many of those they had killed had been boys, and some appeared to be drugged.

'Captured Burma army soldiers claimed that they were forced ahead by NCOs [non-commissioned officers] and officers who threatened to shoot them from behind if they stopped.'

Successive Tatmadaw leaders have continued these ruthless policies. After taking power in 1992, following the downfall of Saw Maung, Than Shwe gradually consolidated his hold on power, and removed potential rivals to his reign, through a mixture of 'patronage and punishment'.[49] The former was achieved in part through military-linked conglomerates established in the 1990s as part of an apparent liberalization of the economy, such as the Union of Myanmar Economic Holdings Limited (UMEHL), which provided an income stream for Tatmadaw officials, who were able to purchase shares. The use of punishment was evident, for example, in Than Shwe's swift action to remove the increasingly powerful Khin Nyunt from power.

Then, to the surprise of many Myanmar observers, following a general election in 2010 that the popular NLD boycotted, and the military's proxy party, the Union Solidarity and Development Party (USDP), resoundingly won, Than Shwe announced he would step back from power, handing the reigns to a 'civilian government' comprised of former generals who had shed their fatigues for suits.

As well as retiring as commander-in-chief of the armed forces, Than Shwe went further, also arranging the retirement of his number two, Maung Aye. The military's top brass were also stood down, assigned to civilian positions. Thein Sein, a former general, was appointed the country's new president.

It was widely expected that Than Shwe would announce his direct replacement as chief of the armed forces as Shwe Mann, who had earned the honorific title *Thura* (brave hero) for leading the 1989 capture of the KNU's headquarters. According to a US cable, he forcibly used civilian porters, including women and children, 'on a massive scale' during the operations.[50]

The same cable, written in 2007, said that Shwe Mann was believed to be Than Shwe's preferred successor, serving 'as his hatchet man on several occasions'.

'Some sources claim Shwe Mann is pro-reform and would move the country back into the mainstream once he consolidates power', it said.

But that never happened. Instead of becoming commander-in-chief, Shwe Mann was made speaker of the newly opened Lower House of Parliament, and the top job given to Min Aung Hlaing.

We'll never know what direction Myanmar would have gone in had Than Shwe chosen Shwe Mann and his replacement, and not Min Aung Hlaing, but there are indications that Shwe Mann may have been genuinely intent on reforms to the Tatmadaw and could have led the country on a very different path to the coup leader. Given this potential sliding doors moment, it's worth at least some reflection.

As well as being made house speaker, Shwe Mann was also the leader of the military's political party, the USDP, tasked with leading it into the 2015 election against the NLD. However, a few months before the vote, in August, security forces dramatically sealed off the USDP headquarters in Nay Pyi Taw. Hours later, a reshuffle of the party's leadership was announced, with Shwe Mann and his allies 'permitted to resign'. Shortly after, Htay Oo, an ally of both Thein Sein and Than Shwe, was announced as the party's new chairman.

'The party needed to be reformed for party unity', a USDP statement said.

As always with political developments in Myanmar, the real issue may have gone much deeper. For some of the more hard-line members of the military, Shwe Mann was regarded as a turncoat who cosied up to their long-time rival, Aung San Suu Kyi, and in his role as house speaker had allowed debates regarding potential amendments to the military's all-important 2008 Constitution.

Information Minister Ye Htut later said that Shwe Mann had made some 'very questionable' decisions in parliament.

'He sometimes tried to force his will on other people. This kind of thing happened again and again', Ye Htut told *Reuters*.

There may have been even more to it. A few weeks after Shwe Mann's ouster, I was approached by a source in Yangon, who claimed to be present at the USDP compound on the night of the incident. The source said they were part of a small group who had been working on a drastically reformed USDP manifesto that was due to be released on 13 August, the day after the crackdown.

After a series of cloak-and-dagger meetings in various venues around Yangon, a colleague and I were able to obtain what we were told was the new manifesto, a 177-page document adorned with the USDP logo. There was also polling analysis of all of Myanmar's constituencies ahead of the election, predicting that, in a worst-case scenario, the party would win just sixteen seats in the upcoming election. Reforms were clearly needed to win over the public. Changes put forward in the manifesto proposed drastic changes to the Myanmar Police Force (MPF), part of the military-controlled Ministry of Home Affairs and therefore an important component of the Tatmadaw's security apparatus. The document also outlined plans to bring the military-owned corporations, which provided huge revenues to generals high up the chain of command, under public ownership. Other proposed policies deemed 'too sensitive' to be included on the document were shown to senior USDP members, we were told.

Whether the manifesto was genuine USDP policy planned to be introduced ahead of the election or a public relations exercise aimed at cementing Shwe Mann's reputation as a genuine reformer, we were never able to fully establish.

Despite being ousted from the party leadership, Shwe Mann ran on the USDP ticket in the 2015 election, losing resoundingly to an NLD candidate. The following year, he and several allies were sacked from the USDP, and Shwe Mann went on to form his own party, the Union Betterment Party (UBP), ahead of the 2020 election.

A year before that vote, I was finally granted an audience with Shwe Mann, at his Yangon home, a heavily guarded compound on the north-western shore of Inya Lake. For Shwe Mann's advisors who'd helped set up the interview, its intended thrust was clear, to publicize UBP policies ahead of the vote. Realistically, however, the UBP was not expected to perform well (it won no seats in the election), and I was more interested in learning about his relations with the military's top brass. In a book published a year earlier, he admitted to sleeping with a gun under his pillow.

But Shwe Mann was guarded in his responses. Softly spoken and smiling throughout, he answered my questions through a translator – which felt like a frustrating power play given I was sure his English was good enough – simply saying that he had 'a good relationship' with the military and was confident he could work alongside his former colleagues should he become president.

'I am very proud to be part of the military, but there are a lot of misunderstandings about it', was as far as I was able to get.

Min Aung Hlaing comes to power

When Than Shwe overlooked Shwe Mann, and announced Min Aung Hlaing as the new commander-in-chief in 2011, at the same time that other political and economic reforms were taking place in the country, many hoped it would coincide with drastic changes also being made to the Tatmadaw, potentially going as far as placing it under civilian control.

Little in Min Aung Hlaing's backstory would suggest a commitment to such open principles, however. Born in the picturesque southerly town of Dawei, he studied at Yangon University, before enrolling at the military's DSA in Pyin Oo Lwin, graduating in the 1970s, at the height of its fierce battles with Communist and ethnic minority insurgencies.

A committed Tatmadaw man, he worked his way up through the organization to command the 44th LID before being promoted to commander of a Regional Command in the border area of the country's east. He was also heavily involved in efforts to convert rival militia groups into Tatmadaw-loyal Border Guard Forces (BGF). In 2009, he led the military's successful offensive against the Myanmar National Democratic Alliance Army (MNDAA) in Kokang, near the China border, an incursion that appears to have been crucial in him being granted the top job two years later. Than Shwe may have also considered Min Aung Hlaing 'too junior' to implement radical changes that may have threatened his own legacy.[51]

Some limited changes were made during Min Aung Hlaing's early days in charge, however, including a mandatory retirement age for all military personnel as well as limits on time-in-rank for high-ranking officers.[52] Generals were permitted to retire after serving four years in rank, lieutenant generals after five years, a major general after six years and a brigadier general after seven. The commander-in-chief and their deputy would be forced to stand down at the age of sixty-five.

During the reform years, the Tatmadaw also worked with international agencies on issues around underage recruitment and improved relations with the militaries of democratic countries, such as Australia, which provided training to the Tatmadaw until the coup.

Min Aung Hlaing also hinted at major changes to the Tatmadaw as an institution, regularly speaking of the need to establish what he called a Standard Army 'with capabilities to conduct conventional operations'.[53] Although Min Aung Hlaing never fully articulated what he meant by a Standard Army, it likely meant changes to its recruitment and training, enhanced relations with foreign militaries and the acquisition of new weapons.

'As the country embarked on this democratic transition, I felt the history of the Tatmadaw ruling the country was in the past, and that it would reform', said Nyi Thuta, the defecting Tatmadaw captain, who is in his early thirties. 'My generation believed that the Tatmadaw would reform, because this was when we had parliaments and elected representatives, and power was transferred to a civilian government. I had very high hopes for my country at this time.'

Min Aung Hlaing, however, appeared more intent on buying new toys, rather than overhauling the Tatmadaw's practices and culture. He instigated a 'wide-ranging scheme to improve the armed forces' order of battle',[54] spending billions on acquiring weapons such as radars, missiles, drones, armoured vehicles and even the country's first submarine, brought from India, and which it displayed for the first time shortly before the coup.[55,56]

He was particularly focussed, however, on the purchase of planes and equipment for his air force, and for this he turned closely to Russia, a relationship that has continued in the post-coup environment. In the few years before the coup, he bought from them air-to-air missiles to kit out the combat planes it already had at its disposal, as well as subsonic fighter jets,[57] while since the coup Russia has committed to fulfilling past orders and struck new arms deals with the Myanmar military.

Although the quasi-civilian government that replaced Than Shwe's junta in 2011 took a more dialogue-centric approach to ending the decades-long conflicts in Myanmar, still the Tatmadaw remained in active conflict with many groups around the country at this time.

In 2011, a seventeen-year ceasefire with the KIA broke, leading to periodic bouts of conflict across the state for the next decade or so, which saw civilians killed, mass displacement and widespread accusations of human rights violations. In 2015 the Tatmadaw became embroiled in a deadly months-long conflict in Kokang.

The Tatmadaw's renowned brutality towards civilians did not cease in this period. This was most apparent in its devastating campaign of violence against the Rohingya in 2016 and 2017, which saw more than nine thousand people killed and which the United States has since declared a genocide, but Myanmar military soldiers also committed human rights violations in a series of conflicts taking place elsewhere in the country.

In September 2018, the Independent International Fact-Finding Mission on Myanmar published an in-depth report into military violations in Rakhine, Kachin and Shan states. It found that the Tatmadaw had 'systematically targeted civilians', including women and children, committing sexual violence, promoting 'exclusionary and discriminatory rhetoric' against minorities and established a climate of impunity for its soldiers. The report's authors said they were struck by how 'similar the Tatmadaw operations and conducts were in all three States'.

With the February 2021 coup, and the violent crackdown that followed, Min Aung Hlaing appears to have given up his pretence of establishing a professional Standard Army. Not only have relations with other – although not all – militaries ground to a halt as a result of the power grab, but no one looking at its behaviour today could see anything remotely resembling a professional outfit.

We'll look more closely at the historic and current violence in the next chapter, but it's worth spending some time reflecting on the current junta leaders in Myanmar and how much they differ from previous military rulers in Myanmar. The truth is, not by a great amount.

Although the SAC comprises a smattering of civilians, including a few ethnic minorities, these are military allies or those whose loyalty to the junta has been bought. When the SAC was originally announced immediately after the coup, it included eight military officers and three civilians. Although the SAC make-up has since expanded, to get a grasp on its way of thinking, it's worth taking a close look at the top six posts in its hierarchy when the coup took place.

As well as Min Aung Hlaing, this included his deputy Soe Win, Chief of General Staff Mya Tun Oo, Tin Aung San and Maung Maung Kyaw, commanders of the navy and air force, respectively, and Moe Myint Tun, commander of the Nay Pyi Taw-based Bureau of Special Operations 6 and who had previously been tipped as Min Aung Hlaing's replacement as commander-in-chief.[58]

All deeply reflected the culture of the Tatmadaw.[59] All were Buddhist Bamar, and all had spent decades being indoctrinated into the Tatmadaw belief system, first at the DSA, where all six attended, then during several decades fighting battles around the country. Four of the six spent years heading one of the Tatmadaw's powerful regional commands, while the other two served as heads of the armed forces and navy. It's clear they were all chosen for their loyalty to the institution.

The Tatmadaw is run according to a deeply hierarchical structure, and the key decision maker in the SAC is Min Aung Hlaing. Anyone who has seen the short, bespectacled general speak will agree that he is not a particularly impressive or imposing figure, but that's not necessarily a desired attribute among the Tatmadaw's leadership. There's a reason Myanmar's earlier dictators didn't build huge sculptures of themselves in the style of Stalin or the ubiquitous Kim statues of North Korea. Leading the Tatmadaw is not about a personality cult but a deep commitment to the belief that the institution is the only protector of the nation. Min Aung Hlaing has that in spades.

One question that was commonly raised in the immediate aftermath of the coup was about the prospects of a 'coup within a coup'. What were the chances, the question went, of a senior member of the junta, upon seeing how deeply unpopular the military's takeover was, choosing to act and oust, or even kill, Min Aung Hlaing, returning the country to the democratic path?

Highly unlikely, and even more so as time wore on. As mentioned above, all of the figures within the top echelons of the SAC were chosen for their deep commitment to the Tatmadaw and will hold roughly the same warped view as Min Aung Hlaing about the military's role and standing. That's before you even get to the junta leaders' deeply entrenched economic interests, which would be put at huge risk in the event of the Tatmadaw's collapse, as well as the risk that a civilian government could pursue transitional justice for the countless crimes committed under the junta's watch. In short, the Tatmadaw will not be giving up power voluntarily.

But that's not to say there aren't potential fault lines to be found in the huge wall the Tatmadaw has built around itself. Afterall, there have been splits among the Tatmadaw leadership in the past. Over time, middle-tier officers may be able to find a way to break into the junta's top brass and take actions to destroy it from within, but admittedly that feels more like wishful thinking at this point. It's clear that efforts to destroy the Tatmadaw as an institution must come from the outside.

As time wears on, and resistance to the coup shows little sign of abating, increasingly important in the movement are the efforts to encourage Tatmadaw soldiers to defect towards the NUG and its PDFs.

The Tatmadaw has somewhere in the region of 350,000 soldiers, and so any efforts to tip the balance of power to impact the conflict will take years, but there is now a concerted effort to encourage troops to switch sides, something that may bear fruit over time.

It's not an easy task, however. Nyi Thuta, the defecting captain, says that many soldiers are worried about the safety of their family if they leave or feel they don't have any other choice.

Nyi Thuta believes that something that would speed up the number of defections taking place would be an understanding among the general public about the difficulties faced by rank-and-file soldiers in the Tatmadaw.

'We have to understand the lives of soldiers. They join for many reasons, but we must understand that life is very difficult for them. Until now, people have only seen the bad side of soldiers, but that is starting to change', he said.

What's clear, however, is that any efforts to put an end to the current situation, and force the Tatmadaw into concessions, will not come from within, unless the military is dramatically depleted. Even then, it appears unlikely. The Tatmadaw has never known the meaning of compromise or negotiation, a mindset based on the fact that it has always done what it wants, never facing consequences for its actions, in particular the campaign of terror and violence it has meted out against the people for several decades.

Ghosts of Rangoon

The first few months after the 2021 military coup saw a wave of peaceful protests across Myanmar.

In remote Chin State, in the country's west, thousands travelled across its vast range of mountains by whatever means necessary to congregate in the picturesque state capital, Hakha. There, they marched through its streets, chanting pro-democracy slogans and calling on the military to stand down.

Out east, at Inle Lake in Shan State, one of the country's best-known tourist attractions, local people from the huge cluster of villages that surround it took part in one of the more scenic mass protests the country has seen, rowing their boats around the famed lake, holding aloft anti-military placards and chanting revolutionary songs.

As the country's largest city, some of the biggest protests took place in Yangon, with demonstrations occurring every day in townships across the city, and its outskirts, over the Yangon River to the south, into the rural impoverished areas to the west, the industrial eastern suburbs and towards the villages and hills further north.

In Shwe Pyi Thar Township, an industrial area in Yangon's northwest, up past the infamous Insein Prison and close to the international airport, one of those leading the protests was Zaw Myat Lynn, an NLD member and a prominent community organizer in the local area.

Since the coup, Zaw Myatt Lyyn, a 46-year-old with a slightly receding hairline and prominent cheekbones, had vocally spoken up against it, leading rallies in the local area and taking to his public Facebook page to urge the people to fight back against the soldiers, who he called 'dogs' and 'terrorists'.

A strong believer in the power of education, Zaw Myat Lynn also worked as a teacher at a local school, the compound of which he lived on with his wife. After taking part in a protest in early March, he returned home to spend the night.[1]

In the early hours of the morning, soldiers broke into the school and arrested Zaw Myat Lynn, bundling him into a truck and driving him away. Later the next day his wife, Phyu Phyu Win, received a phone call from a local official telling her that her husband was dead, and that she could come and see his body.

His body was 'badly bruised', according to a BBC report, and his stomach had been 'cut open by a long, horizontal incursion'. His intestines had also come out.[2]

The *Guardian* also reported it had seen photographs of Zaw Myat Lynn's body, which appeared to show that 'boiling water or a chemical solution had been poured into his mouth. The tongue was melted, his teeth missing. Facial skin was peeling off'.[3]

Almost a week after his death, an article was published in the state-run *Global New Light of Myanmar* saying that Zaw Myat Lynn had 'jumped down from the house . . . and fell on the about two inches high steel pipe of the fence. In the incident, he died of injury at the belly'. The report added that 'severe action' would be taken against those who shared 'fake news' about his death.

It's not exactly clear what happened to Zaw Myat Lynn in his final few hours, but torture at the hands of his captors is the most likely scenario. Around this time, there were other similar incidents of soldiers coming to people's homes during the night and dragging them away, only for them to turn up dead the next morning. For decades, torture has been a grim calling card of Tatmadaw troops.

Another likely victim was Khin Maung Latt, fifty-eight, like Zaw Myat Lynn an NLD member, and living in the heart of downtown Yangon, a few streets from its official centre, the Sule Pagoda.

One evening in early March, security forces arrived at Khin Maung Latt's home, forcing their way in, and kicking and beating him, before taking him away at gunpoint.

The next morning, like Phyu Phyu Win, Khin Maung Latt's family received a phone call telling them to come and recover his body from a military hospital in northern Yangon. His body had severe wounds to the hands and back and was covered in a bloody cloth.[4]

Physicians for Human Rights, a US-based organization, examined the evidence, including photographs of Khin Maung Latt's body, concluding that it was most likely he had died from 'homicidal violence' while in custody.[5]

Since the coup, there has been global shock and outrage regarding the level of violence the Tatmadaw has unleashed against the Myanmar people, including firing indiscriminately into crowds, point-blank executions of random passers-by, air strikes on defenceless villages, burning people alive in the streets and many more. Many of those arrested have been subjected to torture, including kickings and beatings and being burned with cigarettes.

In Mandalay, a young girl of six was shot dead as she ran into her father's arms after soldiers entered the family home. In Monywa, a renowned poet was shot in the head, before his bloody body was callously dragged away. In

Magway, in central Myanmar, an elderly couple were burned alive when they were unable to flee after junta forces burned down their village.

These are just a few select examples of a campaign of violence from the Myanmar military that rights groups have said amounts to crimes against humanity.[6]

Yet these tactics are nothing new and are in fact the modus operandi of the Tatmadaw, which since at least the 1960s has subjected the people to regular bouts of violence and terror, killing an untold amount, but probably somewhere in the hundreds of thousands. Much of this violence has occurred in the country's remote borderlands, where civil war has raged for decades, but it has also been witnessed in the country's centre, particularly during the emergence of anti-military protests.

A culture of impunity

While it has been the soldiers committing these crimes first-hand, it's important to step back for a moment and remember who it is giving them the orders – their commanding officers, which include powerful regional commanders overseeing specific geographical locations, and in an institution that has such respect for hierarchy like the Tatmadaw, all the way to the very top, to the commander-in-chief.

This culture of impunity can most likely be traced back to the 1960s, in particular the Tatmadaw's shift towards a 'People's War' approach to conflict, best defined by the brutal 'Four Cuts' strategy, which aims to cut off insurgents' access to food, funds, intelligence and recruits. This approach to warfare essentially gave soldiers free rein to behave as they wished in a series of battles throughout the country, including killing, looting and raping, a mindset that has clearly been heavily absorbed into the minds of today's soldiers.

This approach was ultimately decided upon by Ne Win, the dictator who ruled the country for decades following his decisive 1962 coup d'état, and it's worth looking a little at this figure whose legacy remains such an important, and troubling, aspect of the Tatmadaw.

Ne Win was born as Shu Maung in May 1911, in a small village just east of the town of Pyay, a few hundred kilometres north of Yangon.

In 1929, Shu Maung began studying biology at the illustrious Rangoon University but dropped out and spent the next few years working in a variety of civil service roles. In 1930, he joined the nationalist *Dobama Asiayone* group, working to overthrow the British colonial rulers, and rose quickly through its ranks alongside Aung San, the country's independence hero.

Shu Maung was chosen as a member of the famed Thirty Comrades by the Japanese, where he took on the *nom de guerre* Ne Win, meaning Radiant Sun. During the Second World War, he developed a reputation for his skills as an intelligence officer,[7] and when independence came he was appointed second in command of the army. When a Karen revolt occurred within the Tatmadaw ranks a year after independence, Ne Win replaced Smith Dun, a Karen, as the military's chief of staff.

Over the next decade, Ne Win played a crucial role in building the Tatmadaw up from the scrappy, anti-resistance force it had been at independence to a more professional and powerful outfit. This came in the form of increased spending on equipment, new and improved training facilities for recruits and numerous 'shopping trips' abroad to learn about and acquire new weapons.

When Ne Win transferred power back to U Nu following the 1960 election, the move was celebrated globally as a victory for democracy. Ne Win was even awarded the Magsaysay Award, sometimes described as 'Asia's Nobel', although he rejected it saying he was merely carrying out his duty (some suspect the real reason was because of its close association with the United States).[8]

But clearly he had enjoyed the taste of power he had sampled over the past two years and believed that it was military rule, not democracy, that could put the country on the right path. In the early hours of 2 March 1962, his tanks rolled into Rangoon's streets, in a coup that would entirely alter the country's history.

The night before, Ne Win and his wife had attended a performance of a musical troupe that was visiting Burma from China. During the performance, Ne Win was said to have got into an argument with a group of youths behind him, who had put their feet on his chair.[9] But he clearly had other things on his mind than the antics of a few unruly kids. After the show ended, Ne Win conducted his coup.

U Nu was one of the first to be arrested at his home in the middle of the night, held incommunicado in Rangoon's north,[10] and over the next few hours about forty others were arrested in the capital, including senior ministers, the chief justice and kings from the Shan and Kayah minorities. The only immediate death in the coup was that of Sao Mye Thaik, who was killed trying to protect his father, one of the Shan kings, Sao Shwe Thaik.

Within days, Ne Win had disbanded parliament, torn up the federal constitution from independence and made himself minister for defence, finance and revenue. He also promoted himself to president of the republic, and later chairman of the newly formed Revolutionary Council, a move that gave him all executive, legislative and judicial powers.[11]

This was the start of Ne Win's 'Burmese Way to Socialism', a hybrid of Marxism, Buddhism and xenophobia that isolated Burma from the rest of the world. Immediately, English-language lessons at the British Council were halted, and renowned institutions such as the Ford and Asia foundations were ordered to leave. Western-style dancing, horse racing and beauty contests were all banned, while the Boy Scouts and Automobile Association of Burma were nationalized.

Despite the overwhelming challenges Burma had faced in the early years after independence, it had at least been a democracy, holding elections and adopting a common law legal system that, despite its flaws, was largely able to dispense justice.

That changed after Ne Win's coup, and the dictator immediately went about abolishing the Supreme and High courts, which he viewed as 'a possible obstacle or even a threat to [the military's] grip' on power. The military now exercised complete control, and under a new 'Chief Court' system 'there was no possibility or opportunity to challenge the validity of the Army's usurpation of power'.[12]

Decades of cruel and relentless rule were only just beginning, and the new military government's version of justice was put immediately on display. Many senior officials in the previous government, including U Nu, spent the next several years in 'protective custody' without trial, while Sao Kyaw Seng, the *Sawbwa (Chief)* of Hsipaw, Shan State, was detained at an army checkpoint in his home state and never heard from again.

Months after the coup, in the July, Ne Win's troops entered the campus of Rangoon University to put down an anti-military protest, killing about 100 students. The next day, to demonstrate the ruthless tactics the military was now willing to resort to, soldiers blew up the historic Rangoon University Students' Union Building, for years a crucial rallying point.

U Thant incident

Twelve years later, in 1974, the same year Ne Win introduced a new Constitution, demonstrations returned to the Rangoon University campus, and those who took part were once again subjected to the military's brutal version of justice.

The protests exploded in the December regarding the final resting place of the Burmese diplomat U Thant, who had died in New York a month earlier. U Thant had been a crucial figure in the politics of newly independent Burma, and after a stint in the UN in New York, in 1961 he was unanimously appointed its secretary general after his predecessor, Swede

Dag Hammarskjold, died in a plane crash in Northern Rhodesia (now Zambia). U Thant was the first non-European to be granted the illustrious role.

Serving two five-year terms that began in November 1961, it was an action-packed decade for U Thant. His most important role came at the height of the Cuban Missile Crisis in 1962, as mediator between US president John F. Kennedy and Soviet premier Nikita Khrushchev, an intervention that went a considerable way to preventing nuclear war.

U Thant stood down in December 1971 and three years later died of lung cancer at his New York home. After his body was laid in state at the UN headquarters, it was flown to Rangoon, with a funeral due to take place in early December.

U Thant, by now a globally recognized figure, had significant support back home but was not so popular among the military regime, in particular Ne Win.

'I don't think anyone had a good idea of what lay ahead', the historian, and U Thant's grandson, Thant Myint-U, wrote in his book *The River of Lost Footsteps*. 'At the root of it was General Ne Win's smouldering hatred of U Thant.'

Ne Win's animosity appeared to come from a speech U Nu had made at the UN's New York headquarters in 1969, which launched an attack on the Rangoon regime and called for an overthrow of the government (U Thant was on a mission in Africa at the time).

'Never before had a call for the overthrow of a UN member state government been made from inside the UN', Thant Myint-U wrote. 'My grandfather later phoned U Nu and told him his action had been inappropriate; U Nu apologised for his indiscretion.'

In his biography of Ne Win, British historian Robert H. Taylor argued that the general's anger towards U Thant would have subsided in the intervening years, but whatever Ne Win's mindset was as the former diplomat's body arrived in the capital, the next few days would bring fresh turmoil to the country and would further showcase the brutal means the dictator was willing to resort to maintain his hold on power.

After arriving at Mingalardon Air Field – today the site of the plush, modern Yangon International Airport – U Thant's body was transported a few miles across town to the old race track at Kyaikkasan. Previously known as the Rangoon Turf Club, before Ne Win banned horse racing as part of his efforts to isolate the country, it had been one of the most high-profile tracks across Southeast Asia and was where the city's wealthiest would often spend their weekends.

Among that clientele was Ne Win himself, who is said to have met his second wife there. Not long before his 1962 coup, Ne Win's antics at the race course led observers to dismiss rumours that he had serious political ambitions. He was described as: 'Good looking, debonair, rather lazy and fond of a good time, he gives the impression of not liking serious business.'[13]

But Ne Win had changed significantly in the decade or so since, and he remained adamant that U Thant would not be granted a state funeral. After the body was kept at the racecourse for several days, it was decided that a small ceremony would be allowed at a nearby cemetery.

The service itself went to plan, but as the body was being transported through the city, student protestors surrounded the car carrying it, carting it away to his old campus at Rangoon University, where they believed he should have been laid to rest.

The students insisted that a mausoleum for U Thant be established at the site of the old Student Union inside the university compound, the building Ne Win had ordered blown up twelve years earlier.

A compromise was eventually reached. The government refused a state funeral but said U Thant could be laid to rest in a mausoleum at the foot of the Shwedagon Pagoda, the country's holiest site, and next to the grave of Burma's last queen, Supayalat.

Although most protestors, as well as U Thant's family, agreed to the compromise, some elements of the demonstrators refused to allow the body to leave the campus.

Shortly after, a heavy-handed crackdown began inside the university compound. Although it has never been confirmed, there are reports that several students were killed trying to protect the body, with many more arrested. The army eventually established some semblance of peace, and U Thant's body was transferred to the mausoleum near the Shwedagon Pagoda, where it remains today.

Anger continued for a few more days, however, and before the military took back control, 9 people were killed, 74 injured and 1,800 arrested, according to the government. A real figure for the number killed has never been confirmed, but there were rumours of more than 1,000 dead with many being buried in an unmarked grave in northern Yangon.[14]

One of the lesser-known heroes of the country's democratic struggles was killed for his role in these protests, and his plight was a further example of how the rule of law had completely eroded under Ne Win's watch.

Salai Tin Maung Oo, from the country's Chin minority, went underground after playing a prominent role in the U Thant protests but was arrested when he re-emerged two years later for celebrations around the birthday of renowned writer Thakin Kodaw Hmaing, who had died a decade earlier. Not long after his arrest, Tin Maung Oo was hanged in secret at Yangon's Insein prison.

More than forty years later, I was researching a story about life inside Insein when I interviewed an elderly man who had been a guard at the infamous jail at the time of Tin Maung Oo's hanging and remembered the day vividly.

'At about 4 am, soldiers came to his cell and began beating him', he told me. 'They gagged him and eventually dragged him to the room where he was hanged. At first, I was proud to work as a government official, but afterwards I felt ashamed.'[15]

Despite his grisly death, Tin Maung Oo was defiant to the end. Authorities had offered to spare his life if he agreed to abandon his political activism and declare that his protests were wrong, but he refused. His final words are etched in the memory of many pro-democracy activists in the country today.

'You can kill my body but you can never kill my beliefs and what I stood for', he said. 'I will never kneel down to your military boots.'

8-8-88 Uprising

By the late 1980s, Ne Win had ruled the country for more than twenty-five years and no doubt believed that he would be able to stay in power for another few years, before passing on the mantle to another army figure who could ensure the military's control for decades ahead.

But a seismic shift occurred in 1988, in protests that swept across the country, and although they fell short of toppling the military junta, they entirely altered the country's direction and laid the groundwork for a pro-democracy movement that would emerge twenty years later.

By late 1987, public anger towards Ne Win's rule was bubbling under the surface. Not only had the army ruled with alarming brutality, and impunity, since taking power, but it had also dragged a once thriving economy into the mud. That anger would spill onto the streets in the middle of 1988, a movement that was triggered by a government announcement a few months earlier.

In September 1987, Maung Win Htoo was a student at the Rangoon Institute of Technology in the city's northern outskirts.[16] On 5 September, a Saturday, he walked the short distance from his halls of residence to a nearby restaurant for lunch. Shortly after arriving, an announcement from the government's Burma Broadcasting Service came over the restaurant's radio. It said that all 25-, 35- and 75-kyat notes were to be demonetized, effective immediately. No reason was given.

'I couldn't believe what I was hearing', said Maung Win Htoo. 'When I arrived at the restaurant, I had three 35-kyat notes, then suddenly I had nothing. I didn't eat my lunch that day.'

It was the second demonetization the military had authorized in less than two years and left an already poor population destitute. Students in particular were affected, as their savings for tuition fees were immediately wiped out. The official explanation for the move was that it would bankrupt black market currency traders, but a more plausible theory was that it was enacted by the ultra-superstitious Ne Win, a theory that was strengthened weeks later, when two new bank notes were introduced to replace those now deemed worthless. The new notes were for 45 and 90 kyats, both divisible by nine – Ne Win's lucky number.

On the night of the demonetization, Maung Win Htoo and some fellow students held a small protest in the city, but it attracted little attention, and although things remained quiet for the next few months, anger was growing.

Around this time, Shein Win was a sixteen-year-old high school student living in downtown Rangoon with his family.

'Growing up, my whole life I saw injustices in our country', said Shein Win, who would come to be heavily involved in the 1988 protests. 'Our country was desperately poor, and I saw people being arrested all the time just for selling things on the street. All my life I had a feeling that something wasn't right.'[17]

The demonetization of September 1987 bankrupted Shein Win's entire family.

'We weren't wealthy, but we had some money saved away, and then suddenly that was worthless', he said.

The situation grew even more perilous in December 1987 when Burma was classified as a Least Developed Country by the United Nations.

'That was a national shame', said Shein Win. 'We had once been one of the wealthiest countries in Asia, now look where we were. Of course, what happened happened.'

As well as the demonetizations, a major factor in *what happened* – namely nationwide protests, thousands of deaths and arrests and the seedlings of a nationwide pro-democracy movement – was a fight that broke out at a tea shop in Rangoon's northerly Insein Township on 12 March 1988 between a group of students and some drunk local residents.[18]

Shortly after the incident, the students called the police, who acted swiftly and arrested the culprits, and when the students returned to their campus digs that night, the matter appeared to have been dealt with.

But early the next morning, word spread around the campus that the accused had been released, and that – even worse – the main instigator in starting the fight was the son of a senior figure in Ne Win's despised government.

Anger erupted immediately. For years, the country's military had acted with complete impunity, and as the country's population sank deeper into poverty under the military's mismanagement, senior figures in the junta were growing ever richer, as a result of the country's bountiful natural resources. The immediate release of the son of one of these figures, therefore, was viewed by the students as yet another insult to the long-suffering people.

Crowds quickly gathered, first at the local government office, then at an intersection close to the teashop where the fight had broken out. Between 200 and 300 students marched to the junction but were met by forces from the dreaded *Lon Htein*, or riot police. It wasn't long before the enforcers began firing into the crowd and at least one student, a 23-year-old named Maung Phone Maw, was killed. Dozens more were injured.

The students' anger festered over the next few days, and several small-scale protests were held, mainly around the leafy campus of Rangoon University on Pyay Road, just south of the city's Inya Lake. On 16 March, after marching around the campus for several hours, the students collectively made a decision to march north, towards the Rangoon Institute of Technology campus where Maung Phone Maw had been killed.

'There were thousands of people there that day, going back as far as you could see. Everybody was cheering and singing songs', said Maung Win Htoo, who joined the march as it made its way alongside Inya Lake.

The procession continued northwards, but when it reached the upper shore of the lake, it was halted by a line of soldiers, who were stood behind barbed wire fencing pointing their guns at the students.

'We began singing the national anthem, and then people sat down', Maung Win Htoo recalled. 'Some people were holding up their books and pens to the soldiers, to show that their protest was peaceful.'

After about thirty minutes, Maung Win Htoo said he looked down the hill towards the back of the huge crowd when he saw something that startled him.

'There were riot police trucks racing up Pyay Road. Then the police jumped out and began beating those at the back of the crowd', he said.

This led to widespread panic, causing the students to flee in fear. Hemmed in by the soldiers at the front and the onslaught of police at the back, Maung Win Htoo joined those who ran west, scaling the walls of what was then a residential compound to safety.

Those who fled in the other direction, up the bank to Inya Lake, were less fortunate. They were chased by the riot police and beaten with batons as they went, with many jumping into the lake out of desperation. It is believed that dozens of people were killed that day, and some of the women were raped. There are reports of soldiers drowning students in the lake.

Today, the incident is ingrained in the memory of those who lived through those years of military junta rule. The area where the march was halted was at a bus stop known then as the White Bridge, and there was so much blood on the ground after the crackdown that it is now remembered as the 'Red Bridge incident'.

Until that point, it had only been students involved the anti-government protests, but word of the military's brutality quickly spread, inspiring members of the general public to join the movement.

Within months, the protests had reached all corners of the country. Authorities had closed universities as part of an attempt to quell the dissent, but momentum kept building. After decades of oppression, anger was finally spilling over onto the streets.

The bulk of the fury was aimed at Ne Win as well as one of his deputies, Sein Lwin. Regarded by most as an uneducated bully, Sein Lwin had become a prominent member of the Myanmar army. He received particular prestige after his unit located and killed the Karen rebel leader Saw Ba U Gyi in 1950, a major blow to the Karen movement. Sein Lwin is reported to have kept Saw Ba U Gyi's gun as a souvenir.[19]

Sein Lwin had developed a reputation as a brutish man and was despised by much of the general public. He headed the brutal army crackdown that led to the destruction of the Yangon Students Union building in 1962, as well as the 1988 Red Bridge crackdown, and is remembered today by the grim moniker, the 'Butcher of Rangoon'.

By July, anti-government protests were breaking out on an almost daily basis, and the anger had built to such a point that there were fears that even the smallest incident could spark a large-scale riot.

It was amid this tense atmosphere that Ne Win called an extraordinary meeting for his BSPP in Rangoon on 23 July, announced his resignation from the party, and promised an election. But it wasn't to be as straightforward as some had hoped. Towards the end of his speech, Ne Win made a thinly veiled threat towards protestors.

'In continuing to maintain control, I want the entire nation, the people, to know that if in the future there are mob disturbances, if the army shoots, it hits – there is no firing into the air to scare', he said.[20]

A few days later, it became clear that there was unlikely to be any real change at all. Ne Win was 'permitted to resign' as chairman of the BSPP but not as a party member. Three days after his speech, on 26 July, came the worst news of all, when the party's committee announced that Ne Win's replacement was to be Sein Lwin, the brutish butcher. As veteran journalist Bertil Lintner wrote in *Outrage*, his book about the 1988 protests, 'at the time of his appointment, Sein Lwin was probably the most hated man in Burma'.

While all of this was happening, a young British journalist caught a plane from London to Rangoon to cover the developing story, immediately finding himself caught up in the midst of it.

At the time, Chris Gunness was a reporter covering Asia for the BBC World Service from its London headquarters and in mid-1988 said 'strange noises began to emerge from Burma'.

'From the vantage point of a young reporter . . . these developments had all the makings of a cracking good story', he told me.[21]

Gunness had been following the story closely from London, and when the BSPP announced its extraordinary meeting in late July, his editor told him to catch a flight to Rangoon and pose as a backpacker to keep an eye on developments.

'People were angry, and they were terrified', he said of his most vivid memories of stepping off the plane at Rangoon's airport. 'I also remember a pervasive military intelligence. They were humourless and fearless, and they knew they were completely beyond the law.'

After landing, Gunness checked into The Strand Hotel ('a rat-ridden hellhole in those days') and kept a close watch on developments. After Ne Win's speech announcing his retirement, Gunness said he remembered taking a taxi through Rangoon, and that the city was 'confused and shell-shocked'.

Despite Ne Win's resignation, public anger continued, with Gunness playing a prominent role in the protests that swept the country about a week later.

After Ne Win's announcement, Gunness's editor in London told him to break cover and begin reporting on the record. Immediately, his dispatches were broadcast on the BBC World Service, most notably the Burmese-language version, one of the only outlets an information-starved population could use to gain any real insight into what was happening.

'Social media didn't exist, and the BBC Burmese Service was the Twitter of the revolution, and I was the person writing the Tweets', he said. 'There was the BBC morning edition, and the BBC evening edition, and you could see the country come to a stop twice a day to listen.'

A few days later, Gunness returned to his hotel room to find a note instructing him to be at the city's Sule Pagoda early the next morning, from where he was taken to a student safe house.

After conducting his interviews in English, Gunness then did the same in the local language through a translator, the recordings of which he planned to pass on to his colleagues on the Burmese-language desk.

'For the Burmese service you always wanted to broadcast in original voices', he told me. Not understanding Burmese, Gunness didn't know that the interviewee had snuck a message into the broadcast. He said: 'The revolution will begin at eight minutes past eight, on the eighth of the eighth, 1988.'

Shortly after, Gunness learned that the interview had been organized by Nay Min, a 45-year-old human rights lawyer who had been informed that the BBC journalist was staying at The Strand. Nay Min also arranged for Gunness to speak with an economist about the dire financial situation in the country, as well as a member of the Tatmadaw, who admitted that the army had committed human rights abuses.

'[The soldier] talked about abuses in ethnic minority areas, and specifically how they were using children to walk in front of them [as human shields]', Gunness said. 'For Burmese people to hear the voice of a soldier admitting this, I think they found it deeply shocking.'

With military officials closing in, Gunness was told to leave the country and continued reporting on the situation from neighbouring Bangladesh but kept in close contact with Nay Min and other sources on the ground. A few days after he left, on 6 August, his interview with the student, announcing the time and date of the revolution, was broadcast on the BBC Burmese Service.

As Gunness later said: 'It was a broadcast that sealed the fate of a nation.'

On 8 August, the meeting point in Rangoon was to be at Sule Pagoda, in the heart of the city. Marches were organized across the country, but by far the largest were held in the then capital, where at 8 am precisely, tens of thousands started marching towards the gleaming, golden shrine in downtown.

Maung Win Htoo remembered being stood on top of a bus close to the downtown area and seeing people filling the streets.

'There was no space anywhere, just thousands and thousands of people', he said.

Momentum had continued in recent months, and the students were joined by people from all walks of life, including government workers and Buddhist monks. The protests attracted people from different ethnic groups too, including Indians and Chinese. It was the biggest anti-government protest the country had ever seen.

By midday, thousands had gathered at Sule, chanting and singing songs. The mood was festive throughout the day as protestors belted out the national anthem, the army song and chants calling for the firing of Sein Lwin and an end to totalitarian rule.

The celebratory mood prevailed until late into the night, when thousands were still gathered around Sule. The soldiers monitoring the protests had largely sat idle all day, but that changed around midnight, when trucks full of troops charged out from behind City Hall – the grand structure next to Sule Pagoda – and began firing shots into the crowd. It's not known how many people were killed in that particular incident, but estimates put it in the hundreds. The killings continued into the early hours of the following morning.

The military's ruthless tactics then came into full force, and the crackdowns increased in intensity over the next few days. Despite this, the protests continued.

On 12 August the short but gruesome reign of Sein Lwin came to an end – he had been in power a total of sixteen days. Shortly after his resignation it was announced that his replacement would be Ne Win's biographer, Maung Maung, the first non-military figure to be the country's president for more than twenty-five years.

Maung Maung has written several books about his country, one of the best-known of which, *The 1988 Uprising in Burma*, was published eleven years after the protests. Largely taking the government's stance on what happened that year, Maung Maung put much of the blame of the crisis on overzealous foreign reporters.

Of the March crackdowns, notably the Red Bridge incident, Maung Maung admitted that some soldiers had been 'rough' with the protestors.

In June, he wrote, the military changed its approach and dealt with the crowds 'without arms'. This, Maung Maung said, led to some of them being beaten and burned to death (this was true, and there are several reports of civilians killing soldiers or suspected government informants – public executions, mainly beheadings, of suspected government agents were an almost daily occurrence at the height of the protests).

Although Maung Maung acknowledged that some of those protesting were sincere, he blamed most of the violence on dishonest looters looking to take advantage of the situation. However, he also wrote that 'less objective and more emotional' reporters had misrepresented what happened.

He claimed that 1988 had been a dull year for international media – perhaps ignoring the build up to that year's US election that saw George H. W. Bush come to power or the Olympic Games in Seoul, South Korea – and 'events in Myanmar drew their full attention'.

Of foreign journalists, he wrote: 'Their sources of information were not reliable, which was not entirely their fault for journalists had not been made welcome and they would often come in under the guise of tourists on a one-week visa. They therefore relied on hearsay and local informers who had their own motives.'

Maung Maung said that the government had made its own mistakes by not making itself available to the international media in order to tell its own version of events.

'In any case, journalists are generally anti-establishment', he continued. 'What was unfolding in Myanmar excited them and made them feel like crusaders, a feeling that nourished them and made their adrenaline flow.'

However dismissive Maung Maung was of the protests, their momentum continued.

Since the demonstrations had started in the March, many of those protesting through the streets had held aloft a framed black-and-white portrait of a young man wearing a military-style hat and a large, thick coat. The image was of Bogyoke Aung San, the country's independence hero who was gunned down months before he could see his dream of a free country fulfilled.

Into mid-August, the anti-government demonstrations had remained leaderless, made up mainly of a passionate but ragtag group of students. That would soon change. Towards the end of August, a young lady held a speech in front of a relatively small crowd on the roof of Rangoon General Hospital; it was Aung San Suu Kyi, Aung San's daughter.

Aung San Suu Kyi was born in June 1945 in Rangoon and was just a few years old when her father was assassinated. She left Burma as a fifteen-year-old in 1960 when her mother, Khin Kyi, was appointed Burma's ambassador to India.

Aung San Suu Kyi went onto study at St Hugh's College, Oxford, and after a stint working at the United Nations in New York met and married British academic Michael Aris, and the couple had two sons.

In the 1980s, Aung San Suu Kyi lived with her young family in the UK, but she returned alone to Burma in 1988 to care for her ailing mother, around the time that the momentum of the protests was building.

She was largely unknown to most people in the country at this point, but those who saw her speak at the hospital grounds in late August were impressed, both with her engaging speaking style and the similarities with her father, who remains an adored figure in the country today. Word quickly spread around the hospital grounds that Aung San Suu Kyi would speak again in a few days' time, at the country's holiest site, the Shwedagon Pagoda.

On 26 August, tens of thousands of people gathered at the western gate of the Shwedagon. Photos of the day show a densely packed crowd filling the entire area that leads to what was then the country's parliament at the bottom of the hill on which the pagoda sits.

Win Htoo was there that day. As an undercover photographer, he had witnessed many of the earlier demonstrations in the country, including the U Thant funeral protest fourteen years earlier, but said he had never felt such excitement as he had on that morning.[22]

'I got there as early as I could, but even by that time you couldn't get anywhere near the front', he told me. 'The crowd stretched all the way back to the parliament building. I have never felt anything like it. It was electric.'

Despite the support, there were those in the crowd who remained wary of this newcomer, and in her speech Aung San Suu Kyi spoke openly of some of the criticisms that had been levied against her – that she had spent most of her life abroad and was married to a foreigner.

'It is true that I have lived abroad. It is also true that I am married to a foreigner', she said, of Aris. 'These facts have never interfered and will never interfere with or lessen my love and devotion for my country by any measure or degree.'

She also challenged those who said she knew nothing of Burmese politics.

'The trouble is that I know too much', she said. 'My family knows best how complicated and tricky Burmese politics can be, and how much my father had to suffer on this account. He expended much mental and physical effort in the cause of Burma's politics without personal gain.'

Those present were impressed and by the end of the speech, the movement that had begun with anger at the army's heavy-handedness, and evolved into calls for an end to military rule and for multiparty democracy to be reintroduced, now had a new leader.

The protests continued into late August and early September. The demonstrators continued their calls for the military regime to stand down, but the army held firm, refusing to give into the demands.

End of the uprising

Then, on 18 September – almost a year to the day since the whole saga had started with the demonetization – an announcement came over the government radio.

'In order to bring a timely halt to the deteriorating conditions on all sides over the country, and in the interests of the people, the defence forces have assumed all power in the state with effect from today', a voice said.

A coup had taken place. Maung Maung was stood down, replaced by Saw Maung, who had previously been the armed forces commander. For the next few years, Saw Maung would oversee a new military apparatus called the State Law and Order Restoration Council (SLORC).

Into late September and early October, further brutal measures from the military brought any lingering protests to a halt, and many of those suspected of having been involved in the protests were arrested. The uprising was over.

Despite the brutal way in which the protests were ended, SLORC officials insisted that the promised election would go ahead, allowing the Burmese people to vote for what sort of political future they wanted. Almost a week after the coup, the NLD was formed, headed by Aung San Suu Kyi, while senior members included former military chief Tin Oo, and Aung Gyi, a prominent politician in the early days of independence.

The number of people killed in Burma throughout 1988 has never been fully revealed, but estimates put it somewhere between 3,000 and 10,000, with thousands more fleeing the country. Some travelled west, into India, but most went to the jungles on the Thai-Myanmar border to plan a second uprising against the government that failed to materialize. Across the country, thousands more were carted off to jails, usually without trials. Those who were granted hearings describe them as shambolic.

Shein Win spent most of the next two decades in prison and laughed when I asked him about his trial.

'Trial? What trial? I suppose you could call it a kangaroo court, but there wasn't really a trial that anyone took seriously', he said.

After taking part in the 1988 protests, Shein Win chose not to flee to the jungles but instead stayed in Rangoon in the hope that the situation might change. Living in the heart of the city, he said the then capital was a ghost town in the months after the September coup.

'People were scared to go outside', he told me in a bustling teashop in the centre of the city almost thirty years later. 'If an army truck went by, they would shoot people in the streets. I saw a pregnant lady walking along the street shot dead. For no reason.'

Shein Win was eventually arrested and, like many who had played a prominent role in the protests, faced torture on a regular basis while inside prison.

'I was beaten by hand, with a stick', he said. 'They beat you a lot, but it didn't matter if you told them the truth. They just heard what they wanted to hear, and if they didn't like what you told them, they carried on beating you.'

The arrests continued into 1989, but those members of the NLD who were still free went on campaigning nationwide ahead of the planned election a year later. They were all aware of the risks they faced, according to Ma Thanegi, a prominent writer who at the time was an assistant to Aung San Suu Kyi.

'Many of the boys and girls had cheerfully gone through the Buddhist rite of blessing the dead, the *Tharangon* ritually normally performed over a corpse, although they were alive at the time', she wrote in her book *Nor Iron Bars a Cage*. 'They said they wanted to make sure they departed this life with all necessary rituals completed, if this should happen in a hurry. Most of them became monks or nuns for a few days ensuring, they half joked, that at least they would have that merit to take with them to the next life.'

Ma Thanegi was with Aung San Suu Kyi when the NLD leader was arrested for the first time, on 20 July 1989, at her home on Rangoon's Inya Lake.

'Ma Suu [Aung San Suu Kyi] and I decided we couldn't be arrested without wearing a dash of French perfume, and she ran upstairs to put on some, while I used a small bottle that I had in my bag. Then both of us, in a cloud of scent, walked out to the gate', she wrote.

Ma Thanegi was carted off to Insein Prison, but Aung San Suu Kyi was immediately placed under house arrest, where she would remain for most of the next twenty years. She remained cut off from her family and only got to see her husband, Aris, once more in 1995, before his death from cancer four years later.

To the surprise of many, the promised election did go ahead, on 27 May 1990, with the military no doubt thinking that their actions had guaranteed them victory. They were wrong. The same fighting spirit people had shown on the streets two years earlier was on display at the ballot box, and the NLD swept to victory, winning more than three-quarters of the seats in the national assembly. But SLORC ignored the result, issuing a vague edict that it had the right to take action to prevent the nation from breaking apart. The country, which the junta had officially renamed Myanmar in 1989, would remain under military rule.

In 1992, Than Shwe became the junta leader, replacing Saw Maung who was stood down citing 'ill health' following a bout of apparently erratic behaviour – including waving a gun at his office and claiming he was a reincarnation of former kings – but little else changed for the country's citizens, apart from the fact that authoritarian rule became even harsher.

During Ne Win's rule, authorities in Myanmar regularly used colonial-era laws to punish those regarded as enemies of the state, including the Unlawful Associations Act and specific sections of the Penal Code. But the approach to quietening political rebels shifted around the turn of the twenty-first century, when cases started to be opened under almost any law.

In 2007, two men were arrested under the 1996 Television and Video Law, as well as being charged with upsetting public tranquillity, for possessing a video of the lavish wedding ceremony of Than Shwe's daughter, Thandar Shwe. The video caused great embarrassment for the military junta, as it showed the offspring of the leader of an impoverished nation wearing what appeared to be expensive jewellery and drinking large quantities of champagne. Than Shwe himself, and other senior figures in the military, can be seen in the video.[23]

In another case, a monk who publicly supported Aung San Suu Kyi was charged with 'insulting religion' for allegedly planning to self-immolate, despite there being no material evidence, while teachers were sentenced to years in prison under a series of laws for holding classes about human rights or drawing attention to the NLD leader's plight.

Those punished for such acts weren't really given trials at all but rather 'administrative processes', in which the outcome – invariably a guilty verdict – had already been decided.

Saffron Revolution and Cyclone Nargis

There were rumblings of discontent for the next few years, but Myanmar largely disappeared from international news until the middle of 2007, due to an uprising led by Myanmar's monks. It is today remembered as the Saffron Revolution, a reference to the colour of the robes worn by the country's clergy, and once again, the military's methods of handing out their version of justice were on full display.

The government had removed subsidies on fuel in the August, causing a rapid rise in transport prices and basic commodities. Over the next month, sporadic protests broke out nationwide, amid calls for the government to lower fuel costs. But it was a heavy-handed crackdown on a monk-led protest in Pakokku, a quaint, riverside town in the centre of the country, that riled up the people's anger.

As the monks walked through the town, soldiers were quickly dispersed to the scene and started firing warning shots into the air. But the determined monks continued their march, after which the soldiers' brutality began. Many monks were beaten, and at least two were tied to a lamppost and beaten with bamboo sticks and rifle butts. There were reports that at least one monk was killed.[24]

Myanmar is a deeply religious society, and the vast majority – almost 90 per cent – are Buddhist. Monks are held in particularly high regard. Each morning, local people can be seen out in the streets, offering *alms*, while visitors to the country are warned not to touch monks' robes, out of fear of causing offence.

News that the military had killed a member of the clergy, therefore, was particularly distressing.

A group representing the country's monks demanded a public apology, but none was forthcoming. In Yangon a few days later, hundreds of monks gathered at the Shwedagon Pagoda and marched peacefully through the city's streets towards Botahtaung Pagoda, on the banks of the Yangon River.

The monks' marches continued over the next few days, and before long they were joined by laypeople. As momentum built, the demands of the protestors grew increasingly political, including calls for the government to free all political prisoners, most notably Aung San Suu Kyi, who was still being held in her lakeside home. A few days into the protests, she made a brief appearance at the gate of her home, giving blessings to the protesting monks.

The crackdown began a few days later. On 26 September, the military finally made its move, first with the announcement of a dawn-to-dusk curfew and the banning of gatherings of more than five people, then a day later with a return of its brutal tactics.

The protests continued for several weeks, and although the military tried to silence international press coverage, an incident that took place in downtown Yangon on 27 September further exposed to the world the army's brutality.

Kenji Nagai was a Japanese photographer who travelled to Burma to cover the protests for the photo agency APF News. An experienced photoman, he had previously reported on sensitive stories in countries including Cambodia, Afghanistan and Iraq and was described by his friends as being a relentless journalist who worked according to the mantra of: 'Someone has to go to the places no one wants to go'.[25]

When news emerged that a Japanese photojournalist had been killed in the protests, the initial reports – no doubt fuelled by the military, who didn't want the truth to emerge – were that he had been accidentally hit by stray bullets.

However, within days a photo was splashed across international newspapers, including the front page of the *New York Times*, showing what really happened. In the photo, taken from a footbridge crossing Sule Pagoda Road, Nagai can be seen lying on the ground holding a camera above his head, apparently capturing his final moments. As terrified protestors flee in the background, a soldier stands above Nagai and callously shoots him in the chest from point-blank range. The soldier has never been identified.

By the end of the protests, at least thirty people were killed, and several hundred were arrested, including about 1,500 monks. Military tribunals sentenced the monks to terms ranging from two years to several decades. Even though all were released in amnesties several years later, many of the monks have been denied the right to rejoin the clergy, often as a direct result of their involvement in the protests. Others continue to face mental health issues from the torture they endured inside prison.

'I have dreams – it is like physical torture. They're not really beating [me] now, but it is not far away', said one of the targeted monks, Gambira, in a 2014 interview with the *Myanmar Times* of the impacts of the torture he endured in prison.[26]

The suffering of those living in and around Yangon was to get even worse just a few months after the Saffron Revolution ended, and the military's cruelty towards its own people was once again put on full display. In late April 2008, a storm began brewing in the Bay of Bengal, off Myanmar's south-western tip. As it evolved into a cyclonic storm, scientists working on weather monitoring in the region gave it a name: Nargis (meaning daffodil in Urdu).

It threatened for several days, before making landfall on the night of 2 May at a speed of 135 miles per hour. The storm ripped straight through the Irrawaddy Delta – an impoverished, low-lying area where most people's homes were little more than tin huts – before passing Yangon and then dissipating in the mountains close to the Thai border. The storm, and the humanitarian disaster that followed, led to about 140,000 people being killed and millions displaced.

The delta was particularly affected, and boats transporting aid were clogged by waterways filled with dead bodies, while confused and desperate survivors congregated in major towns, seeking shelter and food.

Several years later, I travelled to the delta area to research a story about poverty in rural Myanmar. During my visit, I met Thida, who lived in a small bamboo hut on a paddy field south of Yangon. During our interview, her young son would repeatedly interrupt, marching into the room and screaming at the top of his lungs.

'I'm sorry for this', Thida said on one occasion. 'He has never been able to recover from what he saw during Nargis.'[27]

I never got to the bottom of exactly what the young boy saw, but it must have been horrific. As well as a storm surge, the cyclone was so strong that it ripped trees from its roots and threw entire houses several miles across the delta. There are accounts of sheets of corrugated iron severing limbs and tearing away people's skin, while others were crushed by fallen trees or flying planks of wood.

Remarkably (or perhaps not), the military junta did almost nothing to help and in some cases made the situation worse. As word of the devastating scale of the disaster spread outside the country's borders, foreign governments came forward with offers of assistance but were constantly rebuffed. Next door in Thailand, the US government had loaded a plane with relief supplies but was denied permission to land at Yangon Airport. The UN's World Food Programme had planes packed with supplies ready from Bangladesh, Thailand and the Middle East, and although they were permitted to land, they were immediately forced to take off again without unloading their contents.[28]

Foreign relief workers were denied permission to travel outside of Yangon. Luckily, Myanmar had – and still has – a vibrant civil society made up of those who want to help their countryfolk in times of need. As a result, Yangon residents, and others who had travelled from across the country, made regular visits to the delta, handing out supplies, and providing accounts of the realities on the ground, which were invariably bleak. Then UN secretary general Ban Ki-moon attempted to establish meetings with the country's leader, Than Shwe, but insiders within the UN said the general simply refused to return his calls (around this time, according to a US diplomatic cable, Than Shwe was considering an offer to buy Manchester United Football Club for US$1 billion but eventually decided that the purchase could 'look bad'[29]).

The military's lack of concern for its people was on full display. It took the government a week to acknowledge that any disaster had taken place at all and more than two weeks for Than Shwe to visit the affected area. When a senior military official was asked what should be done with the bodies, he replied that there was no need to do anything. 'The fish can eat them', he said.[30]

When the scale of the disaster became better known, authorities did eventually allow international agencies to enter the affected area and begin distributing aid, but the military's inability to coordinate an effective relief effort led to thousands of preventable deaths.

Despite the tragedy and chaos wrought by the cyclone, a week after it hit, the junta went ahead with a referendum for a new constitution it had written and which ensured the military would play a prominent role in the country's politics for years to come.

On 10 May – eight days after Nargis wreaked havoc on almost the entire lower half of the country – the military government conducted its referendum, which it said was approved by 92 per cent of the population. Voting in areas directly affected by the cyclone was delayed by two weeks, but by that point the result had already been decided.

The vote was, of course, a sham, with one research paper saying that the junta 'affirmatively and systematically violated the basic rights of Burmese citizens before and during' the referendum, including through threats, coercion, misinformation, deception and violence to ensure that people voted through the new charter.[31]

In the build up to the referendum, the military's ruling party only allowed media coverage that was biased in favour of the constitution, including a state-run television campaign that said that 'public approval of the draft constitution is the responsibility of every citizen'. Meanwhile, a campaign led by the NLD to encourage people to reject the document was 'systematically disrupted'. Dozens of people who campaigned against the charter were arrested.

The constitution may have been part of the junta's 'roadmap to democracy', but it is not even remotely close to being democratic and was instead written by the military in order to protect their own interests, while loosening some level of control.

The charter was part of a seven-step road map that also included the hosting of a National Convention, which after many delays finally took place in 2004, as well as the holding of 'free and fair elections'. A general election did go ahead in 2010, the country's first since 1990, although it wasn't remotely close to being free or fair and was won by the military's proxy, the USDP, after the NLD boycotted the vote citing 'unjust' electoral laws.

Reforms begin

The next few years would see a period of rare optimism in Myanmar, with the quasi-civilian government led by Thein Sein that replaced Than Shwe in 2011 initiating a series of reforms, including a drastic liberalization of the economy, the loosening of political freedoms and an emergence of independent media for the first time in decades.

As a reward for these changes, the United States, and other countries, lifted economic sanctions against Myanmar, and during a speech as part of a visit to the country, then president Barack Obama expressed confidence 'that something is happening in this country that cannot be reversed'.[32]

Yet amid this hopefulness, away from the public eye, the Tatmadaw's dark arts were continuing, with government critics and journalists still facing threats, harassment and death. Arrests increased in the build up to the 2015 election, and this period also witnessed a dark episode that demonstrated that the Tatmadaw's go-to method of violence and cover-ups were not a thing of the past.

In late 2014, Aung Kyaw Naing, an experienced journalist better known as Par Gyi, travelled from Yangon to Mon State to cover fighting that had recently broken out between the Tatmadaw and a small armed group known as the Democratic Karen Benevolent Army (DKBA) near the Thai border.

Par Gyi was a burly man by Myanmar standards, more than six-foot tall with a mat of thick black hair. He'd started out as an activist, joining the 1988 protests, before turning his hand to reporting. His main beat was the various conflicts in the country's borderlands, particularly in the south-east.

'If you were working on the Karen issue, he was the person you went to for contacts, because he was very strong in this area, and also very helpful', a friend of Par Gyi's told me, referring to decades-long battle between the Tatmadaw and the Karen National Union (KNU).

Par Gyi embedded with the DKBA troops to document fighting at a village close to Kyaimaraw, a small town on the banks of the Ataran River in Mon State.

After covering the fighting for a few days, he was planning to cross the nearby border into Thailand and travel to the northern town of Chiang Mai to attend a ceremony at his daughter's university.

But he never made it. On the morning of 30 September, he was arrested by local police, before being taken into military custody. The chief of police in the area later said: 'It was not that we formally handed him over to the military, they just took him.'[33]

Par Gyi's wife, Thandar, a well-known democracy activist, immediately hosted a press conference in Yangon, demanding that authorities either release her husband or transfer him to police custody. International pressure also increased on authorities to reveal his whereabouts.

Almost a month after he disappeared, the military released a statement saying that Par Gyi had been killed in military custody four days after his arrest when he 'tried to seize a gun from a guard and run away'.[34] The statement also falsely claimed that Par Gyi was a member of the DKBA, implying that he was participating in the fighting and not covering it as a journalist. The statement offered no explanation as to why his death had been covered up for several weeks.

A few days after the statement was published, a fax was sent to Thandar saying her husband's body would be exhumed from a field close to Kyaikmaraw in a few days' time, and she immediately made the day-long trip to Mon State with a group of friends and supporters.

Once there, military officers appeared to toy with Thandar. They told her that her husband's body was in a field about an hour's walk away, but that in order to reach it they would have to walk through an area filled with landmines.

After more than an hour, the entourage reached the field and, in the presence of more than 100 soldiers and police, as well as the media, Par Gyi's body was unearthed.

'[His head] was completely smashed. I could not recognise the body. Although I could immediately tell by the height that it resembled my husband', she said in a documentary by local outlet *DVB*.

After the body was revealed, there were then concerns about how it would be taken back to town, through the minefield. It was then, however, that Thandar realized that the march to find the body had been a devious scare tactic. Soldiers said the body would be taken back by car – the grave site had been accessible by road all along.

'I asked the police chief why they had made us walk through the minefield if we could have driven there. He said he was just following the army detail. I was furious', Thandar said.

Par Gyi's body was eventually taken back to Mawlamyine, the Mon State capital, where an autopsy took place. It revealed that Par Gyi had been shot five times – twice in the leg, twice in the back, and once through his head from under the chin. Months later, the Tatmadaw revealed that two soldiers involved in his killing were acquitted by a military court, and the case was closed. Par Gyi was laid to rest in Yangon.

2015 election

Despite incidents such as these, as the 2015 election approached, a general feeling of optimism could be felt, with all indications pointing to a resounding NLD victory.

I covered the election from Mandalay and on the morning of the vote awoke early and set out to explore. There was excitement in the air, and queues had started forming outside polling stations before sunrise. The first line I came across was outside a school, and the voters were roughly an even split of men and women, ranging from twenty-year-olds to octogenarians. Everyone I spoke to was voting for the first time.

Some were decked out in their finest traditional dress, while others had simply rolled out of bed in their pyjamas. All were wearing a beaming smile and proudly clutching a small piece of paper – the registration that would allow them to vote.

I asked one lady how she was feeling.

'I'm so excited, so happy', she said. 'I never thought the day would come that I would be able to vote.'

I asked her who she was planning to vote for – technically illegal this close to a polling station, but no one seemed to mind.

'NLD of course', she said, and her friends gave a quick thumbs up before a small cheer broke out in the queue.

At 6 am exactly, the gates to the polling stations opened and people began shuffling inside. I crossed the street and sat on a pavement outside a shop, waiting for the first voter to emerge.

It was a young man, who smiled and gleefully raised the little finger of his left hand into the air, which was marked with purple ink – proof he had voted (I had attempted to coin it the 'purple pinkie' but it never caught on). He told me he had voted for 'Mother Suu', a nickname for Aung San Suu Kyi, and merrily made his way home.

After conducting my unofficial exit poll – 100 per cent NLD after thirty minutes – I roamed the city to soak up the atmosphere a little more. By mid-morning, everyone I had spoken to said they had voted for the NLD, and after exchanging messages with a few journalist friends stationed elsewhere in the country, it was clear that the party was on course for a resounding victory.

Despite the excitement, there was still trepidation in the air about a potential coup.

There were also questions about what sort of government the NLD would form. Take Aung San Suu Kyi for example. It was clear that she possessed an incredibly strong will, and although this had served her well during the years of house arrest, there were questions about how this would translate to being the leader of a country that had so many challenges to overcome. And what of the NLD members, most of whom had zero political experience? How effective could they be in leading the country through what was inevitably going to be an extremely challenging period?

But that was all for later, and one thing that was clear to me was that a government chosen by its people was considerably better than an authoritarian regime that had held the country back for several decades.

By midday Mandalay's streets had fallen silent. The polling stations were empty, and those responsible for manning them sat around staring into the distance waiting, like the rest of us, for the moment when the vote counting could begin.

During the break in electoral proceedings, my translator and I travelled to a Muslim-majority area in Mandalay's eastern outskirts. In mid-2014, the city had seen its own ugly outbreak of violence after reports were circulated on social media that two Muslim brothers had raped a Buddhist woman. The claims were later found to be fabricated and related to a business dispute, and those who made the accusations were given lengthy jail terms, but not before two people, a Buddhist and a Muslim, had been killed, and mosques and other buildings in the city burned.

We travelled to the neighbourhood that had witnessed the worst of the violence, where many of the scars remained, including burn marks down the pillar of a mosque that was closed off behind an iron fence.

At a small teashop next to the mosque, three Muslim met were sat at a table sipping tea. The men eyed us suspiciously as we entered, and our questions about the election were met with short, gruff answers.

It was only after my translator mentioned the 2014 violence that the men started to open up. One member of the group – a man wearing a plaid shirt who appeared to be in his early thirties – remained silent throughout, but the two other men, both older, wearing *kufis* and sporting distinctive long beards, grew animated as they explained what they had seen.

'The people who came here in the violence, walking the streets, were not from around here', said one of the men, Thihan.[35] This fit with testimonies by people in other communities in areas affected by religious violence in Myanmar, that people from elsewhere had been bussed in, sometimes quite literally, in order to whip up tensions.

'We were terrified, of course. We thought they were going to burn down our homes', Thihan said.

Amid the 2014 outbreak, the police had eventually arrived and quelled the worst of the violence, but the mental scars clearly remained; the men spoke passionately about the fear they felt for themselves and their families at the time.

Thihan and his friend began to speak more broadly about the political climate and their experiences of being Muslim in Myanmar.

Both men felt that the religious tensions the country had witnessed in recent years had been deliberately driven by the military government in order to distract people from other issues the country was facing, including continued widespread poverty.

'This government has done nothing for us Muslim people', said Thihan, referring to the USDP. 'We still do not have freedom of religion. After our mosques were burned, we were not able to rebuild them', he said, tilting his head towards the still-closed mosque next door.

Both men had been to the polling station that morning with their families and had voted for the NLD. Everyone they knew had done the same. They both had questions about the party, particularly given the fact it had not fielded any Muslim candidates due to pressure from nationalist groups, but they felt certain that a change from military rule was necessary.

'We don't know what the NLD will do if they win, but things can't be as bad as they were before', said Thihan.

After an early afternoon rest, as the sun began to descend over the royal city, my translator and I travelled to the NLD's Mandalay headquarters, to wait for the results from across the region to start trickling in. Out in front of the party office, a few dozen NLD diehards were already set up in front of a large screen.

Inside the office, a flimsy teak structure, serious-looking NLD members and volunteers were frantically speaking on the phone with party pollsters located around the region and scribbling down their findings.

I asked one of the workers, an elderly bespectacled man, how things were looking.

'I can't say for sure right now, but pretty good', he said, a wry smile creeping onto his face.

As darkness fell, the crowd in front of the screen swelled to a few hundred NLD supporters, all who were in a jubilant mood. The first results began to appear, showing resounding victories for the party.

The crowd continued to grow and the results kept rolling in – almost unanimously an NLD victory – and each announcement was met with a cheer and another rendition of the catchy, if slightly irritating, party song. The screen showed a sea of red, with just a few patches of green where the USDP had won a handful of seats in the south of Mandalay Region.

The celebrations continued well past midnight, with revellers singing the party song and continuing their 'Dee-mocracy' chants. It was clear that the NLD had won resoundingly nationwide and would be forming the next government (albeit with some input from the military, who ensured their own role through the 2008 constitution). Shortly after midnight I returned to my hotel room, exhausted but delighted to have witnessed such a historic moment.

Transitional justice

The following morning, Aung San Suu Kyi sat down for an interview with the BBC's Fergal Keane in the leafy garden of her Yangon home. In a wide-ranging discussion, Aung San Suu Kyi spoke about the election results, her plans for the future and concerns about rising nationalism in the country.

Towards the end of the interview, Keane asked Aung San Suu Kyi if she would seek justice for the countless atrocities committed during the years of junta rule.

Her response was clear.

'We're not going in for vengeance, and we're not going in for a series of Nurembergs', she said, a reference to the trials of Nazi criminals at the end of the Second World War, in which a dozen of the party's members were sentenced to death.

She stayed true to her word. Throughout the NLD's term, and before her arrest in the February 2021 coup, Aung San Suu Kyi stuck to her promise of not pursuing any legal action for the crimes committed under military junta rule. In some ways this could be understood as necessary to keep the army on side, but nor did she acknowledge that any of the countless incidents chronicled in this chapter – and there are dozens more that haven't been included – took place at all.

Her party's timidity on the issue angered many, especially those who suffered abuse, or lost loved ones, during the years of junta rule.

Between the 1962 coup and 2011, Myanmar had about 10,000 prisoners of conscience, advocacy groups estimate, while thousands more spent years hiding from authorities because of their role in anti-government activities. While all were released when the reforms began, many struggled to return to everyday life, especially those who were tortured while in custody.

Among them is Shein Win, who was eventually released in a mass amnesty after the 2010 election but struggled to adapt to life outside prison. He immediately buried himself in a photography project, documenting those whose family members had died while in custody, or jail, as political prisoners.

'I had friends who died in prison, so it was important for me to document these families and make sure people know how much they suffered', he told me.

He had no shortage of material – before the coup more than 200 political prisoners had died inside Myanmar's jails, either during imprisonment or interrogation.[36]

I had been told of Shein Win's project by a mutual friend and met him at a meeting room in northern Yangon. As the rain thundered on the room's roof, Shein Win explained his project and began flicking through images on his laptop of the families he had documented.

'There's a lot here. Take your pick of who you want to speak to', he said, grimly.

A few days later, we were in downtown Yangon visiting the family of Maung Min, a former NLD member who had died almost fifteen years before while serving time at a prison in central Myanmar (I've changed his name, as well as Shein Win's, and some details about them both, to protect them and their families from potential repercussions).

Maung Min had been arrested in the late 1990s for holding a meeting with NLD members in Yangon, and sentenced to several years in prison, accused of 'undermining security'.

We met the family at their Yangon home. Maung Min's sister, who I'll call Phyu Thein, greeted us at the door and invited us inside. Entering the house into a room filled with NLD logos and a black-and-white photo of Maung Min, we passed a bed, on which an old lady was lying silently, facing the wall.

We sat down near a window overlooking a large development project. As we waited for Phyu Thein to pour some tea, occasional groans came from the old lady lying on the bed.

'That's my mother; she hasn't moved since my brother died', Phyu Thein told us. She had been there for fifteen years.

The town in which Maung Min was being held is located almost 1,000 kilometres north of Yangon, and the family would visit him once a month.

'As you can see, we are not a very well-to-do family, so it was very difficult for us to go and see him', Phyu Thein said.

The trip would involve a train journey from Yangon to Mandalay, which took anywhere between sixteen and twenty-four hours, followed by a bus journey of many more hours to the prison. The family would spend one day in the town, visiting the prison to see Maung Min, before returning to then capital the following day.

Later, the family was given financial assistance by an international organization, allowing them to fly from Yangon to the prison and back. But the long distance made it difficult for the family to keep track of developments, for which they were reliant on a friend living close to the prison, who was well connected in the town.

It was through that friend that the family found out about Maung Min's death.

Phyu Thein said that her brother had been nursing a fever for about three weeks, but that prison authorities had refused to take him to the hospital until the very last moment. Once there, he collapsed and died after trying to stand up to walk to the toilet, the family was told. Media reports at the time speculated that Maung Min may have died from malaria, due to the high prevalence of the disease in the area, but no autopsy was ever conducted. He was forty-five years old.

The family travelled to the town where the prison was located immediately after hearing about Maung Min's death.

'When we arrived, the authorities isolated us and took us straight to [our hotel]. We were constantly watched by the military intelligence', she said.

Despite attempts by authorities to curb the number of people present at the funeral, Phyu Thein said that the next day the town's streets were filled with hundreds of people dressed in black, paying their respects to Maung Min.

'Even though the military intelligence tried to stop people from attending, the funeral had so many people marching behind the procession', she said, smiling.

At the end of our interview, I asked Phyu Thein if I could speak with her mother, who was in her eighties. Phyu Thein disappeared for a few minutes to speak to the old lady before returning.

'I'm sorry', she told me. 'It's still too difficult for her to speak about him.'

I returned to the house a few months later while in downtown Yangon researching another story. At the door, I asked Phyu Thein how her mother was doing.

'She died last month. She never had justice for what happened to my brother', she said.

Covering this story, examining what transitional justice might look like in the Myanmar context during the reform years, there were many other interviews conducted that were equally as upsetting.

There was the brother of a young man, who was told by a military intelligence officer after his sibling died in solitary confinement in 1999: 'When one dies, they die. Don't complain.'

Or the family of a man who disappeared from a Yangon restaurant in 2005. After filing a missing person's report, the family heard nothing for a week, until a soldier turned up on their doorstep to tell them their loved one had died in police custody 'while resisting arrest' (the same reason given to Par Gyi's family). Or the bereaved family of another political prisoner, who on his death bed at Yangon General Hospital told his family: 'Don't cry. If you do, it means I have surrendered to the government. You must always live with your thumbs up.'

There were a variety of emotions in the people I interviewed, from those who struggled to open up about their experiences to those who easily talked at length for several hours about their deceased relatives.

But one constant in all the people I met was a desire to see justice, or at least some form of recognition, for what happened.

'These military men can't just continue as if nothing happened. There's still so much pain in this country', said one of the relatives, who asked not to be named. This conversation took place before the coup.

But justice for these crimes never happened during the reform years and appears impossible in the current context. Afterall, it was members of the military who stand accused of conducting some of the most heinous crimes during the earlier junta years, and they've rarely shown the desire to prosecute their own.

It was even something the military wrote into its transition process, with Clause 445 of the 2008 Constitution ruling that no legal proceedings could be initiated against members of the pre-2011 military government 'in respect of any act done in the execution of their respective duties'. The clause was essentially an amnesty for past crimes.

The NLD is not entirely blameless in this, however, and after taking office Aung San Suu Kyi in particular never expressed any desire to pursue justice.

In a speech in August 2017, she said that the 'victims of the past, those who can't shatter the shackles of the past' had 'caused a lot of hindrances' in Myanmar's transition.

'The past is only about learning lessons. The most important thing for us is the present', she said.[37]

What lessons were they, if people's losses could not even be recognized? Her comments were unusual, particularly given the oppression that she, and those close to her, had and continue to suffer at the hands of the military. Added to that, many of the same abuses she asked people to ignore continued in the country under her leadership, especially in border areas.

Her argument was that the country needed to look forward in the name of 'national reconciliation', particularly as she navigated a tricky relationship with the military during the reform years. Yet, thousands suffered horrendous abuses under the first iteration of military rule. Those who lost loved ones as political prisoners are at the extreme end of the scale, but countless others were arrested, had their land stolen or witnessed violence against friends or family.

Myanmar has thousands, perhaps millions, of people who have never received justice, or even recognition, for what they went through. Having no outlet for seeking justice, or even speaking openly about these experiences, doesn't bode well for any country that hopes to move towards a prosperous, more equal future.

The human psyche is a fragile thing, and these experiences are not easy to recover from, no matter how small. Anyone who has experienced what they perceive to be an injustice knows how strongly the feeling of resentment can linger.

The February 2021 coup in Myanmar was one built heavily upon the Tatmadaw's culture of impunity. Since the 1960s, and perhaps before, almost none of its soldiers have faced any form of accountability for their actions, and those who have are typically tried in secretive military-run courts, where few details are provided to the public.

For example, when seven Tatmadaw members were tried for the massacre of ten Rohingya men in northern Rakhine State in early September 2017, their trial was shrouded in secrecy, and it later transpired that the soldiers had spent less time in prison than the two *Reuters* journalists, Wa Lone and Kyaw Soe Oo, who exposed the gruesome murders.

When the BBC journalist Chris Gunness travelled to Burma at the height of the 1988 crisis, speaking to me more than thirty years later, he said his standout memory was the military personnel dotted around Rangoon that 'knew they were completely above the law'. This mindset hasn't changed. Weeks after the February 2021 coup, when authorities began their brutal crackdown on protestors, gunning down dozens of unarmed people in the streets, Tatmadaw soldiers took to the popular video application TikTok to boast about killing demonstrators.[38]

'In 1988, we had to load the gun once . . . but today's gun can shoot 30 bullets at once', said one soldier in a video.

This is not something that happens in an institution whose members know they could eventually be held to account for their actions.

This is evident in the crimes Myanmar military soldiers have committed before and after the coup. Since February 2021, junta forces have shown a 'flagrant disregard for human life', according to a report submitted to the UN Human Rights Council more than a year after the coup.[39] Their actions have included shooting peaceful protestors in the head, burning people alive in the streets, bombarding populated areas with airstrikes and heavy weapons, torturing prisoners to death and using them as human shields. Sexual crimes have also been committed by security forces, including rape. Detainees have been also suspended from the ceiling without food or water and electrocuted.

Although the wheels of international justice are slow to turn, and often require painstaking patience, some steps are being made in the right direction when it comes to accountability for the Tatmadaw's actions, particularly regarding its 2016 and 2017 campaign of violence against the Rohingya, which in early 2022 the United States officially declared a genocide.

In 2019, the Gambia filed a case at the International Court of Justice (ICJ) in The Hague, alleging that Myanmar's atrocities against the Rohingya violated the Genocide Convention, which Myanmar has been a party to since 1956. In 2019, the International Criminal Court (ICC), also in The Hague but which is separate to the ICJ, authorized its prosecutor to open an investigation into certain crimes against humanity, notably the forced deportation of more than 740,000 Rohingya to Bangladesh in 2017. While Bangladesh is an ICC member state, Myanmar is not, and this case can only look at alleged crimes committed in Bangladesh. A full investigation into crimes committed on Myanmar soil could only occur through a referral to the ICC by the UN Security Council, which has so far failed to do as part of its dismal response to the Myanmar coup. The vetoes held by Security Council permanent members China and Russia have contributed to this inaction, but nor has any other member put forward a resolution, arguing it would automatically be vetoed. But as one activist said to me: 'Let China and Russia veto it, and let them argue why they are defending this murderous regime.'

In addition to these cases, Rohingya and Latin American human rights organizations have filed a criminal complaint in Argentina requesting an investigation of Myanmar's military leaders for crimes committed in Rakhine State. That case has been brought under the principle of universal jurisdiction, which says that some crimes are so serious that all states have a responsibility to address them. Argentina was chosen in part because of its efforts to confront its own dark past, of exacting accountability for the thousands disappeared during its own era of junta rule in the 1970s and 1980s.

Some encouraging steps have also been made in this area by the NUG, the shadow government in Myanmar formed largely by MPs-elect from the November 2020 election.

Six months after the coup, the NUG announced it had lodged a declaration with the ICC 'accepting the court's jurisdiction with respect to international crimes' committed in Myanmar since 2002.[40] The statement also expressed solidarity with the Rohingya, in sharp contrast to the policies of the NLD, which vilified the group, peddling the narrative they were illegal interlopers from Bangladesh, while refusing to join the ICC or respect its ruling. While the NUG's announcement was encouraging, should it ever come fully to power, this policy and others it has announced deserve considerable scrutiny to ensure they are fully implemented, and not mere lip service paid to the international community for its support in the efforts to remove the military regime.

These campaigns for justice are all important steps on the path towards accountability for the many wrongs the Tatmadaw has committed over the decades. These crimes have seen countless numbers killed, displaced, tortured and terrorized, and yet the military has never faced any real consequences. The military is certainly not going to investigate itself from within. If international actors really want to help end the current bloodshed, dread and hopelessness in Myanmar, and assist the people's efforts to remove the military from power, then lending support for international justice is one of the most important steps they can take.

The US Rohingya genocide declaration was a welcome step on that road, but the United States and its democratic allies need to go much deeper than a mere announcement. It should turn this historic announcement into action and formalize an international concerted campaign for accountability for the Tatmadaw's actions, historic and current. This can come in the form of increased financial and legal assistance to the cases mentioned earlier, recommending the UN Security Council to adopt a resolution referring the situation in Myanmar to the ICC, as well as exploring the possibility of pursuing more cases under the principle of universal jurisdiction, including in Southeast Asia – the generals shouldn't be allowed to even make a shopping trip to Bangkok or Singapore.

Short of a concerted international campaign to exact accountability, the Tatmadaw will only continue acting as it has for the past several decades, terrorizing and killing the people with absolute impunity.

This violence is the most obvious example of the measures the Tatmadaw has taken to oppress and silence the people, but there have been other, more subtle steps taken too to try and mould a population that is subservient to it.

One of those is its control of the education system.

Teaching control

In June 2021, a few months after the coup, images were widely shared on Myanmar social media showing Tatmadaw troops patrolling a school.

In the photos, a group of soldiers, decked out in full military gear including fatigues and an assortment of accessories attached to their hip, are inside a classroom. As young children, who look to be less than ten years old, are sat at their desks, their study books open in front of them, a soldier can be seen handing his gun to a child, encouraging him to hold it.

They were troubling images, and also came amid reports that since the coup the military had occupied dozens of schools and university campuses, while more than 100 schools had been 'attacked and damaged by explosives', including Improvised Explosive Devices (IEDs) and hand grenades.[1]

'Armed soldiers have no place in schools or other learning spaces', said Save the Children, in the sort of comment you'd think really shouldn't need saying out loud.

Even before the coup, more than twelve million children had already lost more than a year of education as a result of school closures caused by Covid-19, Save the Children said, two million of which were already out of school before the pandemic.

As disturbing as the developments were, they also provided a stark level of symbolism about the Tatmadaw and its legacy on education in Myanmar. After a period of relative optimism in the country's education sector during the reform years, developments since the coup indicate a return to the practices of the dark days of previous iterations of junta rule, with the regime attempting to use the system to create generations of subservient subjects.

In large part due to the policies introduced by Ne Win and his successors, Myanmar's education system has a bleak reputation compared to its regional neighbours, with issues including poorly trained and underpaid teachers, outdated facilities and resources and a by-rote learning system that discourages free and critical thinking.

Widespread neglect of Myanmar's education system by successive military governments has led to high drop-out rates, creating a knock-on effect of fewer job prospects for future generations, while outdated teaching methods – as well as mindsets from teachers, administrators and even parents – meant that those who completed their studies often did so without the necessary skills required in the working world.

It's worth noting that, in part due to the poor state of government-run schools in Myanmar, as well as the deeply pro-Bamar bias in its practices and the curriculum, many ethnic armed organizations operating in the country's border areas have established their own parallel education structures. These systems, which have been developed by groups including the Kachin Independence Army, Karen National Union and the New Mon State Party, typically teach classes in a student's native tongue, and have curriculums that focus on their own histories, rather than the pro-Bamar narrative taught in central government schools.

During the reform years, as Myanmar recovered from decades of military-enforced isolationism, the nation-building project required a new generation of young people trained to a high standard in subjects as diverse as medicine, engineering, English and economics. The system in Myanmar, however, did little except develop millions of students who – through no fault of their own – only ever learned by repeating back what has been said to them.

'It's not the sort of system that prepares students for a life outside the school or university compound', said a foreign education specialist who spent years working on initiatives to develop Myanmar's education system.

Before the coup, things were rapidly changing in this area. Major education reforms were initiated under Thein Sein's quasi-civilian government, and continued under the NLD administration. A plan was underway to overhaul the system from top to bottom, but those efforts have drastically halted since the coup.

It's commonly claimed that around the time of independence, Burma had one of the strongest education systems in Southeast Asia, boasting high literacy rates as well as internationally recognized universities, with things rapidly deteriorating after Ne Win's power grab, when the dictator nationalized schools to further his chauvinistic agenda and implemented policies that led to a drastic drop in standards.

While the military, and particularly Ne Win, deserve their fair share of blame for the current state of Myanmar's education system, it doesn't tell the entire story. In 1948, the British left behind a hugely unequal education system that rewarded those who had contributed to the empire effort – effectively, the country's 'elite' – but created negligible opportunities for almost the entire rest of the country. It was an apparatus that Ne Win was more than happy to adapt to suit his own needs.

History of education in Myanmar

Education has a long and proud history in Myanmar. Around the eleventh century monastic schools were introduced by King Anawrahta, founder of the Bagan Empire, after he embraced Theravada Buddhism. They emphasized learning and reciting religious Pali scriptures that prepared students to become monks.

Funded through voluntary donations, monastic schools were free to attend, and as a result often acted as the great leveller in Burmese society, catering to the sons of farmers, as well as royalty (Burma's final king, Thibaw, attended a monastic school in Mandalay).

'To begin a school in Burma is the easiest thing in the world', wrote John Ebenezer Marks, a Christian missionary teacher in Burma in the second half of the nineteenth century. 'The Burmese have a natural love of being taught. It has come to them through many generations.'[2]

Marks spent much of his time in Burma in Mandalay, becoming a trusted aide of King Mindon, Thibaw's father, and the penultimate leader in the Konbaung Dynasty before his death in 1878. The pair formed a close relationship, with Marks describing the king as a 'good Burmese scholar, a gentleman with much of king dignity', as well as a 'pleasant, low and musical voice'.

However, Marks was critical of Mindon for having 'narrow ideas' of his kingdom, particularly the fact that he viewed himself 'to be at least an equal of the most powerful monarch in the world', seemingly a reference to Queen Victoria.

Mindon may not have ruled half of the planet, but he was certainly more hands-on than the British empress. While Victoria spent her later years in self-isolation, grieving the loss of her beloved husband Albert, Mindon's entire reign saw drastic reforms made in his realm. Major changes introduced under his watch included an overhaul of the tax and financial systems, the introduction of a royal mint, and a telegraph system linking Upper Burma with the outside world.[3]

Mindon also viewed education as crucial to modernizing his country, introducing subjects such as science and English to the curriculum, and sending missions to Europe and the United States to learn about the advances made as part of the Industrial Revolution.

When the British annexed the country in 1885, one of their many priorities was to overhaul the education system to suit their own needs in this new colonial project. They had initially planned to achieve this gradually, by introducing secular subjects to the network of monastic schools, but the idea failed when it became clear that the monks running them had no interest in changing their curriculum.

Instead, the British established a three-tier structure. At the top were the English-language schools, established typically in commercial centres, and serving the children of Europeans living in the country. These schools, which aimed to produce the next generation of colonial leaders, had support from Christian missionaries, and received considerable funding from the colonial government. The next tier down were schools aimed at the children of Burma's 'elite', offering classes in Burmese and English, and acting as a feeder for lesser 'native' jobs in the colonial order. At the bottom were the Myanmar language schools for the masses, which 'lingered under dismal conditions'.[4]

This tiered structure, particularly of Burmese schools, inevitably led to divisions in society. One well-known taunt from Myanmar students who attended the higher-quality schools said that students of English schools were superior, while those attending monastic schools were 'mere beggars'.

The education system the British introduced assisted them in their colonial project, allowing them to supply staff for an administration that would capitalize on Burma's rich natural resources and fill the already heavy coffers of the empire. Burma saw huge economic growth during British rule, particularly after the opening of the Suez Canal, mainly through the export of rice from the lush Irrawaddy Delta, oil production from Upper Burma as well as other deposits including teak, rice and rubies.

These riches, however, largely stayed in the hands of the British, barely trickling down to local people.

John Furnivall, a British civil servant in Burma at the start of the twentieth century, later wrote that this division created a plural society 'comprising numerous groups living side by side, but separately and meeting only in the market place'.[5]

In this plural society, dominated by what he called 'economic forces', Furnivall wrote that the Burmese had few prospects of capitalizing on the opportunities presented by their country's economic growth.

'Because industry, commerce and the scientific professions offered no opportunity for Burmans, the doors leading to the modern world were barred against them', he said.

These 'economic forces' were even felt in the schools of colonial Burma, with local students discouraged from taking courses such as economics and science, which were 'two main pillars of all that is distinctively modern in the modern world'.

'Thus, although foreign rule brought Burma into economic contact with a larger world, Burmans were halted at the threshold, and could not learn to live in it', Furnivall wrote, adding that the options for Burmese were also narrowed by the fact that the British had actively encouraged the migration of Indian labourers to help boost the economy.

This inequality in the education system became an important component of the anti-colonialist movement that emerged in Burma at the beginning of the twentieth century. In fact, one of the first major protests against British rule occurred in November 1920, when students from Rangoon University demonstrated against a new University Act, which critics said aimed to limit the access local students could have to higher education. Those protests, commemorated today as Myanmar's National Day, are regarded as a major turning point in the anti-colonialist movement.

An argument is often made that when Burma achieved independence in 1948, the education system left behind by the British was one of the region's best. Yet this isn't entirely accurate. It's certainly true that the higher education system created by the British was one of the finest in Southeast Asia, and Rangoon University in particular had a strong international reputation. But this prestige didn't necessarily filter down into the overall school system, particularly in rural parts of the country that had been neglected by the colonial rulers. Much like today, Burma's rural poor were ignored by the central government, and many families sent their children to work instead of school, out of economic necessity.

Post-independence

After independence, any plans to overhaul the education system were thwarted by the many issues the young country was facing, most notably the series of civil wars that ignited almost immediately. As a result, the school system in the early years of independent Burma closely resembled the structure under colonial rule, with wealthier Burmese families sending their children to Christian missionary and private institutions, and government schools regarded as inferior.

Burma's education system witnessed major changes following Ne Win's 1962 coup. His Revolutionary Council came from a place of deep xenophobia, aiming to prevent Burmese people from being exposed to outside thinking. Influences from capitalist Western countries were particularly targeted, with internationally renowned institutions ordered to leave.

Most international books, magazines and journals were also banned, and those permitted were heavily scrutinized to ensure they were 'free from foreign domination'.[6] Libraries that had been established by diplomatic missions of other countries were ordered closed, while any international news that the population was exposed to became controlled by the newly established News Agency Burma.

Ne Win's new government attempted to entirely alter the mindset of Burmese people, justifying such a drastic measure by claiming the country had been 'dominated by the feudalists for over a thousand years, by the foreign imperialists for over a hundred years and was also dominated by the landlords and capitalists after it had attained independence'.[7]

Education, naturally, was crucial to changing this way of thinking. The Revolutionary Council viewed the existing system as laying 'under the shadow of the foreign system which it had copied', with the primary purpose of producing officers and clerks for administrative purposes. To the Council's credit, they weren't exactly wrong, although the changes they implemented did little to improve the system that was already in place.

After 1962, all public and private schools were nationalized, and the government enacted the Law on the Registration of Private Schools, which had the explicit aim of altering 'thinking in the country, to prevent the domination of foreign habits, customs, ways of thought, opinions and culture', which had apparently infiltrated the Burmese psyche.[8] Buddhist monastic schools were also eventually forced to close.

An insight into the government's thinking at the time comes from Dr Nyi Nyi, who was deputy-minister for education under Ne Win. He justified the need for Burmese as the language of instruction in schools by saying that local people had been 'slaves' during colonial rule, contributing to a 'slave mentality'.

'We tend to think highly of foreign language, foreign literature and foreign culture, while we looked down upon our own products and our own culture', he said. 'This has led to the development of inferiority complex, and that is a major damage to our nationals.'[9]

Under the new system, Burmese replaced English as the language of instruction, while no foreigners were permitted to hold positions as teachers or school administrators. A new curriculum was also established in line with the new socialist ideology of the Revolutionary Council, and students were required to pay daily homage to the 'Five Gratitudes' – Buddha, Dhamma (Truth), Sangha (Buddhist clergy), parents and teachers. This would drill into students the belief that no authoritative figure is to be challenged.

As well as socialist ideals, the Revolutionary Council also pushed a fiercely nationalistic narrative that billed the Bamar as the key group in building the nation state of Burma. The new curriculum, introduced under the 1966 Basic Education Law, played into this revisionist version of history, downplaying the roles of the kingdoms of groups including the Mon, Shan, Rakhine in building the Myanmar nation state, and glorifying those of groups such as the Pyus – regarded as the earliest inhabitants of Burma – as well as 'great' Burmese kings such as Anawrahta, Bayinnaung and Alaungpaya. This was an added insult to many ethnic minorities, whose own cultures had been supressed, and often destroyed, by many of these monarchs as they went about building their own empires.

As well as major alterations to the curriculum, Ne Win also rewarded those who were loyal to him with top positions in the education ministry. As a result, career educators who had ideas about improving standards were out, and sycophantic yes men were in.

Than Oo, a career educator who advised Ne Win on educational affairs, said that the dictator's lack of knowledge on the subject became a running joke among intellectuals. He said that when the renowned poet Min Thu Wun expressed a desire to create a Burmese dictionary, Ne Win dismissed the idea, comparing it to 'a loaf of bread that had not been baked properly'.

'This upset [Min Thu Wun], who confided in me', Than Oo said many years later. 'I told him not to get discouraged by the words of Ne Win, who knew nothing, and to only suffer if an intellect like Saya Zawgyi [another renowned writer] criticised him.'[10]

A lecturer of English at Rangoon University during the 1970s and 1980s, who asked not to be named, told me that it was impossible to escape the influence of the military if you were teaching at universities across the country.

'There were so many restrictions during Ne Win's rule. Education was so strictly controlled, and we had to follow whatever rules the military told us', she said. 'You could be fired if you didn't join pro-military groups on campus, or if you in any way questioned the military's authority. It was very difficult, but there were so few jobs available, and despite the troubles, I enjoyed it', said the lecturer, who fled into exile during the 1988 pro-democracy demonstrations.[11]

Aung Min Soe was a student in eastern Myanmar at this time, graduating from high school in 1981.

'Ne Win heavily controlled the education system, and because of him we only learned through memorization, while critical thinking and analytical skills were unheard of', he told me.[12]

'We just had to memorize all of our subjects, and were taught nothing about critical thinking', he said. 'So, people passed their matriculation exams, or even their university exams, but actually knew nothing about the subject they were learning. They [the military] systematically destroyed our education system, which produced a mass of people who don't know what actual education looks like.'

An example of Ne Win's mismanagement of education affairs came in the early 1980s when he suddenly changed the language of instruction for subjects including mathematics and science from Burmese to English. A prominent theory persists that the decision was made after his favourite daughter, Sandar Win, failed to be admitted to a medical school in the UK because of her poor English skills. Although never confirmed, this would go a long way to explaining such a drastic measure taken by a renowned xenophobe like Ne Win.

The anonymous Rangoon University lecturer said that around this time resources for English teaching at universities drastically improved.

'Suddenly everything got better. We had more money for books, and we had professors coming in from abroad, including the UK. It was like night and day', she said.

Textbooks and exams in certain subjects were immediately changed from Burmese to English. If the move was aimed at improving Myanmar's education system, however, it had the opposite effect, as neither teachers nor students had the English proficiency to teach or study classes, particularly the more technical subjects, in their non-native tongue. With Myanmar's exam system rewarding rote learning, teachers would therefore prepare students for their exams in these subjects by composing the material into songs or poems, resulting in the students never actually learning anything they could use in the real world.

'The change of the language of instruction from Burmese to English remains a major problem', said a foreign teacher who worked in Myanmar for several years.[13] 'Because of the low level of English, students cram and memorize what they need to learn in English in order to pass their exams. There's no space for innovative and meaningful teaching, and this is a major problem as the whole point of universities is to prepare students for the outside world.'

In essence, Burma's education system under Ne Win became a political tool that allowed him to push his socialist agenda, while aiming to prevent students from learning to think for themselves or challenge authority, and to automatically reproduce any information that was presented to them. Over the next few decades of junta rule, the military would attempt to craft a pliable population that it hoped would not challenge its authority.

It wasn't always this way, however.

Yangon, or Rangoon, University has long been regarded as the most prestigious institute in the country, with alumni including independence hero Aung San, former UN secretary general U Thant, Ne Win and a host of other renowned politicians, writers and academics. As an example of its respected regional status at the time, in 1958, just as war was breaking out in his homeland, Vietnamese revolutionary Ho Chi Minh visited Burma, where he was granted an honorary doctorate in law by Rangoon University.[14]

The institution was established by the British in 1878 as Rangoon College, affiliated to the University of Calcutta, the then capital of British

India. Around the turn of the twentieth century, its name was changed to Government College, then later University College. In 1920, it merged with the Baptist-affiliated Judson College to become Rangoon University, then Yangon University in 1989 when the city's official name also changed.

1988 crackdown

As well as its impressive roll-call, Yangon University is also renowned for playing a prominent role in the major protests that have swept the country in the past century, including the 1920 demonstrations against the University Act, those against Ne Win's coup in 1962, as well as the on-campus chaos regarding the body of U Thant in 1974.

But by far its most important contribution came in 1988, when the university's leafy Inya Road campus became a key rallying point in the early days of that year's anti-government protests that swept the country. The deadly 'Red Bridge' incident, which took place in March and is regarded as the trigger for the nationwide movement that emerged months later, occurred just outside the university's gates.

After the movement ended and the military re-gained control in September, it was the students who were targeted with some of the harshest punishments.

Authorities had long viewed the country's student population with deep suspicion, and were angered that they had lit the spark for a movement that had come so close to toppling the regime. They also wanted to thwart any potential uprising in the future.

Resigned to this inevitable crackdown, thousands of students fled to the jungles on the Thai-Myanmar border to plot a revolution against the Rangoon government that never materialized. Thousands more had been gunned down in the streets or carted off to jails around the country; many of them moved to prisons thousands of miles from their families in order to destroy their morale. Many more who had played a role in the protests remained in-country, keeping a low profile in the hope they'd be overlooked in the crackdowns that continued long after the protests ended.

By early 1989, the Rangoon University campus, which had played such a crucial role in lighting the torch-paper for an unprecedented nationwide movement a year earlier, sat empty.

Although schools re-opened in 1989, university students were not able to return to their campuses until May 1991, under the watchful eye of uniformed and plain-clothed police officers. This re-opening was short-lived, however. In the December of that year, universities nationwide were closed once more when pro-democracy protests broke out at Rangoon and Mandalay universities during the ceremony in Oslo that awarded the Nobel Peace Prize to Aung San Suu Kyi.

A *Reuters* report at the time said that between 40 and 500 people were arrested for their role in the protests, the range in figures indicating how difficult it had become for foreign journalists to report on developments inside the country.[15]

Writing in 1992, British journalist Martin Smith said that the recent upheavals to the education system had led to a deep demoralization of many students and teachers.

'Increasing drug-related problems, including heroin addiction, are being reported in student circles and many parents blame the [government] for deliberate inaction or even tacit involvement in the growing narcotics trade', he wrote.[16]

Due to the closure of universities, a huge backlog had built up of students unable to complete, or even start, their university education. The government appeared willing to sacrifice an entire generation of trained graduates – including doctors, teachers and engineers – if it meant holding onto power.

'The consequences for Burma's future development are incalculable', Smith wrote.

It wasn't only the students who were targeted, but teachers and university lecturers as well. When the universities and schools re-opened, professors were ordered to fill in forms describing their involvement in the protests, and those found, or suspected, to have taken part were dismissed, replaced by officials who could prove their loyalty to the regime.

In April 1991 a new decree was issued banning public servants, including teachers, from engaging in politics of any kind. They also had to fill out a 33-question survey on a range of topics, including their views on the NLD, the Communist Party of Burma and the CIA. Those who gave answers that displeased the authorities were sacked.[17]

The 1991 protests related to the Nobel Peace Prize ceremony also led to harsher sanctions against teachers and lecturers. With universities closed once more, they were sent away to 're-education' boot camps overseen by the military.

'Please do not think that the SLORC [government] is conducting the course in order to torture the teachers', Khin Nyunt, a senior general in the junta, was reported as telling the trainees. 'Education is more effective when it is based on patriotism and the interest of one's race and religion. No matter how educated a person is, if that person lacks patriotism, that person cannot contribute to the nation and its citizens.'

The camp consisted of a four-week course comprising three priority areas: 'promotion of patriotism', upholding 'national unity', and the 'systematic management of student affairs and the enforcement of rules and regulations'. According to some estimates, more than 7,000 teachers and hundreds of university lecturers were sacked for not adequately proving their patriotic credentials.

When the universities re-opened again in September 1992, academics found they had new roles to play, conducting surveillance duties of their students and being made responsible for the actions any members of their class took.

The continued protests into the 1990s, even after thousands had been arrested, forced to flee or killed, demonstrated to the authorities that the student movement was by no means finished. A new approach was needed to quell it. In July 1992 the government announced that a new correspondence course system, 'The University of Distance Learning', would be prioritized, the knock-on effects of which would be keenly felt in Myanmar's universities for decades.

Distance learning for higher education in Myanmar started in the 1970s, with a system based on printed materials and radio lessons, before students sat their final exam at the end of the academic year. In 1992, the government scaled up the system, ostensibly to 'make higher education accessible to all students at minimal cost'. In reality, however, the measures were aimed at preventing students from congregating on campuses and potentially organizing further protests.

At the time of the 2021 coup, about 60 per cent of the students in higher education in Myanmar learned by long distance. The concept of studying from home is of course nothing new – one of the world's best-known distance-learning institutions, the Open University in the UK, was established in the 1960s – but the way it is conducted in Myanmar is problematic. Even today, classes do not take place online, and students are instead sent books at the beginning of term, which they are expected to read throughout the year, with almost no guidance from their teachers. The only interaction they have with any authorities at all is a two-week face-to-face 'revision session' ahead of their final exam.

'A lot of people see distance education in Myanmar as a waste of time. It's as if the degree is not worth the paper it's written on,' said a university lecturer in Myanmar.[18] 'Of course this has impacts on wider society. A developing country like Myanmar needs people who can contribute to the nation's growth. You can't achieve that if people aren't actually learning anything.'

Authorities resorted to other measures to prevent students from gathering in urban centres, including by establishing university campuses in hard-to-reach areas far outside city limits. For example, Yangon's Dagon University was established in 1993, and its campus is tucked into an uninviting industrial area in far north-eastern Yangon, several miles from any sort of development in the commercial capital.

Ko Lwin studied for a distance-learning bachelors' degree in English at Dagon University between 2007 and 2010. Students were only permitted to attend the campus in-person for ten days during an academic year, plus on exam days, and Ko Lwin said the journey from his home to the campus would typically take one and a half hours' each way by bus (that may not seem like the longest commute for those living in other cities, but this was when there was almost no traffic in Yangon, because the majority of the population couldn't afford cars).

Ko Lwin disliked distance learning. At the beginning of each term, students were given books that they were expected to read before sitting for an exam.

'That's not a good way to learn. You need a teacher', he said. However, even when classes did take place, he said the teaching ability of lecturers was poor.

'I would have much preferred to have the option of learning in classes, but we weren't given that opportunity', he said.[19]

The legacy of the military's involvement in Myanmar's education affairs could not be clearer. The most prominent issues today, including packed classrooms, undervalued teachers and a system that doesn't prepare students for a future outside the classroom, can all be traced directly to Ne Win and his SLORC successors.

The attempted impact on society is clear. If it hasn't exactly indoctrinated the population into believing the Tatmadaw is needed to 'crush all enemies', a system that encourages unbridled respect for authority and has discouraged free thinking for generations has at least contributed to a reverence for authoritative figures that the military has benefitted from. It should, however, be pointed that the remarkable sacrifices made by the people since February 2021, which has upended many people's previously comfortable existence and come with monumental threats to their safety, demonstrates just how much anti-military sentiment was bubbling under the surface all along, as well as an example of how this mindset can be shifted in certain circumstances.

Respect for authority is not unique to Myanmar, of course. From a young age I was taught by my parents to listen attentively to, and heed the advice, of my elders – to learn the lessons they themselves have acquired throughout life.

The concept is a healthy one to live by, but it should have limits. Around the world, we have witnessed those in positions of power – whether in religion, politics or corporate institutions – regularly take advantage of the level of control they have over a person or group. With that in mind, it's just as crucial to constantly question why we have so much respect for a particular figure or entity.

In a country like Myanmar, where institutions such as the judiciary and police are pliant to the military, and corruption is rife, abuse of power by authorities is everywhere you look, and the Tatmadaw is one of the worst culprits.

'It's ingrained in us completely to respect authority, no matter who they are,' a Myanmar colleague once told me. 'You learn it at school, and you learn it from your parents. You hear it so often throughout life that you don't question it.'

The education system is not the only reason for this mindset in Myanmar, but it contributes heavily towards it.

When the horrendous attacks against the Rohingya by the military hit international headlines in late 2017, one of the most surprising aspects for many outside observers was how these atrocities attracted so much support from the majority of Myanmar people (although it's important to note that some people in Myanmar always stood by the Rohingya, often at great risk to themselves). Despite overwhelming evidence to the contrary, most believed the narrative pushed by the military, and supported by Aung San Suu Kyi's government, that it had committed no wrongdoing, and that the violence had been initiated by the Rohingya, the entire population of which was billed as 'terrorists'. According to the official version, and one supported by much of the population, the Rohingya burned their own homes in order to trick the world into believing their level of suffering was much worse than it actually was.

There's little doubt that an education system that glorifies 'national unity', belittles outsiders and demands unquestioned respect for those in power, has contributed to this way of thinking. As the response to the coup has displayed, however, things look to be rapidly changing on this front, a welcome development as far as I'm concerned.

Until as recently as 2019 some schools taught a jingoistic poem that urged students to 'maintain the dignity of one's own race' – a reference to the Bamar – and avoid having one's race 'swallowed' by another. The offending extract, taken from a teacher's manual, also said: 'We hate mixed blood, it will make a race extinct'.[20]

As well as non-Bamar, Myanmar's religious minorities also face issues in an education system that prioritizes Buddhist practices and beliefs. Each morning, students are expected to recite Buddhist prayers (in some schools, adherents of other religions are not forced to take part, although it depends on the teacher), while priority in the curriculum is granted to Buddhism –

a recent plan to introduce a curriculum to civic education classes covering
the fundamental values of four major religions, Buddhism, Hinduism, Islam
and Christianity, was strongly opposed by nationalists who viewed it as an
attempt at 'Islamisation' of the country.[21]

Soe Naing, a Muslim who grew up and went to school in downtown Yangon,
said he believed that the military junta had deliberately created discrimination
against non-Bamar and non-Buddhists in the country's education system.

'We [Muslims] weren't forced to pray during Buddhist prayers, but we
had to listen to them each morning, and of course we knew them by heart.
Also, the syllabus was predominately Buddhist, and in certain classes we
were taught about Buddhist values, but no other religion', he said. 'We had
to recognize Buddhist holidays, or if an army general came to our school –
we were in downtown Yangon remember – then we had to greet them with
the traditional Buddhist prayer. It didn't bother me, but some Muslims were
very sensitive about this, because they were made to worship someone [who
wasn't Mohammed]'.[22]

He added that the discrimination witnessed in Myanmar's schools can
also be seen in everyday life. For example, he said it was rare for Muslims,
or non-Buddhists, to be employed in government jobs such as the police,
military or administrative roles.

As a result, he said that non-Buddhists from his father's generation, who
attended school around the 1970s, often dropped out early, because they saw no
point in staying in a system that wouldn't reward them with a job at the end of it.

'People started their own businesses instead, and left formal education
entirely', he said. 'My father had a textiles business, and as far as I know, most
of his friends who were Muslim had their own businesses too.'

Soe Naing said things were different for his grandparent's generation, who
had attended school before Ne Win's coup, and that he had many Muslim
friends whose grandparents worked in government jobs.

'It was Ne Win who changed everything. He hated foreigners, or non-
Buddhists, and everything changed under him', he said. 'I have to be blunt
– Ne Win fucked everything up.'

Reforms begin

After 2011, however, major reforms started to be seen in Myanmar's
education system, initiated by Thein Sein's quasi-civilian government and
then continued under the NLD. An indication of the importance Aung San
Suu Kyi placed on reforming the sector came when her party took office in

March 2016, and she briefly gave herself the education portfolio – one of four – before handing it to Myo Thein Gyi, a career educator.

During his inauguration speech in 2011, Thein Sein spoke of the need for Myanmar to have 'more and more human resources of intellectuals and intelligentsia in building a modern, developed, democratic nation'.[23]

'Therefore, we will promote the nation's education standard to meet the international level and encourage human resource development', he said in a speech in Nay Pyi Taw, adding that his government would focus on providing free primary education for all, improving the standards of schools and universities, and enhancing the 'socio-economic status' of educational staff.

For anyone familiar with the rhetoric of Tatmadaw members it would be easy to dismiss these remarks as yet another empty gesture. Yet, real efforts were made to improve the education system during Thein Sein's term, resulting in a drastic increase on education expenditure, contributing to improved resources, new legislation and an increase in the number of schools, particularly in remote areas.

But there were controversies too, including indications that despite the change of government, authorities still held a deep-rooted distrust towards students.

A major change to education during Thein Sein's tenure was the passing of the 2014 Myanmar National Education Law, viewed by its supporters as a major step forward in the much-needed reform process, for example through the teaching of ethnic minority languages in schools for the first time. However, the new law had its critics too, who said it failed to protect the right to form student unions, and didn't go far enough in decentralizing decision making.

Despite this opposition, the law was enacted by parliament in September 2014, and immediately after a student-led protest movement was established against it. Several months of negotiations with the government aimed at amending the law had no impact, and in January 2015 hundreds of students began a protest march from Mandalay to Yangon. They aimed to complete the 400-mile journey in just over two weeks.

By late February, about 200 protestors had made it to Letpadan, 75 miles north of Yangon, camping out at a monastery on the southern edge of the town. After a week's rest, the final push for Yangon was supposed to begin on 2 March, but when the students attempted to leave the monastery compound that morning, they found their path blocked by barbed wire fencing and a heavy police presence.

A week-long standoff ensued, and on 10 March desperate protestors tried to break through the barricade. A brutal crackdown followed.

A photographer who was in the monastery and covering developments said that what followed was 'a complete breakdown of police discipline'.[24] Security forces, who greatly outnumbered the students, split into two groups, he said, with one exercising restraint and the other indiscriminately attacking anyone who tried to flee the violence. Police stormed through the monastery's buildings and nearby homes, dragging out protestors to arrest them, said another witness. Some of those who turned themselves in were viciously beaten by police, and dozens were arrested.

As ugly as the episode was, it didn't derail the education reform agenda, and progress continued under the NLD after it came to power in 2016. Major victories during that period include the provision of free school uniforms and textbooks to students, and an extension of the education structure from eleven to thirteen years to bring it in line with international standards. The elimination of school entrance fees also led to a drastic increase in school enrollment figures.

Government expenditure on education in 2017–18 was more than six times higher than the amount allocated in Thein Sein's first year, and this upward trend in spending looked set to continue until the coup.

However, it's one thing spending money, and another thing entirely spending it in the areas where it's needed most. The deep-rooted structural issues in Myanmar's education system meant that those tasked with leading the reform process faced difficulties in choosing where to prioritize their resources.

Successive governments took a systematic approach to the reform process, starting with the Comprehensive Education Sector Review (CESR), a survey launched in 2012 that identified three major issues with the system: access to education, quality of education and the real-world value of learning.

Next came the National Education Strategic Plan (NESP), described as a roadmap for sector-wide education reforms that aimed to 'dramatically improve access to quality education for students at all levels of the national education system'. The NESP highlighted the need for major changes in many of areas of education, including expanding access to pre-school services in remote and rural areas, improving the quality of distance learning, and overhauling the examination system away from one that rewards rote learning.

It also recommended a complete restructuring of the curriculum, towards one that focuses on '21st century skills, soft skills and higher order thinking skills'. The curriculum changes were introduced according to a year-by-year schedule, starting with kindergarten in 2015–16, Grade One in 2016–17, building to changes to the Grade 12 syllabus by 2028–29.

Many of the curriculum changes were welcomed, including the removal of content deemed offensive to minority groups – for example the poem that criticized those of 'mixed blood'. However, some subtle biases favouring certain groups remained, particularly Burmese Buddhists and men, said Rosalie Metro, an American anthropologist who has studied Myanmar's education system for the last twenty years.

'On the rare occasions where more space is devoted to ethnic minorities, stereotypes are on display', Metro told me in an interview conducted before the coup. 'For example, a story on ethnic minority people in the Morality and Civics curriculum shows them enjoying nature in a small village. Because this is one of the only portrayals of ethnic minority areas, it has the potential to reinforce stereotypes that non-Bamar live in a pre-modern world.'[25]

For future curriculum changes, Metro recommended that those involved in the process conduct interviews with a broad range of students, teachers and parents, to represent their views and experiences.

'It is my hope that future textbooks will include more substantive coverage of women as well as ethnic religious minorities', she said. 'The new curriculum does not yet reflect the identities and needs of all children who will use it, and in that regard, its potential to act as a force for social inclusion and peace is limited.'

The Bamar-centric aspect of Myanmar's education system under military rule has also led to conversations about reforms allowing ethnic minorities to be taught their own languages, and about their cultures, at school.

Some encouraging moves were made in this direction, and the 2014 National Education Law allowed regional and state governments to introduce the teaching of ethnic minority languages alongside Burmese at primary school, and expanding to higher grades.

'In the past, ethnic [minority] languages were totally neglected, and our schools and learning institutions were too heavily Burmanised', said a friend, who is a member of the Naga minority in north-western Myanmar. 'The young generation didn't know about traditional customs and practices because Naga only had them in oral form.'

However, he said that the decision to introduce Naga languages to schools in an area known as the Naga Self-Administered Zone, which hugs the border with India, was a hugely important step in helping to preserve these traditions.

'It helps us to research our folktales, culture and traditions, from our food habits to handlooms, handicrafts and festivals', he said. 'Now almost every Naga tribe is bringing their dialect into written form, which didn't happen in the past. We are also working on orthographies, grammar and dictionaries, besides textbooks.'[26]

Another crucial area of reform is to improve the quality of teacher training. The NESP recognized that one of the issues with teacher deployment and promotion in Myanmar was that it was not linked to performance, but instead years of experience. In addition, teachers were typically promoted upwards through the levels of the education system, and away from primary schools.

'This drains quality teachers from primary schools when they are needed most', the NESP said. 'Recently recruited daily wage teachers, who receive less formal training, are often sent to the most remote primary schools, meaning that these schools have the least experienced teachers.'

The increased spending on the education sector allowed the government to recruit teachers, bringing down the country's student-to-teacher ratio, although it remains one of the worst in Southeast Asia. Between the 2011–12 and 2015–16 academic years, the number of basic education and higher education teachers both increased by 20 per cent.

Despite the increased investment, even in pre-coup Myanmar life was still incredibly difficult for most teachers, especially those living in rural areas.

Myat Kyaw Thein is a secondary school teacher close to the town of Monywa, in central Myanmar.

'We have so many things to worry about as teachers, especially our safety and salary', said Myat Kyaw Thein, who told me in an interview conducted before the coup that he earned the equivalent of about US$150 per month. 'It's not enough, especially when you compare it with other countries in Southeast Asia. No wonder so many people leave teaching to go to better paying jobs.'[27]

'It's a rotten salary, but whenever we raise it with authorities, they tell us it's because of the low budget for education. Well, if you want to improve the education in this country, then increase the budget', he said.

A similar story was told by a teacher in a remote village of Myanmar's Nagaland. The teacher had worked at a school in her local village for more than ten years, and although the resources had improved in recent years, life was still difficult for her and her colleagues. She told me they often used their own money to provide things such as pens and books for their students.

'It's difficult for us because we don't have much salary, and sometimes have to use our family's [money]', she said. 'But then we want [the students] to be happy and to come to school. That's why we provide these things for them.'[28]

Even before the coup, it was clear that those tasked with overhauling Myanmar's education system had an unenviable task ahead of them, including bringing together the dozens of different stakeholders – national and foreign – involved in such a monumental task and forming a cohesive strategy that pleases everyone.

Even what some may regard as the successes of the past decade in terms of reforms to education did not please everyone. For example, a recognition by the government about the need to switch from a teacher- to a child-centred approach was a welcome step for those hoping to encourage more critical thinking, but parents who have only ever been exposed to the former their entire lives were understandably sceptical.

'When a parent passes a school and doesn't hear students chanting in unison what the teacher has written on the board, they think, "What's going on in there? They aren't learning", said an educator involved in the reforms.[29]

Since the coup, however, much of the progress made over the last decade or so in Myanmar's education sector has gone swiftly into reverse. With many teachers refusing to work under this junta, and parents not wanting to send their children to schools – either due to legitimate security concerns or because they don't want them taught under this regime – the SAC has resorted to many of the tactics of past military juntas to try and portray an image of normalcy in schools and universities.

Like in 1962 and 1988 it has closed universities and fired teachers not supportive of the coup. Thousands of teachers have been sacked, and hundreds jailed, for participating in the CDM against the junta.[30] To fill these teaching ranks, the military-controlled education ministry has encouraged applicants with lower qualifications to apply for jobs, and even been accused of dressing up army wives and female members of pro-military organizations in teachers' uniforms and transporting them to schools.[31] Like under the SLORC government, teachers have been sent on month-long 'refresher courses'[32] where they are urged to 'pay attention to the preservation of Myanmar culture and traditions' as well as 'speak and behave respectfully and to be disciplined', almost certainly euphemisms to discourage teachers from imbibing any form of revolutionary thinking into their students.

Before the coup, despite some bumps, the general trajectory of the education system in Myanmar was on a positive path. The changes were also made largely free of the military's sphere of influence, an indication of the potential Myanmar has as a whole if the Tatmadaw's own interests are not directly threatened.

Like almost everything in Myanmar, however, the 2021 coup has created considerable concerns about what happens next. If the current situation continues, and the military manages to maintain an albeit loose grip on power, it is the next generation of young people in Myanmar, and others beyond that, who will be the ones to suffer the most, through a lack of investment, or care, in their education, a lack of capabilities to think critically and problem solve, and a lack of skills to prepare them for the working world. This could well manifest, as it has in the past, of creating a general feeling among the population that Myanmar's remarkable diversity is something to be feared, not celebrated.

Life on the margins

A few months after the 2015 election in Myanmar, I flew from Yangon to Kale, a dusty town in the country's west, close to the Indian border.

Months earlier, the town had been devastated by flooding, brought about by heavier than usual monsoon rains. The entire town and surrounding area had been swamped, with thousands displaced, and residents forced to move around on makeshift boats, or climb aloft flimsy structures to escape the rising water levels.

I planned to travel to Kale to write about how the town had recovered from the flooding, but I also had, I confess, an ulterior motive. I wanted to travel to Chin State, which Kale sits on the cusp of, and which had been described to me as the most beautiful corner of Myanmar, an already exceedingly picturesque country.

Convincing my fellow editors that the flooding aftermath story needed to be covered, I flew to Kale, where I spent a few days conducting interviews around the town about the floods, before catching a bus that would take me to Falam, a small town high up in the Chin hills.

After leaving Kale's ramshackle bus station pre-dawn, the road out of town was initially smooth, and we journeyed westwards at an impressive rate. But within minutes, the flat surface gave way to a bumpy track, immediately cutting our travelling speed in half.

Kale is located in Sagaing, one of the seven regions in Myanmar, where the Bamar comprise the majority, while Chin is one of seven states, where ethnic minorities make up the largest number of people. The border between Sagaing and Chin is just a few miles west of Kale, and the drastic change in road condition happened almost exactly at this boundary.

Many ethnic minorities in Myanmar, including the Chin, will tell you that this is not a coincidence, and this drastic contrast in road condition between the regions and states is the perfect metaphor for the neglect they have been subjected to by the Bamar-majority government for decades. In Myanmar's borderlands there's a strong perception that while the country's centre has seen development in the form of roads, bridges, jobs, schools and hospitals, the groups living at the country's periphery have witnessed few changes, ignored by authorities because they are not Bamar, or Buddhist, or both.

Next to me on the bus from Kale was Jessica, an English student who was travelling back to Falam, her hometown, after completing her studies in Yangon. Kale and Falam are less than 100 kilometres apart, but the journey was expected to take anywhere between four and eight hours, such was the poor condition of the only road between the two towns.

'It's better than it used to be', said Jessica, who told me the road had recently been upgraded, and that previously the journey took about a day, with travellers often stopping overnight to sleep along the way.

Shortly before we started our ascent into the Chin hills, the bus stopped by the side of the road, and everyone onboard fell silent.

'What's happening? We haven't broken down, have we?' I said to Jessica, a little louder than I'd anticipated.

'Shhh', she said, giving me a swift dig in the ribs with her elbow. 'People are praying to God for a safe journey', she whispered.

It was a reminder that we were leaving the Buddhist-majority heartlands of Myanmar and entering Chin State, one of the few parts of the country where Christianity is the dominant religion, a result of mainly American missionaries arriving here in the nineteenth century. One of the most influential, Reverend Arthur Carson, is buried in Hakha, the state capital, and today about 90 per cent of Chin people identify as Christian, mainly Baptist. The term 'Chin' is in fact disputed, and is a blanket term for various subgroups with similar ancestry, some who refer to themselves as Zomi.

After the missionaries came the British, who invaded the Chin hills in the late nineteenth century as part of their annexation of the country. Under the 1886 Chin Hills Regulation Act, they governed the area separately from the rest of Burma, allowing traditional Chin chiefs to hold onto much of their authority.

The Chin people, like many ethnic minorities in today's Myanmar, played a crucial role in helping the Allies win the brutal Burma Campaign of the Second World War, but received little reward or recognition. After independence they were neglected by the central government, and for the last several decades this picturesque, but hard-to-reach corner of the country saw little change or development. This scenario, felt in almost all corners of the country, has led to resentment of the central government, and distrust of the Bamar majority.

Following our prayer pit-stop, our bus began its climb into the Chin hills, as Kale and the colourful plains of central Myanmar loomed below us. For the next few hours, we bobbed and bounced along the mountain path, at times perilously close to the edge before the driver jerked us back to safety.

The prayers must've worked. We passed looming valleys of jungle below us, and up above were mountains with the slightest frosting of snow, set against the backdrop of a deep-blue sky. At 3.30 pm, eight and a half hours after setting out from Kale, we arrived in Falam.

Falam was one of the most agreeable towns I'd ever visited. There wasn't much to it – some elaborately painted churches, a handful of guesthouses and restaurants and a school – but the crisp, clean air and striking mountain views, coupled with the easy way of life, made for a wholly enjoyable experience.

After checking into my guesthouse – named Holy, an indication of just how devout the Chin people are – I arranged to meet a Falam resident I'd been given the contact of back in Yangon.

Nathan, as he preferred to be called, was the editor of a local newspaper, which he published out of his tiny newsroom on the edge of town.

'Here's my state-of-the-art printing press', he said, laughing as he pointed to a battered HP printer.

Nathan was born in Falam, but spent many years working as a journalist in Yangon after media restrictions were lifted in 2012 as part of the country's widespread reforms. He returned to his home state ahead of the 2015 general election.

I met Nathan in early 2016, a few months after the election and around the time the NLD was coming into office. He was an articulate and passionate person who cared deeply about the many issues facing the Chin people, including a lack of jobs, poor education as well as alcohol and drug use. When I asked if he felt the NLD would bring improvements to people's lives in the Chin hills after decades of being ignored by successive military governments, Nathan dismissed my question with a flick of his wrist, calling the party 'a dictatorship'. I asked him where his hatred for the NLD came from.

'It's not the NLD I don't trust; it's the Burmese [Bamar]. Historically, we have been oppressed by them', he said. 'Look around, there's nothing here for the people. They have no jobs, and so many are on drugs. The government, whoever they are, don't care about us.'[1]

Unprompted, he continued.

'We call it the double C virus – Chin Christian. If you are double C, you cannot do anything in this country', he said. 'You cannot find work, you cannot get scholarships for schools, and you cannot move up in government jobs.'

Over the next few days in and around Falam, I heard many similar complaints about the lack of development in Chin State, which people blamed on the central government. One afternoon while travelling out of Falam into the interior of Chin State I was on the back of a motorbike being ridden by

Isaac, who acted as my translator. As we weaved around the mountain road, Isaac pointed up to a pylon sat on a hill overlooking Falam.

'The government tell us we will be connected to the national grid soon. But nothing yet', he said, laughing.

Certainly, the feeling among Chin people that they have long been neglected by the government is reflected in the statistics.

Before the coup, it was the poorest of Myanmar's fourteen states and regions. Data from the country's 2014 census shows that three-quarters of Chin's half a million people live below the poverty line. The second poorest state was Rakhine, where about half of the population live in poverty (although this figure didn't include the state's Rohingya population, who were not included in the census because they refused to be identified as 'Bengali').[2]

Chin State, one of the least populated states or regions, consistently ranked near the bottom in other social indicators in the census, the country's first since 1980, including rates for literacy, infant mortality and life expectancy at birth.

Ask most Chin people why they think they have so often been ignored by the government, and there is one simple explanation: their religion.

On my final evening in Falam, I joined Isaac and his friends for a few too many bottles of rice wine at a barbecue outside town. Most parts of Myanmar have their own version of rice wine, often concocted in a clay pot and mixed with an array of ingredients, but it's my view that Chin State has the best (with Kayah a close second).

As I swayed a little on my bamboo mat, and Isaac pulled out yet another bottle, I mentioned to him the 'Double C' theory that Nathan had told me about a few days earlier.

'Everyone knows about that', Isaac said. 'Look around, there's nothing here for us. No work, and nothing to do. If you want to find a job, you have to leave.'

As the local hooch continued to make its presence felt in my bloodstream, I asked Isaac why he thought that was the case.

'It's our religion, no doubt. Look up there', he said, pointing towards one of the many mountains that surround Falam.

'Do you see that pagoda?' he said.

Squinting through a drunken eye, I could just about make out the golden glint of a pagoda glowing in the dark.

'We are Christian. Everyone in Falam is Christian. Why do we need these pagodas above the town? There are two of them', he said. 'It's a message from the government. It's their way of reminding us that they're the ones in charge.'

There's more to this theory of religious persecution of the Chin people than the rantings of an otherwise placid man, and even before the coup there were countless reports of Tatmadaw soldiers, who are majority Buddhist, destroying churches in Chin State, tearing down crosses to replace them with pagodas, and forcing Chin Christians to contribute money and labour for the construction of new pagodas and monasteries.

According to local residents, in some cases monks were appointed as military intelligence operatives in parts of the state.

'The monks . . . rule the communities', a local pastor said in a 2009 report published by the Chin Human Rights Organisation. 'Anyone who doesn't abide by the monks' orders are reported to the [military] and he/she is punished by the army. The monks give judgement on all cases. For those who become Buddhist, they are free from any persecution such as forced labour, portering [or] extortion of money.'[3]

The Tatmadaw heavily increased its presence in Chin State after 1988, following the formation of the Chin National Front (CNF), which aimed to secure self-determination for the Chin people in the wake of that year's popular uprising.

The Tatmadaw's increased presence in Chin State led to the widespread use of sexual violence by soldiers against Chin women.

'There is a clear pattern of impunity for military sexual violence', said a 2007 report by the Women's League for Chinland.

In none of the cases in the report were the perpetrators prosecuted. Military authorities mostly ignored reports of sexual crimes, or actively sought to cover them up, and even threatened survivors. 'The soldiers committing rape displayed extreme brutality, sometimes torturing and murdering victims, irrespective of the presence of local witnesses. One woman was stripped naked and tied to a cross, in a savage act of mockery against the people's Christian beliefs,' it said.[4]

With just a few hundred troops, during those early years the CNF had limited success against the Tatmadaw, and in 2015 it was one of eight ethnic armed groups to sign the Nationwide Ceasefire Agreement (NCA), which it was hoped would pave the way for peace at last in Myanmar, but achieved nothing of the sort.

Still, given the legacy of distrust created by the decades of civil wars in Myanmar, the agreement was at the time at least a step in the right direction, and for many years the guns of war fell silent in the Chin hills. The area, however, has witnessed some of the largest resistance to the February 2021 coup, with armed groups operating across the remote state, including the CNF returning to conflict, alongside the newer Chinland Defence Force. This has brought with it a return of the Tatmadaw's violent and often shocking tactics in Chin, where it has been accused of burning churches and killing religious figures. The once peaceful town of Falam and others around it have witnessed some of the deadliest violence since the coup.

Decades of conflict

Myanmar's civil war is one of the world's longest running, and certainly one of its most complex. Ever since independence in 1948, various different groups – mainly, although not exclusively, formed along ethnic lines and operating in border areas – have taken up arms. The fighting has usually been against the central government, although there have been bouts of fighting between different groups.

The ethnic armed groups, known as EAGs, operating in Myanmar include some of the Tatmadaw's fiercest rivals, either historically or more recently, such as the Karen National Liberation Army (KNLA), the Kachin Independence Army (KIA), and the Arakan Army (AA), as well as smaller groups such as the Kayan New Land Party (KNLP), the New Mon State Party (NMSP) and the Wa National Army (WNA). Myanmar's dizzying array of acronyms would bring tears to the eyes of even the most avid supporter of the Judean People's Front.

The complexity is, in part, explained by the vast array of ethnicities in Myanmar, differences first exacerbated by a 'divide and rule' strategy by the British that the Tatmadaw continues to use, with varying degrees of success. Officially, there are 135 recognized ethnic groups in Myanmar, but the situation is significantly more complicated than the government is willing to admit.

Given the country's location, it should be no great surprise that there is such ethnic diversity in what is today the Myanmar nation state. The country is located between India and China, has access to and from the sea and is along the north-south route of great rivers including the Irrawaddy, the Salween and, to some extent, the Mekong.

These factors have resulted in the constant flow of people to and from Central Asia, and even further afield, since time immemorial. I've heard Myanmar described as 'an anthropologist's dream'.

Some of the earliest inhabitants of the area Myanmar comprises include the Mon of Lower Burma, as well as hill tribes including the Palaung and the Wa, who are now living in what is today Shan State. Other early arrivals include the Chin, Rakhine and the Shan, but it was the Bamar king

Anawrahta, ruler of the ancient city of Bagan, who is credited with founding the earliest incarnation of what is today Myanmar.

Anawrahta's kingdom fell to Kublai Khan's marauding Mongols in the late 1200s, and over the following centuries several empires ruled the land, including Mon, Shan and Rakhine realms, before a return of Bamar kings in the late eighteenth century under the Konbaung Dynasty. This was the final line in centuries of kingdoms in Myanmar, before it fell to the British guns and steamboats in 1885.

Many of the issues Myanmar faces today with regard to ethnicity can be traced back to the British, who gathered some of the most extensive information on the different groups inhabiting the country, but which it used to play different groups off against one another.

'Nation building was never a British priority', said journalist Martin Smith. 'The British annexation of Burma was piecemeal and always peripheral to the main British concern which was India. Rather, the twin motives were of security and profit, and colonial administrators were to display a destabilising readiness to trade territory.'[5]

The system they introduced to govern Burma was to split it in two: Ministerial Burma, or 'Burma proper', which comprised the mainly low-lying plains of the country's mainland, and the Scheduled Areas (or Frontier Areas), of the Shan, Chin and Kachin hills.

Ministerial Burma was their main priority, due to the lucrative rice trade of the Irrawaddy Delta and booming oil production in the country's centre, and it was here that the British introduced a formal structure of governance.

In the hills, the administration was less formal and in many parts of the Frontier Areas, particularly in Kachin, Chin and Shan, traditional rulers were allowed to maintain control of their respective areas.

The thinking behind this system is explained in a letter Lord Dufferin, the governor general of India, sent to his seniors in London in October 1886.

'The Shans, Kachins and other mountain tribes live under the rule of hereditary chiefs, whose authority is generally sufficient to preserve order amongst them', he wrote.

Here, then, we have to deal not with disintegrated masses as in Burma Proper, but with large organized units, each under the moral and administrative control of an individual ruler. If we secure the allegiance of these rulers, we obtain as far as can be foreseen most of what we require and all the premonitory symptoms give us reason to hope that this will not be a difficult task.[6]

As a result of this two-tiered system, colonial Burma became 'a curious patchwork of oddly different administrative islands'.

This skewed structure became part of the 'divide and rule' strategy that the British used to such great effect in Burma, and elsewhere, the impacts of which are still being felt today. Even before annexation, the British had harboured Arakanese rebel leaders and encouraged a Mon uprising against the Bamar rulers, but the tactic came into full force after they took power.[7]

Not only did the British allow the groups living in the hills to hold on to their traditional power structures, creating resentment among the lowland Bamar whose administrative systems were entirely re-ordered, but they also gave preferential treatment to minorities, particularly those its missionaries had successfully converted to Christianity. In particular, Karen troops were regularly recruited into the British armed forces and played prominent roles in quelling Bamar-led, anti-colonial protests, such as the Sayar San Rebellion of the 1930s, creating further distrust between the groups. By 1939, there were just 472 Bamar in the British Burma Army, compared to 886 Chins, 881 Kachins and 1,448 Karens.[8]

This feeling among the Bamar that minorities had been granted special favours by the colonists continued long after the British left.

'In order to separate them culturally from the Burmese, they [the British] converted the Karens to their religion and also created a separate literature and privileges for them', said U Ba Shwe, a prominent Bamar nationalist a decade after independence.[9]

British, as well as American, attempts to convert the Karen to Christianity were reasonably successful, with about 20 per cent today practising the religion, and did help to convert their language into written form, but the colonists did little to actually improve the lives of most minorities in Myanmar.

Under British rule, the Karen for example were divided into different areas across both Ministerial Burma and the Frontier Areas, while the calls from minorities for separation, or some form of autonomy, from Burma at the time of independence were ignored.

These areas also saw little economic development. A handful of projects were developed in Myanmar's hills, including the lead and silver mines at Bawdin and Namtu in Shan State, but these projects were few and far between (and the riches went into British pockets, of course).

'The picture that emerges from the British administration of the hill tracts is not so much one of benign paternalism as of chronic neglect', Smith wrote.

Not everything the British brought to Burma was bad, one might argue. There was economic growth, infrastructure development and governance structures, but they left behind a deeply divided country that had the added challenge of dealing with the aftermath of the Second World War, which had decimated large parts of the country, while leaving it strewn with discarded weapons.

One of the few British officials to understand this was Noel Stevenson, who was born in Rangoon and later became director of the Frontier Areas. In October 1944, Stevenson wrote to the Royal Anthropological Institute in London, criticizing the British for their lack of knowledge of the border areas, warning that the war had 'increased a hundredfold the ancient animosity between the hills and the plains'.

'Can we become successful co-planners with the hill men to guide their future if we do not start by knowing their existing way of life?' he wrote.[10]

The answer was a resounding no. The country the British left behind bore little resemblance to the one it had conquered seventy years earlier. Apart from religion, in particular Buddhism, which is practically indestructible in Myanmar, almost every other institution that existed before the British arrived had disappeared, including the monarchy, education and all forms of administration.

The borders of this new country were also arbitrarily decided, no doubt by some British officer back in London who had no knowledge of, or interest in, the complexities of such a crucial judgement. The decision to make the Salween River a boundary between Burma and Siam (now Thailand), for example, meant that previously free-roaming groups such as the Akha and Lahu were hemmed into one place by these new frontiers, not to mention the impacts it had on the other side of the country, close to the Bangladesh frontier.

The mess left behind by the British created difficulties for all ethnic minorities in Myanmar, but one of the worst affected was the Karen. During British rule, the Karen had been granted privileges denied to other groups, including senior positions in the military as well as administrative roles.

Karen forces, as well as other minorities, contributed heavily to the Allied victory over the Japanese in the Second World War, and when the British left Burma shortly after the war ended, many Karen believed they would be rewarded for their loyalty with a country of their own, or at least a say in their future. They were wrong.

Karen conflict

After the war, senior Karen officials made numerous attempts to engage the British on their request for sovereignty, but their overtures were ignored. This included a 'goodwill delegation' comprising four Karen lawyers, including the charismatic Cambridge-educated Saw Ba U Gyi, which travelled to London in August 1946, but was told by officials that there 'would not and could not' be any British support for an independent Karen State.[11]

Instead, as independence approached the British focussed their attentions on Aung San and his Bamar-majority AFPFL as the leaders of the new nation, leading to further divisions with the Karen and other minorities.

The aforementioned Noel Stevenson, once leader of the hill areas and sympathetic to the demands of those living there, warned British officials to take the concerns of the Karen leaders seriously, saying they had 'the guns, the skills, and the allies necessary to wrest control from the Burmese by force, if other means will not prevail'.[12]

'The only thing that restrains them is the belief that we will repay their loyalty by giving them a homeland', he said. 'I have come to the regrettable conclusion that the present Karen quiescence means simply that they refuse to quarrel with us. But when we go, if we do go, the war for the Karen State will start.'

Stevenson's warnings, however, were once again ignored.

In January 1947, Aung San travelled to London to sign an agreement with British Prime Minister Clement Atlee that guaranteed Burma independence within a year, and allowed the AFPFL to form the interim government. From that moment on, the concerns of ethnic minorities, including the calls from Karen leaders for their own state, were never seriously brought into consideration.

The British were confident that Aung San could appease the concerns of minority groups in Burma, a belief strengthened by the signing of the celebrated Panglong Agreement a month after Aung San's UK visit. In a famed speech at the event in the Shan hills, he said to the minorities present: 'If Burma receives one kyat, you will also get one kyat'.

The agreement's signatories elected to work with Aung San's interim government to achieve independence and agreed, in principle, to the formation of a 'Union of Burma'.

Pre-coup, the 'spirit of Panglong' was still celebrated by Myanmar's leaders – the principle of all of the country's ethnic groups coming together for the good of the country – but the Panglong Agreement was problematic even when it was signed.

For a start, only leaders from the Shan, Kachin and Chin communities attended, while the Karen sent observers but took no part in proceedings. There were no representatives from the Karenni (Kayah), the Mon and the Arakanese (Rakhine), while other minority groups from the Frontier Areas, including the Pa'O and the Wa, were overlooked entirely and shoe-horned into Shan State, which was reconstituted as one state, despite its remarkable diversity.

In addition, the final Panglong Agreement, signed on 12 February 1947, was a flimsy document of just a few pages that made no meaningful promises. For example, the Frontier Areas were promised full control of their area 'in principle', but it wasn't made clear what this would mean in practice. Shan State was granted the right of a 'ten-year trial' period, apparently adapted from the Constitution of the Soviet Union, as were the Karenni, while the Kachin abandoned this right in exchange for the towns of Myitkyina and Bhamo to be included in the new Kachin State. The Mon and Rakhine were granted no recognition.[13]

As problematic as the agreement was, the promises it made were effectively made null and void a few months later, when Aung San was assassinated in downtown Rangoon. The man supposed to lead the country into independence, and apparently sympathetic to the concerns of ethnic minorities, was dead.

Even before Aung San's death, Karen officials knew they would have little say in the newly independent country, and began their own moves in the hopes of achieving an independent Karen homeland in the southeast of the country, eventually leading to the formation of the Karen National Union (KNU). Within months of independence the Karen resistance, through the Karen National Defence Organisation (KNDO), had taken up arms against the Rangoon government.

By early 1949, the KNDO had built up a heavy presence – filled with battle-hardened veterans, as well as weapons, from the Second World War – and taken control of towns in the southeast of the country, in the Irrawaddy Delta to the west, as well as Mandalay in the centre. It also had a presence at Insein, at the time a small town a few miles north of Rangoon. It was here that one of the most crucial battles in the country's early years of independence took place, with Karen forces coming within a whisper of overtaking the capital.

Fighting broke out at Insein in January 1949, a year after independence, with Karen forces quickly seizing control from Burma Army soldiers, before making an advance on Rangoon. They got within a few miles of the capital, but would require significant support in order to capture it.

The Karen leader, Saw Ba U Gyi, made contact with regiments from the Karen Rifles, who were involved in battles elsewhere in the country, but none made it to Rangoon in time to help with the assault on the capital. Most notably, the Second Karen Rifles, located at Prome a few hundred miles to the north, reportedly refused to believe that the Tatmadaw commander-in-chief, a Karen called Smith Dun, had been removed from his post and replaced by

Ne Win, and as a result delayed a decision to rush to the capital. This pause allowed government troops the opportunity to replenish their supplies, disarm Karen forces elsewhere in the country and swing momentum of the conflict back in their favour.

The Karen fighters reconvened to Taungoo, a town they held 300 kilometres to the north, on the cusp of the Karen hills. Here they had a choice: move south towards Insein and make a fresh attempt on the capital, or head north to Mandalay and release Karen troops and civilians who were being held by the Bamar. They took the second option, successfully freeing several Karen prisoners in the city, but missing their opportunity of taking Rangoon.

Chaos ensued over the next several weeks, during which Saw Ba U Gyi held talks with U Nu and Ne Win in Rangoon regarding a potential ceasefire, but no agreement could be reached.

Further attempts by the Karen to take Rangoon were thwarted, and by April things had entirely swung in the government's favour, and pressure increased on the Karen forces.

'By contrast, the relief in Rangoon was tangible', Smith wrote. 'Each evening office workers would travel nine miles from the capital to take pot-shots at Karen lines'.

On 22 May, more than 100 days after the siege had started, it was over. Defeated Karen forces beat a retreat from Insein, with many crossing over the Hlaing River and disappearing into the countryside of the Irrawaddy Delta.

But the KNU still had control of much of Lower Burma, as well as allies in the hills of the country's east. The grizzled veterans of the brutal Burma Campaign of the Second World War felt confident they could win any war against the Bamar Army.

Shortly after the Insein defeat, the KNU held a summit in Taungoo, where a re-organization of the armed forces was announced, and a new Karen government formed with Saw Ba U Gyi as its prime minister.

Travel to Karen State today, or Kayin as it's officially called, and you'll still see pictures of Saw Ba U Gyi dotted about the place. The most famous portrait of him shows a hirsute man wearing a beret staring intently into the camera, not dissimilar to the famed image of Argentinian revolutionary Che Guevara.

During colonial rule, Saw Ba U Gyi had been part of the country's elite, born in 1905 into a wealthy Karen land-owning family in the Irrawaddy Delta, before studying at Rangoon University. He spent several years in the United Kingdom, training to become a lawyer at Cambridge University, before returning to his homeland to play a prominent role in the pre-independence government.

As independence approached, Saw Ba U Gyi had lobbied hard for an independent Karen homeland, including as a member as the interim government, but when it became clear his calls were being ignored, he joined the Karen resistance. His grandson, Paul Sztumpf, told me that he believed that the killing of Saw Ba U Gyi's close friend Saw Pe Tha and his family by soldiers from the Burma Independence Army during the Second World War contributed to his distrust of the Bamar people, and his passionate calls for an independent Karen State.[14]

On 7 July 1950, a year after Saw Ba U Gyi was installed as the Karen people's new leader, the KNU held a congress at Papun, its new capital. At the event, Saw Ba U Gyi revealed a plan towards gaining independence for the Karen people, as well as what have become known as Saw Ba U Gyi's 'four principles of the Karen revolution':

There shall be no surrender.
The recognition of the Karen State must be complete.
We shall retain our arms.
We shall decide our own political destiny.

Shortly after the congress Saw Ba U Gyi and other KNU leaders were travelling near the border with Thailand – possibly en route to meetings with international dignitaries in Bangkok – when they were caught in a Tatmadaw ambush and killed. After his assassination, by a group led by Sein Lwin – remembered as the 'Butcher of Rangoon' for his role in the crackdown of the 1988 protests – Saw Ba U Gyi's body was taken to Moulmein and put on public display, before reportedly being thrown into the sea.

In his early days in politics, Saw Ba U Gyi, like many before him, had developed a reputation as a playboy, but had grown more serious as the stakes for a Karen homeland got ever higher.

Many of the British officials who worked with him before independence, as well as those who dealt with him as he fought for the Karen cause, were impressed.

This included former Governor of Burma Reginald Dorman-Smith, who wrote to *The Times* after his death:

'Saw Ba U Gyi was no terrorist . . . I, for one, cannot picture him enjoying the miseries and hardships of a rebellion. There must have been some deep impelling reason for his continued resistance. . . . The major tragedy is that Burma is losing her best potential leaders at far too rapid a rate.'[15]

His death dealt a major blow to the Karen movement, but still it fought on. Over the next several decades, the Karen rebellion and the Communist Party of Burma (CPB), formed by those who'd split from Aung San's faction around the time of independence, remained the two biggest nuisances to the Rangoon government, regularly engaging their troops in intense fighting around the country.

Conflict escalates

In 1959, the two groups joined forces to form the National Democratic United Front (NDUF), aimed at overthrowing the government. However, the coalition ultimately failed because of ideological differences. Not only were the more hardcore Christian leaders of the KNU opposed to the CPB's communist stance, but the latter was also viewed as yet another group of Burmese chauvinists who didn't take seriously enough the calls for Karen self-determination.

To add to the numerous headaches of the government, a number of other insurgencies broke out around the late 1950s, as ethnic minorities grew frustrated that the promises made to them at independence hadn't been fulfilled.

The Shan nationalist movement had grown throughout this period, particularly in response to the increased build-up of Tatmadaw troops in the state. They had been stationed there in response to the influx into northern Burma of Kuomintang troops who had fled there following their defeat to Chairman Mao's Communists in the Chinese Civil War.

The official start point of the Shan revolution is November 1959, when about a thousand Shan launched attacks at Tangyan, southeast of Lashio, killing dozens of government troops and officials.

Two years later, the Kachin insurgency started. Despite promises made to Kachin leaders at independence, the northerly state had been ignored by the central government for more than a decade. The Kachin movement was again launched by a raid led by nationalists, and eventually led to the formation of the Kachin Independence Organisation (KIO), then its armed wing the KIA, which remains in conflict with the Tatmadaw.

As well as the broken promises of independence, ethnic minorities who were Christian were also angry at plans by the Rangoon government, led by the deeply religious U Nu, to make Buddhism the state religion. In 1961 he succeeded, passing the State Religion Promotion Act, which ruled that Buddhist scriptures should be taught in all government schools.

Ne Win's 1962 coup was effectively conducted to bring an end to the conflicts. However, instead of quelling them, Ne Win's heavy-handed approach – a tactic the Tatmadaw continues to use – achieved the exact opposite, strengthening the resentment minorities felt towards the majority Bamar, a mindset commonly referred to as 'Burmanisation'.

After taking power, Ne Win claimed to be creating a united nation that was 'one homogeneous whole'.

'A Chin, for instance, can go wherever he likes within the Union and stay wherever he likes. So, too, a Burmese. Everyone can take part in any of the affairs, whether political, economic, administrative, or judicial. He can choose his own role.'[16]

But this was not the reality in Ne Win's Burma. Almost no senior members in the military throughout his rule came from a minority group, while shortly after taking power he initiated his brutal 'Four Cuts Strategy' – another ugly Ne Win legacy that remains in use by the Tatmadaw – which aimed to sever links between insurgents and the local population by cutting access to food, funds, information and recruits. As civil wars continue to rage across the country, it's clear that the uncompromising stance of the Tatmadaw is the primary – although admittedly not only – reason that conflict continues in Myanmar today.

But Ne Win did make some attempts at initiating peace shortly after his coup, writing to the leaders of ethnic armed groups saying that the civil war had been a 'disaster for our country', adding that real peace could only be achieved through 'mutual cooperation and personal relationships'.

The attempts at negotiation failed, however, and Ne Win changed course, to a much more heavy-handed approach. Both sides have varying versions as to why the peace talks were unsuccessful. The Tatmadaw accused its rivals of 'insincerity' and 'duplicity', while the EAGs have said they were nothing more than a ploy by the Tatmadaw to justify an escalation of war.

The failed talks set off a new wave of insurgencies around the country, including the formation of new armed groups including the KNLP and the Shan State Army (SSA).

KIA operations escalated too, from a small guerrilla group formed of a few dozen troops to a highly organized army that took control of large swathes of the country's north.

'Here in the Kachin hills some of the heaviest fighting in Burma occurred as the Tatmadaw, in an early rehearsal of its Four Cuts strategy, embarked on a drastic scorched earth policy', wrote Smith. 'Thousands died unreported in the world outside.'

Other insurrections were growing in the Shan hills too, as larger groups combined to try, unsuccessfully, to overthrow the Rangoon government, while Wa, Pa'O and Lahu militias were also formed.

As militaristic means failed, Ne Win attempted to resolve the situation by allowing armed groups to reform as 'Ka Kwe Ye' (KKY) government defence militias, yet another disastrous policy of which the impacts are still keenly felt in Myanmar. Notably the arrangement saw the government grant 'business' concessions to war lords, many that used their immunity to build up huge profits from the drugs trade. About twenty KKYs were formed, and although they stifled some of the ambitions of the armed groups operating in the hills, fighting continued.

A drastic shift in Myanmar's conflict landscape occurred in 1989, when the CPB, one of the Tatmadaw's fiercest enemies since independence, collapsed following a mutiny by ethnic minority troops against the party's mainly Bamar leadership.

The mutineers, comprised mainly of those from the Kokang and Wa minorities, disliked the CPB's Politburo, which was almost exclusively Bamar, and felt they were being used as 'cannon fodder' in the conflicts, with no benefits for their own people.

'The CPB style looked very good, they said they were serving the people', said Pheung Kya-Shin, a Kokang who led one of the first rebellions against the party leadership. 'But actually, they destroyed the culture and history of Kokang. During CPB time, not one house was constructed, and there were no roads or cars; we were still riding horses.'[17]

There were other factors in the party's demise. For decades, the CPB's main backer had been the Chinese Communist Party (CCP), particularly as relations between Beijing and Ne Win's government soured after anti-Chinese riots hit Rangoon in 1967. In the power struggle that followed Mao Zedong's death, the CPB's leadership had supported the more hard-line faction, criticizing the 'revisionist clique' led by Deng Xiaoping.[18] The move backfired. When Deng later emerged as China's new leader in the post-Mao era, Ne Win moved quickly to mend ties with his administration, resulting in Beijing's support for the CPB drastically dwindling.

The depleted resources resulting from China's lack of support led to the CPB allowing its officials to begin taxing opium, by now a hugely bountiful resource in the Shan hills. As a result, many local CPB commanders grew reliant on the trade, using it to expand their influence in the areas they controlled. When the party's leadership began introducing tougher policies on the opium trade to try and control the situation, this led to further resentment from those further down the party's pecking order.

With the old CPB leadership ousted into China, the mutineers began forming new organizations, based mainly along ethnic lines. Groups formed around this time included the Myanmar National Democratic Alliance Army in Kokang, the United Wa State Party in Wa and the National Democratic Alliance Army (NDAA) in Mong La, of eastern Shan.

The new SLORC government in Rangoon sensed an opportunity to nullify these groups, which had the potential of linking up with the huge resistance that was forming at the Thai border in the wake of the 1988 protests. It immediately dispatched a negotiation team to the region, led by spy chief Lieutenant General Khin Nyunt, who negotiated a series of peace truces with these groups, in exchange for 'government assistance in health, education and other facilities'.[19] Groups such as the MNDAA and UWSP were also granted the rights to hold onto their arms, and administer control of their own territory, and used this new-found immunity to raise vast funds through the lucrative drugs trade.

These ceasefires also had a knock-on effect with other armed groups operating in the region, many who had relied on the CPB for arms and ammunition, and who were now coming under increased military pressure from the Myanmar army. Between early 1989 and mid-1995, the SLORC government signed more than a dozen ceasefires with armed groups operating in northern and eastern Myanmar.

Yet this didn't mean that the guns of war would fall silent at last in Myanmar. One group that refused to sign any agreement with the government around this time was the KNLA, the KNU's armed wing, which had been fighting the central government since independence.

In fact, the Karen conflict heavily escalated throughout the 1990s, when the ceasefires the Tatmadaw had signed with various groups further north allowed it to funnel more troops and resources into its fighting on the eastern front.

Nationwide Ceasefire Agreement

Then in 2012, following a particularly intense period of fighting, the Karen rebels stepped out of the jungle and signed a bilateral ceasefire with the government, now headquartered in Nay Pyi Taw. Three years later, in October 2015, the KNU was the largest of eight ethnic armed groups to sign the NCA, a much-hyped accord that many hoped would pave the way for peace at last in Myanmar.

After decades of attempting to win the wars by force, Thein Sein's quasi-civilian government had taken a fresh approach, putting dialogue ahead of conflict (although fighting certainly continued, as did Tatmadaw atrocities). This new strategy included inviting former rebels fighting in the jungles to join the government, and try to encourage armed groups to sign peace deals.

In early 2016, I interviewed one of these former rebels, who had taken part in the 1988 protests, before fleeing to the jungles at the Thai-Myanmar border. He spent eleven years there, before returning to Myanmar in 2012 at the invitation of Thein Sein's government.

'You develop a thick skin if you work in the peace process', the former rebel told me in early 2016, in response to criticism that he and other former rebels were too close with ex-members of the military.[20]

'We are a highly polarized country. We have the [Thein Sein] government, who many people think are an extension of military rule. But for us, peace is bigger than anyone', he said. 'For people who do not understand the complexity of the peace process, it's easy to blame this side or that side, but we cannot blame anyone. We are trying to bring an end to armed conflict.'

Even during that period of relative optimism, it wasn't easily achieved. When the NLD came to power following their landslide victory in the 2015 general election, Aung San Suu Kyi promised to make the peace process her number-one priority through a series of conferences known as the 21st Century Panglong.

Under her leadership, however, the peace process went swiftly into reverse. Some conferences were organized under the NLD's rule, and although two more groups signed the NCA in early 2018 – bringing the total number of signatories to ten – during this time, fighting continued in large parts of the country.

The lack of progress on the peace process is hardly Aung San Suu's fault alone, of course. As has been well documented, she held no control over the Tatmadaw, who continue their aggressive campaigns against the insurgencies, including in the form of likely war crimes. However, neither did she contribute to the efforts of trust-building with the minority groups.

In what may go down as one of the most tone-deaf moments during her time in office, at an event held in Nay Pyi Taw in mid-2017 to commemorate the country's peace process, Aung San Suu Kyi arrived at an evening dinner wearing an elaborate necklace covered in jade stones.[21] While no doubt intended to show empathy with the country's ethnic minorities, it instead demonstrated a striking ignorance of their grievances, particularly for the Kachin. One of the main drivers of the conflict in the country's north is Kachin State's vast natural resources, particularly jade, the mining of which has decimated the environment and communities.

She also disappointed many ethnic minorities in Myanmar by refusing to condemn the Tatmadaw's atrocities during its series of conflicts in border areas – including against the Rohingya, but also elsewhere – and often dismissing the concerns that these groups had.

She urged ethnic armed groups to sign the NCA and take part in the peace process, but such an attitude ignored the ongoing belligerent behaviour of the Tatmadaw, who don't seem to have learned the lesson over several decades that the use of brute force and intimidation will not bring an end to the civil wars. Let's not forget, in more than sixty years, the Tatmadaw has never militarily defeated any of its major rivals in Myanmar.

This is certainly true of the Karen conflict, which has raged since the February 2021 coup, with the Tatmadaw using its superior air power to launch strikes on defenceless villages, displacing thousands, including across the nearby border into Thailand.

Conflict continues

In early 2019, I travelled from Yangon to Bangkok for treatment for a minor health complication. While recuperating post-surgery in my hotel room in the Thai capital, I got in touch with a friend who had spent the last few years working in Mae Sot, on the Thailand side of the border with Myanmar, where about 100,000 Karen have fled in recent decades to escape the conflict in their homeland.

There had been rumblings that in the coming days a ceremony was to take place to commemorate the seventieth anniversary of the Karen uprising, and I contacted him to ask if he knew anything about it. He did, and told me that if I made it to Mae Sot by the following morning, I could join him and his Karen colleagues in travelling back over the border into KNU-held territory to attend the ceremony. I headed straight to the airport and reached Mae Sot that evening.

Pre-dawn, the next morning, my friend and his colleagues collected me from my hotel, and we drove several miles north out of Mae Sot towards the Myanmar border. As we wound through the dark mountain roads, the van was silent, which I put down to tension about the trip ahead, in particular the plans to sneak over the Moei River into Myanmar. The roads were silent too, and for most of the journey we didn't see another car until, at one point, a checkpoint appeared on the road ahead, manned by two Thai soldiers. I sank back into my chair, as the driver stared straight ahead, and the soldiers waved our car through.

Before boarding my flight from Bangkok the previous day, I'd got in touch with an editor I regularly worked with, who gave me the go-ahead to write a story on the trip. As we passed through another few military checkpoints, I began to form the story lead in my head, of overcoming a health scare (it was a root canal, but the reader didn't need to know that), and evading Thai soldiers to sneak into rebel-held Myanmar.

It turned out the trip was nothing of the sort.

At about 7 am, three hours after setting out from Mae Sot, we arrived to a road packed with people and pickup trucks. There were a few hundred people present, most of them dressed in traditional Karen costumes, and among the crowd were a handful of bored-looking Thai soldiers. The checkpoints had been nothing but a pretence.

The silence I had mistaken for tension in the car had in fact been fatigue brought about by the early start, and Thai authorities had even laid out a makeshift bridge to cross the Moei River into a KNU-held part of Myanmar.

After walking for thirty minutes, we arrived to a mountaintop, where a few hundred Karen people were gathered around chatting. The valley below us was filled with mist, from which muffled sounds could be heard emanating from a crackled speaker. Eventually the mist cleared to reveal a large sandy parade ground, at the far end of which was a stage where speeches were being held, including from KNU leaders and members of the Myanmar government, who had been invited to the ceremony.

As the speeches came to a close, military displays began to be held on the parade ground, and I took the opportunity to walk around the compound and conduct some interviews.

Among those I met was a Karen pastor who had travelled more than 100 miles to the ceremony from Mae Hong Son, in northern Thailand.

'I came here because I wanted to celebrate with my Karen brothers and sisters, and because I want to see us all united', he told me, as we stood below a large photo of Saw Ba U Gyi, the Karen revolutionary leader who was killed in a Tatmadaw ambush in 1950. 'Things are good for the Karen people living in Thailand, but those in Myanmar still face many problems', he said.

The biggest problem they faced, even at the time, was continued conflict. Although the KNU signed two ceasefires with the government in the past decade, even during the reform years, fighting continued between Karen forces and the Tatmadaw in the state. Tensions at the time were related to a large build-up of government troops in the state regarding a road-building project that the Tatmadaw said was crucial for development, but which the KNU regarded as a violation of the NCA, resulting in armed disturbances that led to the displacement and killing of civilians.

The complex journey towards peace in Kayin State has been further exacerbated by the presence of Border Guard Forces there, and one in particular. BGFs are similar in design to the KKYs created by Ne Win in the 1960s and 1970s to try and put an end to the armed uprisings across the country, but drastically backfired to create even more insecurity, including contributing heavily to the proliferation of the drugs trade.

In 2009 and 2010, the government established dozens of BGFs around the country, which involved integrating Tatmadaw soldiers into EAGs or existing militias. Before the coup, there were about two dozen BGFs in Myanmar, in Kachin, Shan, Kayah and Kayin states.

One of those formed around this time was the Kayin State BGF. Formerly known as the Democratic Karen Buddhist Army, which had broken away from the KNU in the 1990s, it came under the control of the Tatmadaw in 2010. In exchange for loyalty to Nay Pyi Taw, the DKBA was allowed to develop its own major economic interests, including a mix of legal and illegal operations.

But by far the group's most notorious investment was a base it made for itself at Shwe Ko Ko.

Not so long ago, Shwe Ko Ko was a remote and quiet village hugging the Thai border. In recent years, however, it has developed into an enormous 'economic zone' replete with casinos, a gun range and the sort of questionable activities you'd expect in a shady border town. The centrepiece of the project, according to developers, is the Yatai New City, billed as a US$15 billion 'smart city'.[22]

The project may never be completed, however. In mid-2020, the Tatmadaw began cracking down on activities around Shwe Ko Ko, including by forming a panel to investigate apparent irregularities surrounding the Yatai project, and ordering construction activities to cease.

As of early 2021, the developments had created further insecurities in Kayin State, particularly after the BGF's chief, a notorious figure known as Saw Chit Thu, was seemingly 'forced to resign' by the Tatmadaw.

It remains to be seen how the saga will unfold post-coup, but the last thing an already volatile area like Kayin State needs is yet another hostile group, one with access to huge financial resources, and with that arms.

Among the Karen, and other ethnic minorities, there are also questions regarding a future model of federalism, and what that might look like in Myanmar. Since independence, the country has only ever been ruled from the centre, with minority groups having almost no say in their future, a major factor in the distrust many groups feel towards the Bamar.

After the Karen seventieth anniversary ceremony ended, we returned to Mae Sot and that evening went for dinner and drinks with a group of Karen activists. Next to me at the table was a man in his early thirties who told me he'd been part of the rebel forces in the final years of the Karen war, before the 2012 ceasefire, but now worked for civil society groups in Mae Sot.

Naturally, conversation turned to the current situation in his home state.

'People celebrated the ceasefire when it was signed, but people are not as confident about this one holding', he said. 'Unless there's a drastic change in how the Tatmadaw, and the [NLD] government, views the Karen people, there won't be peace in Karen State.'

'As well as peace, what Karen want more than anything is federalism. That's what Saw Ba U Gyi was fighting for, and Karen people will not stop until we achieve this', he said.

The Karen are not the only minority in Myanmar calling for a federal future, and most of the country's smaller groups have their own vision of what that might look like.

The demands among the Karen, for example, are likely to be considerably different from the Kachin, the inhabitants of Myanmar's most northerly state, by virtue of the latter's richness in terms of natural resources. Kachin produces amber, jade, teak and gold, and many other valuable products in between. However, easy access over the porous border to China has meant that these goods have been a crucial driver in the Kachin conflict, with officials from both the Tatmadaw and the KIA, as well as Burmese and Chinese businessmen – and no doubt many more – benefitting from the area's insecurity. It's a situation an activist once described to me as the 'Kachin curse'.

Kachin State has so many resources that the area should have a thriving economy that benefits local people, but since the days of colonial rule these goods have been dug out of the ground with alarming regularity and shifted to areas elsewhere in the country and abroad, and the rewards gone into the pockets of corrupt members or allies of successive military regimes, and other armed groups.

The most obvious example can be witnessed at Hpakant, an area of Kachin State renowned for the quality of its jade deposits, where mining of the precious stone has seen the once lush, green forests stripped away and replaced by mountain after mountain of brown dirt. Thousands of freelance miners have been killed at Hpakant in recent years by deadly landslides caused by the companies, usually with links to the military junta, but also of groups including the KIA, dumping their waste on mountainsides, and which often collapse during times of heavy rain.

But the civil war in Kachin State didn't start as a battle over its resources, and instead for the opposite reason – because it was being ignored by the Rangoon government. Kachin leaders were among the signatories to the Panglong Agreement in 1947, but in the first few years of independence the northerly state saw almost no development, and the Kachin movement gradually built up throughout the 1950s.

For its first few years the movement had largely comprised a group of Kachin ex-students from Rangoon University, but in March 1961 attacks were launched on a bank in Lashio, which is part of neighbouring Shan State, but home to a large number of Kachin people.

This led to the formation of the KIO and its armed group, the KIA. As Ne Win's troops responded to this new movement with the notorious brutality it is renowned for, most of the KIA's leaders went underground and over the next few years became 'one of the most successful and best organised of all the armed opposition movements in Burma'.[23]

Fighting continued in Kachin throughout most of the second half of the twentieth century, until 1994 when the KIA signed a ceasefire with the government after losing control of many of the lucrative jade mines in the state, a crucial source of income for its insurgency.

That deal held until 2011, when fighting broke out close out to the town of Bhamo after Tatmadaw troops attempted to seize KIA-controlled areas. For the next few years after that, sporadic incidents broke out across the state, leaving thousands displaced and many killed.

Some of the heaviest fighting during this period took place in mid-2016, when Tatmadaw troops overtook several outposts close to Laiza, the KIA's headquarters on the China border.

Until the 1994 ceasefire, Laiza was a non-descript border village, but quickly boomed after the KIA's administrative wing, the KIO, moved its headquarters there. Today it is a bustling town that is not only an important place of commerce – and funds for the KIO/KIA – but also a symbol of resistance for many Kachin people in their battle against the Tatmadaw.

In Laiza, the KIO is responsible for administrative duties such as tax collection, policing and vehicle registration and also provides hospital and school services. Classes are taught predominately in the Kachin language.

But the peaceful existence many of the residents enjoy was put under threat in 2016, and worries rippled around Laiza that it would soon be overrun by Myanmar army troops, particularly after the Tatmadaw took the crucial outpost of Gideon towards the end of the year.

'They will never take Laiza', a Kachin activist proudly told me in Yangon at the time. 'The town means so much to Kachin people that they will do everything they can to keep it from falling into the Tatmadaw's hands. Believe me, if the Tatmadaw come close to Laiza, many Kachin people will go back and defend it with everything they have.'

But the takeover never happened, and with the Tatmadaw now stretched like never before in its history, an imminent assault on Laiza appears unlikely.

Yet, following the February 2021 coup, so does any progress on the peace process, with conflict flaring in almost every corner of the country. The NCA, as flawed as it was before the military's takeover, is now dead in the water. A few weeks after the coup, the head of a team representing the signatories to the NCA, said the military had 'continually committed violations' against the NCA in its brutal post-coup crackdown.

Fighting has resumed with ethnic armed groups who have been fighting the Tatmadaw for decades, but whose conflicts dissipated somewhat during the reform years. Myanmar army troops are also facing regular battles with hundreds of newly established armed groups, known as People's Defence Forces, which ballooned in the country in the wake of the coup.

Officially, the PDFs are the armed wing of the shadow government, the NUG, although few are actually integrated into its command structures. Those that are are divided into five regional commands – Northern, Southern, Central, Eastern and Western – and typically receive training in rural parts of Myanmar that are under the control of ethnic armed groups.

The other PDFs are an amalgamation of different groups, ranging from well-organized militias with access to weapons and their own command structures, to outfits focussing on guerrilla attacks against Tatmadaw positions and personnel, including targeted killings.

In September 2021, the NUG called for a 'people's defensive war' against the junta, urging armed groups to 'immediately attack' the military and take control of areas they controlled.[24]

In a video address, Duwa Lashi La, the NUG's acting president, ordered the PDFs to 'target to control the military junta and its assets', urging military-appointed administrators to resign.

Immediately after the announcement, the country saw a spike in violence, with clashes being reported in areas including Kachin and Kayin, while a police checkpoint in Mandalay was targeted in a bomb attack.

As time wore on, the PDFs' tactics grew increasingly daring, and deadly, even setting off a bomb in a military facility in Nay Pyi Taw, which was supposed to be the generals' safe haven. Meanwhile, attacks continued almost daily in major cities including Yangon and Mandalay, including a naval base, police stations and a court.[25]

Elsewhere in the country, some of the largest seats of resistance, and therefore fighting, have been seen in the west, in mountainous Chin State, in the plains of central Myanmar in Sagaing and Magwe regions and in easterly Kayah State, near the Thai border.

In the immediate aftermath of the coup, Chin State – where the people have long been resentful of the central government, as discussed at the beginning of this chapter – saw huge anti-military demonstrations. This quickly evolved into an armed resistance, and Chin has seen the emergence of new armed groups, one of the most influential of which is the Chinland Defence Force (CDF), which has established cells in numerous Chin townships. The CDF has used a mixture of traditional hunting rifles and imported weapons, as well as its strong knowledge of Chin State's hilly and remote terrain, to launch numerous deadly attacks on Myanmar army troops stationed in the state, although it has at times struggled against the Myanmar military's superior firepower, including in the form of helicopter gunships.

Kayah State, in the east of the country, has also witnessed huge resistance to the coup, notably through the more established Karenni Army and the Karenni Nationalities Defence Force, a merger of various PDFs formed in the aftermath of the coup. Sagaing and Magwe regions, sprawling and largely agrarian areas that cover the plains of central Myanmar, have also seen a huge escalation of fighting. The Myanmar military has been forced to deploy large numbers of troops to these areas, where they have been accused of torching villages, looting homes and livestock and generally bringing devastation to the lives of the people living there.

It's impossible – and probably foolish – to predict whether or not the various PDFs can unify and militarily defeat the Tatmadaw, which has advanced weaponry and more experienced (if less motivated) fighters at its disposal. However, there's little doubt that the thousands who have taken up arms under the PDF banner have performed infinitely better, and caused bigger damages to junta troops, than the military's top brass could have ever anticipated. According to the NUG's Defense Minister, Yee Mon, the armed opposition now numbers 'between 50,000 and 100,000 soldiers' formed into more than 250 military battalions across about three-quarters of the country.[26] If resistance forces can continue to encourage high-level defections from the Tatmadaw, and improve its supply lines to acquire more advanced weapons, then there's every chance it can cause an even bigger threat to the junta's top brass, potentially forcing them into concessions they would not have even considered when they launched their coup. Will it be enough to remove them from power? Maybe, maybe not.

Calls have been made for international governments to provide weapons or defence funding to the PDFs or the NUG as part of their efforts to defeat the military, but democratic countries have so far publicly refused to do so, saying it would add to the cycle of violence. Although unlikely, if this way of thinking changes – or if they choose to do so privately – it would go a long way to helping these groups militarily defeat the Tatmadaw and therefore hasten the military's demise.

Amid the almost nationwide misery in the country, there is the occasional bright spark, and the coup has opened an opportunity for some form of reconciliation among Myanmar's hundreds of ethnic groups, who have been divided since before independence.

In the early days of the protests, the calls being made by demonstrators were largely for the release of political leaders, most notably Aung San Suu

Kyi, and for the result of the 2020 election to be respected. As time went on, however, new calls were heard and placards were made calling for the 2008 constitution to be revoked, and a new federal charter enacted.

The main reason for this new-found unity has been a recognition that the real hindrance to progress in Myanmar for the past several decades wasn't someone from a different ethnic group, but the Tatmadaw itself.

Particularly among many Bamar, there has been an acknowledgement that the violence the Tatmadaw has resorted to in streets across the country since the coup were almost the exact same tactics it has used for decades against ethnic minorities in its series of civil wars.

'What is happening has really given the Bamar people a chance to reflect on the struggles and hopelessness faced by the ethnic [minority] people in the past', a Bamar friend told me within a few weeks of the coup. 'We understand now what they experienced under this military. So there really is this empathy and sympathy for the [ethnic minority people] that things were very hard for them. This new-found unity gives me hope.'

Encouragingly this mindset has been embraced by those most likely to emerge as the nation's new leaders in the aftermath of any post-Tatmadaw Myanmar. Within months of the coup, the National Unity Consultative Council (NUCC) – a broad group that includes the NUG, ethnic armed groups, strike committees and civil society organizations – published a new constitution that places federalism and democracy at the forefront.[27] The vision of this new charter is to build a 'peaceful Federal Democracy Union which guarantees freedom, justice and equality', prioritizing issues such as gender equality, human rights, equality and self-determination, social harmony and non-discrimination.

Admittedly, implementing this constitution in a new Myanmar free from the Tatmadaw's tyrannic rule will come with a whole host of challenges, but the fact the conversation is happening at all is an encouraging step, and couldn't be further from the vision the Tatmadaw has of the country.

That's not to say that all of the tensions between ethnic groups in Myanmar will disappear overnight. Many of the grievances ethnic minorities feel towards the centre in particular are deep-rooted, and will likely take many years, and possibly generations, to heal completely. But the current unity we are witnessing between the different groups is an encouraging step, and if the people are able to successfully rise up and oust the military from power, then there is real hope that Myanmar in the future could be more inclusive of its minorities.

What's been particularly striking about the unity Myanmar is witnessing has been a recognition by many about the suffering of the Rohingya. In the early days of the protests, placards were held aloft with messages of apology to the Rohingya for their support of the military's deadly campaign of violence against them in 2016 and 2017. Apologies have also been made online, and when the NUG released a policy in support of the Rohingya, saying it would grant members of the group citizenship, there was barely a whimper.

This could not be in sharper contrast to how things looked just a few years previously.

6

A desperate state

In the centre of downtown Sittwe, the Rakhine State capital in western Myanmar, is the Jama Mosque. Next door is the sprawling, dusty State Culture Museum, and across the road lies U Ottama Park, named after a Buddhist monk born in the town and who played a prominent role in Burma's anti-British movement of the early twentieth century.

With its elaborate black-and-white façade, and distinctive minarets and domes, in almost any other part of the world, the Jama would be a popular tourist draw.

But in Sittwe it is off-limits, hidden behind a stone wall covered in moss. During my most recent visit there, in mid-2018, the mosque's rusty iron entrance gate was guarded by a rough, bleary-eyed man in a stained vest and tattered longyi, who barked obscenities at my colleague and I as we stopped to take photos.

From just a few metres away across Sittwe's main street – where the traffic drowned out the guard's bellows – we could make out only a few small parts of the mosque's exterior, such was the dense foliage that had sprouted up around it.

Sittwe overlooks the Bay of Bengal, and heavy monsoon rains batter its coast every year. They've contributed to such dense vegetation on the mosque that a visitor could be forgiven for thinking it has lain abandoned for several decades.

But the Jama has only been closed for a few years – since 2012 to be exact.

It was that year that Sittwe and many other parts of Rakhine were convulsed into violence, after which most of the town's Muslim residents were removed by the military to camps outside town that they couldn't leave, and where most remain.

Mohammad Anul, a Rohingya, was sixteen at the time of the violence. He grew up in the town's Nasi quarter, a short distance from Sittwe's downtown, where he lived with his siblings and mother. The family ran a small shop selling odds and ends in Sittwe market.

'We used to love to go to the Jama Mosque', Mohammad Anul told me several years later. 'For most of the week, only people from the downtown area went there, but for Friday prayers people came from all across Sittwe. It was a very important place for us', he said.[1]

Tensions had existed between the Rohingya and mainly Buddhist Rakhine, the two largest ethnic groups in the state, for decades, but there had largely been a peaceful coexistence before the 2012 outbreak. Since then, however, Rakhine has witnessed violence and devastation on a massive scale, leaving thousands dead, hundreds of thousands displaced within the state and almost a million people – overwhelmingly Rohingya – fleeing over the border to Bangladesh, where they are living in the world's biggest refugee camp.

Like elsewhere in the country, the military coup of February 2021 has created even more complexities and confusion in Rakhine. In addition to a relatively new insurgency, the Arakan Army, which fights for self-determination for the Rakhine people, widening its sphere of influence since the coup, there are still hundreds of thousands of Rohingya living under apartheid conditions inside Myanmar. The million or so refugees in Bangladesh are also unlikely to return home given that the architects of the decades-long oppression against them – which the United States officially declared a genocide in March 2022 – are back in power.

The catalyst for the 2012 violence was an incident in late May when a young Buddhist seamstress, Thida Htwe, was raped and killed while walking home from work in a village on Ramree Island, in southern Rakhine. The culprits, three Muslim men, were immediately arrested, found guilty and sentenced to prison. However, anger among the Rakhine community towards the state's Muslim population simmered.[2]

Five days after Thida Htwe's murder, a public bus was travelling from Thandwe, a picturesque beachside town hugging the Bay of Bengal, to Yangon. Onboard were a group of Muslim men returning to their homes in central Myanmar after visiting Thandwe for a religious pilgrimage.

When the bus reached Toungup, a few miles north of Thandwe, news spread among the local community that some Muslim men were onboard. A large group mobbed the bus, and forced themselves onboard, before dragging ten Muslim men off and killing them. The murdered men were not Rohingya, but the gruesome attack appeared to have been a retaliatory act for the killing of Thida Htwe.[3]

Tit-for-tat violence escalated. Shortly after the Toungup incident, Rohingya mobs in Maungdaw, in northern Rakhine, attacked Buddhist properties in the town, and within days the state had been swept into violence, before relative peace was restored around the middle of the month.

In that initial violence, according to the government, 98 people were killed and 123 injured across both communities. In addition, more than

5,000 homes, the vast majority belonging to Rohingya living in Sittwe, were destroyed.[4]

After a period of calm, violence returned to the state in late October of that year. While the fighting in June had been more or less sporadic, in this second wave the attacks 'appeared to be well-coordinated and directed towards Muslims in general and not just Rohingya'.[5] Kaman Muslims, one of Myanmar's officially recognized ethnic groups – a status not extended to the Rohingya – were also among those targeted.

By the time the October round of violence had come to an end, at least 200 people had been killed and 140,000 people – overwhelmingly Rohingya – displaced, from the beachside towns in the state's south to the forests and mountains near the Bangladesh border in the north.

'I saw my own home burned in front of my eyes, and four men killed', said Mohammad Anul of the violence. 'For the Rakhine and Rohingya, things were peaceful [before 2012]. I never thought this would happen.'

The overwhelming majority of those displaced in 2012 were Rohingya, but other groups were also affected, including the Kaman, as well as the Rakhine, and a host of smaller groups that call the state home.

Despite its association with so much misery and violence in recent years, Sittwe is not an unpleasant town. Overlooking the Bay of Bengal, each evening its vast beach is filled with families and residents enjoying fried snacks, fresh coconuts and beers. Groups of kids run around the sand playing raucous games of football, while lovers line up along the beach wall, huddled under umbrellas.

But these leisurely activities are no longer available to most of the town's Rohingya population, who are contained in squalid camps they cannot leave on the outskirts of Sittwe and where they are denied access to education, healthcare or jobs. Most are entirely reliant for their survival on handouts from international agencies.

After the 2012 violence started, Mohammad Anul and his family hid for several days. When it ended, they emerged from their hiding place, only to be rounded up by authorities and taken to an area outside Sittwe where they were told they would be safe.

'They told us it would be temporary, but it wasn't', he told me in an interview in the camp several years after the violence.[6]

I first visited the camps on assignment in July 2016, in the middle of Rakhine State's relentless rainy season. During a five-day visit, the rain fell insistently, flooding the streets, making it difficult to walk a short distance without being drenched to the bone and leaving an even gloomier mood hanging over an already desperate place.

The camps were manic, with dozens of people passing in every direction. Even in heavy-set trekking boots, I was slipping and sliding in the mud, while the camp residents expertly navigated the slippery ground in nothing more than flip-flops, their longyis hoisted above their knees.

Shortly after arriving at the camps we set out to explore and soon reached a narrow alley packed with about a dozen people making their way through water that came up to their knees. Then the intensity of the rain stepped up a level, and everyone ran for cover. We found shelter in a bamboo hut and waited for the storm to pass.

The rain continued for almost an hour, and as we waited, I found myself watching a pair of old men standing under a shelter opposite us. Both were sporting distinctive long beards and dressed in traditional Muslim clothing. The entire time we waited, the men stared glumly ahead, saying nothing.

Then, just a few metres down from where they stood, I noticed three teenage boys taking shelter in a makeshift chemist. All were dressed in Western-style clothing of T-shirts and jeans, with one sporting a Manchester United football shirt. Like the old men nearby, they were staring idly into the distance, waiting for the storm to pass.

Then a depressing thought crossed my mind: what were they waiting for?

I felt guilty for thinking it, but that didn't make it any less true. The young men looked to be about fifteen years old, meaning they were probably starting secondary school when the violence started four years earlier and when they and their families had been forcibly moved to this camp, no doubt – like Mohammad Anul – under the promise that they would soon be allowed to return home.

But that hadn't happened, and several years after I visited, there has been no progress on efforts to allow the Rohingya in these camps to return home. In fact, with the military's coup d'état of February 2021, those hopes of returning to a life of freedom look more distant than ever.

I knew nothing about the young men or their desires, but it seems reasonable to assume they had harboured ambitions to go onto further education – at Sittwe University, for example, located just outside the camp we were in, and which had educated many Rohingya before 2012 – or to move to other parts of the country, or even abroad, to work or to study.

'It was my dream to study at Sittwe University', Mohammad Anul told me. 'I would have been the first person in my family to do so. But now I have no hope to', he said.

I have no idea what became of those young men, but the chances are they're still idly roaming around that camp, surviving on handouts from international agencies. Or perhaps they attempted to flee via the dangerous journey by boat to Malaysia or Indonesia in search of a better life.

The Rohingya's plight is today familiar to much of the world, largely as a result of the deadly campaign of violence committed by Tatmadaw soldiers in northern Rakhine in mid-2017, which saw at least 9,000 killed, the burning of homes and villages to the ground and about 740,000 Rohingya fleeing to Bangladesh.

Before the coup, there were about 600,000 Rohingya still in Rakhine State, unable to move or access basic services, as well as an estimated one million in southern Bangladesh, mainly at Kutupalong, which in the last few years has grown to become the world's largest refugee camp.[7]

A long-oppressed minority

Although the issues facing the Rohingya have only become well known to the world at large in recent years, they have faced oppression at the hands of the Myanmar state, in particular successive military regimes, for several decades. The roots of the crisis, however, go back centuries, to a time when varying dynasties ruled the land, before international borders were established, and when populations flowed freely.

Rakhine State is separated from the rest of Myanmar by a vast mountain range known as the Rakhine Yoma. As a result of its isolation, the state developed separately from the rest of the country and had many of its own kingdoms that controlled this land for centuries.

Its last independent kingdom – a point of pride many Rakhine still refer to today – was established with its capital at Mrauk U in the early fifteenth century. Famed for its array of temples dating back to the height of that empire, Mrauk U was a prosperous town, attracting traders from across the globe. Mrauk U's close connections with the Sultan of Bengal next door in what is today Bangladesh led to the free flow of people between the neighbouring empires, in the form of traders, as well as slaves, regularly going in both directions.[8]

Mrauk U fell in late 1784, when the Burmese king Bodawpaya, of the Konbaung Dynasty, conquered and sacked the city. The new king inflicted 'wanton cruelties' on the Rakhine who rose up against his rule, and an estimated 200,000 fled westwards to Chittagong, at a time when there was no hard-and-fast border between today's Myanmar and Bangladesh.[9]

This would change with the arrival of the British who, through the East India Company, made their first foray into Burma in 1824, in what became known as the First Anglo-Burmese War. Over the next six decades, Britain gradually took control of the whole country through successive wars, ruling it first as a province of British India before establishing an independent colony. When the British left for good in 1948, they marked part of this new country's western frontier with Bangladesh (then East Pakistan) by the Naf River, which spills into the Bay of Bengal a few miles north of Sittwe.

More than thirty years after the colonialists exited, Myanmar's military government, led by Ne Win, decided that the First Anglo-Burmese War would be the cut-off when it came to recognizing the country's *taingyintha*, or 'national races'.

In 1982, Ne Win introduced the citizenship law, replacing an act that had existed since independence. Under this new law, only members of ethnic groups that had, according to the government, settled in Myanmar before 1824 would automatically be granted citizenship.

In October of that year, Ne Win stood in front of Government House in Rangoon – a building he ordered demolished three years later – and conducted a speech explaining why the new law needed to be introduced.

During the colonial period, 'foreigners, or aliens entered our country unhindered under various pretexts', he began. 'The first to come were the English who ruled our country. After them came many of their camp followers. Let us say only that much.'[10]

In the decades of colonial rule, the country had been 'subjected to the manipulation of others', he said, and the people had been unable to shape their own destiny.

Many 'guests' and 'mixed bloods' had entered the country – effectively those who had arrived between 1824 and 1948 – and were therefore not 'pure blood' people of Myanmar, he said.

Ne Win said the country could accept these people as 'citizens, say', but argued that the country's leniency on 'humanitarian grounds' should not lead to the country endangering itself.

'We can leniently give them the right to live in this country and to carry on a livelihood in the legitimate way. But we will have to leave them out in matters involving the affairs of the country and the destiny of the State. This is not because we hate them. If we were to allow them to get into positions where they can decide the destiny of the State and if they were to betray us, we would be in trouble', he said.

The new law therefore introduced three categories of citizenship: citizens, associate citizens and naturalized citizens. Full citizenship was granted to those regarded as being from one of the country's 'nationals' – one of the eight 'main' ethnic groups, Kachin, Kayah, Karen, Chin, Burman (Bamar), Mon, Rakhine or Shan – although those not from these groups can be granted full citizenship on other grounds, for example, if they are descendants of families who have lived permanently in Myanmar since before 1824.[11]

Associate and naturalized citizens are granted the rights of full citizens 'with the exception of the rights stipulated from time to time' by the government, a clearly ambiguous use of language. Their limited rights can also be taken away for vague reasons, such as 'in the interest of the State' or for 'showing disaffection or disloyalty to the State by any act or speech or otherwise'. In short, those granted associate or naturalized citizenship are essentially second-class citizens in the country, leaving them exposed to all sorts of manipulation.

At least before the 2021 coup, the dominant narrative in Myanmar was that the term 'Rohingya' is a recent invention, and that those claiming to belong to this group are the descendants of those who arrived in the country after the British annexation began. Therefore, the argument went, these people could not be accepted as one of the country's 'national races'.

However, there is in fact documentation of the word in the country before the 1824 cut-off. Almost a quarter century earlier, in 1799, a Scottish geographer and zoologist by the name of Francis Buchanan published his *A Comparative Vocabulary of Some of the Languages Spoken in the Burma Empire*, one of the first major Western surveys of the languages of Burma.

Having documented the main languages of this 'great eastern nation', towards the end of his study Buchanan added three dialects 'spoken in the Burma Empire, but evidently derived from the language of the Hindu nation'.

'The first is that spoken by the Mohammedans, who have long settled in Arakan [Rakhine] and who call themselves Rooinga [*sic*] or natives of Arakan', he wrote.

As Spanish journalist Carlos Sardiña Galache writes in his recent book *The Burmese Labyrinth*: 'Those who deny Rohingya ethnicity are keen to point out the uniqueness of that document; but its existence is undeniable, and the rare appearance of the term should be understood in light of the fact that scholarship on Arakan was almost nonexistent at the time.'

The origins of the Rohingya are a heavily disputed and emotive issue, but whatever their roots are, there's no doubt that the vast majority of the Rohingya living in Myanmar today, as well as those who have fled in recent years, were not only born in the country but are also deeply connected to the land they call home. Further to that, I have interviewed dozens of Rohingya over the years, and all have been fiercely proud to refer to themselves as such, no doubt a direct result of the persecution they have faced. What's more, there can be no justification for the horrendous violence and oppression hundreds of thousands of Rohingya have had to endure for decades.

This rigid classification of ethnicities is also unrealistic. As discussed in the previous chapter, the constant ebbing and flowing of different peoples for centuries in what is today Myanmar means that mixed heritage among its populace is nothing unusual. In fact, during my daily strolls in downtown Yangon I saw people whose facial features displayed traits from across

Southeast Asia and further afield – dark skins, lighter complexions, small noses, large snouts, lightly coloured eyes and those that are piercing black.

Travel around the country and the distinctions are even more prominent. During my time in the country, I travelled to northern Shan State and saw people who clearly had Chinese lineage, while a few miles further south in the state I heard conversations that sounded remarkably similar to Thai. On the other side of the country, in remote Chin, I met those whose features made it likely their ancestors hailed from India or even further afield.

What is different about the Rohingya however, and why there are so few champions for their cause inside the country, is that they are not included on Myanmar's list of 135 'national races'.

The origins of the list are not entirely clear, although in a press conference in September 1990, Khin Nyunt, at the time a major general in the Tatmadaw, spoke of there being '135 national groups' in the country.[12] Four years later, British journalist Martin Smith wrote that the State Law and Order Restoration Council, which ruled the country after 1988, 'refers to the "135 national races" of Burma, but has produced no reliable data or list of names'.[13] The move from 8 to 135 races is regarded by some as a strategy to divide and rule the country's non-Bamar groups further, while there is also speculation that the number was considered auspicious because the digits (1 + 3 + 5) add up to 9, an astrologically important number for the junta leaders.

2014 census

One of the first times I came across the list was shortly before the 2014 census, the country's first in decades, when many of the 135 groups were shoe-horned into the eight 'major' groups of Kachin, Kayah, Karen, Chin, Bamar, Mon, Rakhine and Shan. For example, the Kokang, a Han Chinese group living in Myanmar's borderlands, were included in the Shan section, while the Salon people, a sea-faring group with almost no links to the mainland, were classified as one of the Bamar subgroups.

The Rakhine section of the list included seven groups: Rakhine, Kaman (who are Muslim), Kwe Myi, Daignet, Maramagyi, Mro and Thet. Absent from this list is, of course, the Rohingya, and the roughly one million people who refused to be labelled as 'Bengali' – the term the government used to refer to them, implying they were interlopers from Bangladesh – in the national count were omitted from the final result.

The census, which was supported by international actors including the UN Population Fund, was highly flawed and certainly went some way to heightening the already tense atmosphere between ethnic groups in the country.

This was particularly obvious in Rakhine, which still maintained a nervous air around it following the violence a few years earlier. Many in Rakhine, and elsewhere in the country, expressed concern that the census would be used as an opportunity to recognize the Rohingya as one of Myanmar's 'national races', which they were adamant was not the case.

The tensions reached their peak in the late March, a few days before counting for the census started, when a crowd of hundreds of Rakhine protestors surrounded the office of an international humanitarian agency in Sittwe, demanding action after a European staff member was accused of removing a Buddhist flag and putting it in her pocket. The move, which came at a time of huge distrust of international actors, particularly those working in Rakhine who were viewed as being too sympathetic towards the Rohingya, was perceived as a deliberate insult of Buddhism.

'She wrapped [the flag] over her buttocks and threw it away when some eyewitnesses saw her', a government official told media at the time.[14]

To quell the anger that followed, police in Sittwe were forced to fire warning shots into the air, a night curfew was put in place and nearly all of Sittwe's international workers were evacuated to Yangon.

A few nights after that episode, I went for drinks with colleagues in Yangon's Chinatown, when the Sittwe incident was raised. Our conversation inevitably turned to the plight of the Rohingya, and when I raised the dreadful conditions they had been subjected to in the camps, and elsewhere in Rakhine, a Myanmar colleague responded angrily.

'You foreigners don't understand Myanmar', he said. 'You talk about human rights and the Rohingya, blah blah blah. But there is no such thing as the Rohingya in Myanmar. They are Bengali.'

His viewpoint was certainly not unique, and there was at the time a commonly held opinion across much of the country that the Rohingya – or 'Bengali' – were foreign interlopers from Bangladesh, who either deserved no sympathy for their plight or were exaggerating the extent of their suffering in order to gain international sympathy.

There are a few reasons this is the case. Firstly, the portrayal of the group as outsiders, taking the country's already negligible resources for themselves, goes back decades, including to the pre-independence era, and the rule of Ne Win, who could use the narrative of troublesome interlopers to push his own agenda that the military was required to protect the country and prevent it from falling into the hands of these intruders.

The Rohingya are also an easy scapegoat. They are typically dark-skinned, playing into the belief that they are different from the rest of the country (despite, as mentioned earlier, the complete variety of appearances in Myanmar), a viewpoint exacerbated by the fact they are also a different religion. Although there is no official state religion in Myanmar, the vast majority of its population practices Buddhism, and the religion is heavily baked into much of the country's cultural identity, especially in the Bamar heartlands. The Rohingya as Muslims heightens this view of them as outsiders. Other factors include the country opening up, heightening anxieties about foreign interference, the role of social media, particularly Facebook, in furthering untrue and hateful narratives about the Rohingya and Muslims more generally, as well as a siege mentality among much of the population amid international criticism of its treatment of the group.

Since the February 2021 coup, there have been indications that this mindset may be slowly changing. Some members of the public, particularly from the Bamar majority, have publicly apologized for their earlier vilification of the Rohingya, saying that the behaviour of the Tatmadaw since the coup had made them realize they had fallen for the propaganda campaign against the Rohingya.

History of Islam in Myanmar

Islam has a long history in Myanmar. Muslim traders have been arriving in what is today Myanmar since at least the ninth century, mainly as traders from India and Persia, with some establishing their own communities in the country's coastal regions, including Rakhine State.[15] Two Muslim men, the sons of an Arab merchant saved from a shipwreck off Myanmar's southerly coast, served as horsemen under King Anawrahta, while his son, King Sawlu, appointed the descendant of his teacher, a Muslim Arab, as governor of Ussa (today's Bago, or Pegu).[16]

The Arakan Kingdom, established at Mrauk U in the early fifteenth century, had a close relationship with the Bengal Sultanate to the west, particularly as the Burmese Court of Ava strengthened to its east, while the Muslim Kaman – today an 'official' ethnic group of Myanmar – are reported to have descended from a unit of archers that helped protect the kingdom at Mrauk U.

Various Muslims also played prominent roles in the courts of the two final kings in the Konbaung Dynasty, Mindon and Thibaw, and although Muslims were not necessarily at the forefront of political life in Myanmar, for centuries relations between different religious groups had largely been peaceful, and there's little evidence of the sectarian tensions that have engulfed the country in recent years.

A major shift occurred when the British colonized the country. Indians had been travelling east into today's Myanmar for centuries, but typically in small numbers, and most quickly assimilated with the local population.[17]

After Burma became a province of India in 1886, Indians could freely enter the country and move around with few restrictions. The British considered them harder working and more loyal than their Burmese counterparts, granting them the bulk of jobs in the new colonial order, including as labourers, civil servants, office clerks and soldiers.

The opening of the Suez Canal in the late nineteenth century helped boost Burma's economy, particularly through the trading of rice, and this industry growth required more and more cheap and efficient labour, much of which could be found next door in India.

By the beginning of the twentieth century, Indian immigrants were arriving in Burma at a rate of 250,000 per year,[18] and although some would stay only temporarily for seasonal work, others began to build up their economic influence. Many Indians were able to buy up huge parts of land around Rangoon and the surrounding delta area, which had become Burma's hugely lucrative rice bowl during colonial rule. Rangoon in particular grew rapidly as a result of Indian immigration, who comprised more than half of the city's population during the 1930s.[19]

Unsurprisingly, this major demographic shift led to resentment from many Burmese towards their new neighbours, but there were other factors too. By the 1920s and 1930s, the country was connected to the global economic chain and as a result not immune from the effects of the Great Depression. As the cost of living rose, so did public anger, and these new arrivals, who were perceived as taking economic opportunities away from the Bamar people, would become an obvious scapegoat.

This period also witnessed the rise of a nationalist, anti-colonial movement that put Bamar Buddhist culture at the forefront of national identity, demonstrated through their rallying cry – *Amyo, Batha, Thathana* (race, language/religion and teaching of Buddha). In addition, Indians were increasingly coming to be viewed as stooges of the hated colonists, particularly as many were drafted into institutions such as the police and the army.

These tensions would spill over into major violence in Rangoon at least twice during this period. The first incident occurred in 1930, when race riots broke out between Indian and Burmese labourers, escalating into anti-Indian riots across the country that led to hundreds of people, mainly Indians, being killed.

In his book *Trials in Burma*, Irish author Maurice Collis, who was a district magistrate in Rangoon at the time, documented an incident where he was called to protect a group of petrified Indians hiding in a house in the city.

The house had been surrounded by 'a band of Burmese roughs armed with swords', he wrote.[20]

Collis, who spoke fluent Burmese, tried to calm the mob, which was responding to rumours about attacks on local women, a motivation that had many parallels with the 2012 violence.

One of the men told Collis: 'Those Indians inside have murdered Burmese women. A Burmese woman has had her breasts cut off. We cannot stand that.'

The police eventually arrived and took the Indian men to safety. 'I have never seen men accept arrest with greater pleasure', Collis wrote.

Similar riots broke out in Rangoon eight years later, after the writings of a Muslim man were unearthed that were deemed to be critical of Buddhism.

Around this time, religious tensions were also rising elsewhere in the country, including in Rakhine. In 1942, as the Second World War reached Burma's shores, the Japanese advanced into Rakhine as the Burma Campaign got underway.

Rakhine's Muslim and Buddhist communities were heavily divided, with most Muslims remaining loyal to the British, while the Rakhine supported the Japanese as part of the wider strive for independence from the Brits. Both sides established their own armed units, launching attacks and massacres, the legacies of which are still keenly felt in the state today.

Return to Rakhine

During my 2016 trip to Rakhine, the day after our visit to the Rohingya camps, our contingent – made up of myself, a photographer and a Rakhine translator – travelled across town to another camp hosting people displaced by the violence four years before. This camp, however, was not home to the Rohingya but to ethnic Rakhine as well as a handful of Hindus.

In contrast to what we had seen the day before, this camp was much more ordered. Rather than a mishmash of crumbling huts, here the houses were constructed in neat, ordered rows, and generally bigger and of a better quality than those we had seen the day before.

Although not well-paved, the roads running through the camp could, despite the recent rains, be traversed without losing half a leg in the quagmire. Many residents had set up small shops outside their homes, and we saw a few people moving freely between the camp and downtown Sittwe, which was a short walk away over a nearby bridge.

At the far end of the camp, next to a small river that offered a view of a gleaming pagoda on the horizon, we were invited inside a home to watch a small Hindu wedding. Particularly given the gloom we had witnessed the day before, it was a sweet and uplifting experience, although we politely excused ourselves after realizing that the timid bride wouldn't emerge while we were present.

Shortly after leaving the ceremony, the heavens opened and we found shelter in a makeshift restaurant. As we waited once more for the rains to pass, I stared out over the camp and found myself reflecting once more. There was one thing not present here that we had witnessed everywhere we looked the day before: out-and-out desperation.

The camp was in no way the height of luxury, but life seemed to go on fairly normally here. During our few hours in the camp, we saw a relatively brisk movement of people in and out. We witnessed a handful of people seemingly returning from a day's work in nearby areas, presumably with some sort of modest income for their family: an option not available to the Rohingya we had met.

This didn't matter to Maung Maung Win, a Rakhine man who lived at the camp. He was living in Yangon when the 2012 violence started but travelled back to his home state a few days after it ignited out of what he said was a sense of duty for his people. He strongly believed that the Rakhine were deeply under threat from their 'Bengali' neighbours.

When we spoke, he was working as a driver for an international NGO and was angry about how the international community was handling the issue. He said he had sat on the sidelines of many meetings, in Yangon and Rakhine State, and said international actors didn't understand the issue.

'The international community, they come, they meet the Bengali, they see they are poor. But we are poor too', he told me inside his home that he shared with his wife and children, two sweet young girls who stared confusedly at me throughout the interview. 'We are one of the poorest countries in the world, and one of the poorest states of the country. Most of these international groups, they go to the Bengali camps, but they do not come here.'

The grievances Maung Maung Win expressed were felt by many Rakhine people. Rich in oil and with direct access to the Indian Ocean, Rakhine has huge economic potential, but still it languishes in desperate poverty, and most of the funds it has received goes into the pockets of generals or businesspeople with close connections to them. Rakhine is one of the poorest of Myanmar's fourteen states and regions, with most of its people surviving on meagre incomes made from farming or fishing.

During our conversation, Maung Maung Win briefly acknowledged the government's role in the current crisis, but his dislike for the Rohingya was obvious. His comments towards me were heated but not unfriendly; clearly he was extremely passionate about the topic. I didn't agree with everything he said, but how could I? I hadn't had the same experiences as him.

Several times he referenced the fall of the Arakan Empire more than three hundred years before, intense fighting between Muslims and Buddhists in Rakhine in the 1940s as well as a sadness about what had happened in 2012. 'I had Bengali friends, but we don't see each other anymore', he said.

After a pause, his face ignited with passion as he spoke about the violence between the Buddhist and Muslim communities of the 1940s.

'My grandmother, she saw friends killed by them [Muslims] and she lost her land to them. Tell me, how would you feel if this happened to you?'

Like elsewhere in the country, independence didn't bring peace to Rakhine. The violence during the Second World War had divided the communities even further, with Muslims fleeing to the state's north, where they formed the majority, and the Rakhine moving increasingly further south. Muslims escaping the south of the state for northern Rakhine came with stories of deadly attacks at the hands of their Rakhine neighbours, incensing the local Muslim population and leading to tit-for-tat violence towards the Buddhists living among them.[21]

Amid this cauldron, a Muslim mujahadin movement emerged immediately after independence, which hoped to separate the northern Rakhine area around Maungdaw from Burma entirely, either creating an independent Muslim state or annexing the area to East Pakistan (now Bangladesh).[22]

Several negotiation attempts by the post-independence government of U Nu ultimately failed, and throughout the early 1950s government forces conducted large-scale campaigns against the Mujahids. In November 1954, after Buddhist monks in Rangoon conducted protest fasts against the group, the government launched Operation Monsoon, which would capture rebel-held areas and kill many of their leaders. The Mujahid threat was no more.[23]

In May 1961, partly in response to the demands of the people living in the area, the government established the Mayu Frontier Administration in northern Rakhine, administered by military officers. However, this new administration was to be short-lived and was dissolved less than a year later, when Ne Win launched his coup d'état in March 1962, bringing the entire country under his control.

Today, the roughly 600,000 Rohingya still living in Myanmar, mainly in central and northern Rakhine, have few rights. Nearly all of them are stateless, while most do not have jobs, cannot go to school, access healthcare or even travel beyond a limited area outside their home or village. I remember meeting a Rohingya man in central Rakhine State who from his home could see a brand-new hospital that had opened a year before. A few weeks before we spoke, his father had died at home from an unknown illness, as he had not been allowed to enter the hospital for treatment. It's a miserable existence that no human should have to endure.

Erosion of rights

The desperate situation facing the Rohingya did not come about suddenly but instead is the result of a series of policies put in place over decades that steadily eroded their rights.

By the 1970s, the mujahadin movement may have been brought to an end in the hills of northern Rakhine, but the area still witnessed major insecurity throughout this period, first with the Bangladesh War of Independence in 1971, which saw thousands of refugees flee into Rakhine,[24] then towards the end of the decade when the military government – whose suspicions of 'foreign invaders' had been heightened by the turmoil in Bangladesh – launched its notorious Operation Nagamin, or Dragon King.

Officially, the aim of the operation was to scrutinize those living in northern Rakhine, to establish whether they were citizens of the country or 'illegal immigrants', but the Tatmadaw's deeply held disdain for this group, coupled with their culture of impunity that continues today, led to a deadly campaign of brutality, rape and murder that saw roughly 200,000 Rohingya flee over the border into Bangladesh, although most returned.[25]

Another large-scale exodus occurred in the early 1990s, shortly after the 1988 protests, which heightened the military's paranoia of 'outside influencers', and around the time the Rohingya Solidarity Organisation was building a sizeable presence at the Bangladesh border. Violence meted out by government troops led to more than 250,000 fleeing to Bangladesh, and this time many did not return.[26]

The reforms that got underway in 2011 brought great hope for people across the country, with prospects of enhanced economic opportunities and greater freedoms.

This optimism was also felt in Rakhine State, including by the Rohingya and Rakhine.

'Of course, we didn't believe the promises about democracy at first, but changes started to happen, and we hoped the situation would improve for us', a Rohingya living in one of the camps outside Sittwe told me in 2016.[27]

Yet the changes also brought with them anxieties, especially for the Rakhine, whose suspicion against their Muslim neighbours lingered from the violence around the Second World War.

Ahead of the 2010 election, which paved the way for Thein Sein's government, the military-linked Union Solidarity and Development Party deliberately courted the Rohingya, issuing many with Temporary Registration Cards (TRCs), better known as 'white cards', which allowed them to vote. Such a move exacerbated tensions between the groups and contributed to the 2012 violence.[28]

The Rohingya's right to vote in the 2015 general election was removed months before the poll when Thein Sein ordered the revocation of the 'white cards', a move made in response to protests against the Rohingya's political inclusion.

The years prior to the 2015 vote saw a rapid rise in Buddhist nationalism in Myanmar, in part brought about by the tensions in Rakhine State, notably concerns that the Rohingya and other Muslims were plotting to 'take over' the country. This may have been an illogical and dangerous narrative that led to the loss of many innocent lives, but it's one that should be explored a little deeper.

First, after decades of isolationism, the country's opening up created an anxiety among some – particularly older generations or those with more traditional mindsets – that its 'traditional' values and culture were being lost (most who viewed things this way regarded those values to be mainly Bamar and Buddhist). References I remember being pointed out to me in interviews across the country included the rise of young people wearing jeans instead of the traditional longyi as well as increased mobile phone use, in particular the watching of YouTube videos, such as music videos, from abroad.

It was often a stick used, particularly by those from the military establishment, for political leverage over Aung San Suu Kyi and her NLD, who appeared on course to resoundingly win the 2015 election. During her time in office, we may have learned that she holds many of the traditional values shared by her countryfolk of the same generation, but at the time critics pointed to factors such as her having had a British husband, the considerable time she had spent abroad as well as the fact she spoke English with such a distinctive accent as apparent evidence that she was an outsider. The election of her party to power, the argument went, would lead to the rapid erosion of traditional Myanmar values, and that included concerns for some that she would allow Muslims to take over the country.

International media also played a role in the rising nationalism. Given the deplorable conditions they faced, it is understandable that the bulk of media reporting on the crisis in Rakhine focussed on the plight of the Rohingya, but this wasn't the only side of the story. The Rakhine also faced very legitimate grievances of their own, including economic marginalization, discrimination by the state and restrictions on their own language and culture, but this was barely covered in international media coverage, contributing to the siege mentality many Rakhine felt.

It was a tense time to be in Myanmar. There was still considerable optimism about the direction the country was going in under the still-continuing reforms, but the euphoria of the 2012 by-election had dissipated somewhat, and there was a rising tension on Yangon's streets.

It was particularly bad if you were Muslim. The nationalist movement growing around this time came to be symbolized by the 969 symbol – representing the nine attributes of the Buddha, the six of his teaching and the nine of the Sangha, or monastic order – a multicoloured and distinctive sign that quickly became ubiquitous in the commercial capital around mid-2013. Almost overnight, it came to be seen everywhere, on bumper stickers, betel nut stands, shops and restaurants, and its underlying message felt clear – Muslims aren't welcome.

And the fear wasn't just an abstract idea but was starting to be felt in real bouts of violence, mainly against Muslim communities, in towns and cities across the country.

One of the deadliest was at the central Myanmar town of Meiktila in March 2013, when a deadly riot started following an argument between the Muslim owner of a gold shop and a Buddhist customer in the town's market. The violence flared after a Buddhist monk was killed, and over the next few days, dozens more were slain, before a state of emergency was declared.

At the time I lived in an apartment just north of Yangon's downtown. Tensions in the city had been high after the Meiktila incident, and for successive nights I travelled with a friend to a Muslim quarter in the east of the city to try and get a grasp on what was happening. Each night, we met large groups of men who were huddled outside their homes, often holding makeshift weapons, worried they would come under attack from the Buddhist mobs they said were roaming the area after dark, often threatening to attack 'the kalar'.

'We don't trust the police to help us. They're on their side', one man said.[29]

About a week after the Meiktila violence, I woke to the news that a mosque in downtown Yangon, just a few streets from where I lived, had burned to the ground. Early reports said that some children had died, and I took a taxi the short distance.

The area around the mosque was heavily guarded by police, and I didn't have much luck trying to interview witnesses, who were understandably guarded.

A few hours later, after the police had dispersed, I returned to the scene and stood in front of the mosque. The once-attractive blue structure still stood in place, but the windows had been destroyed, and the frames around each were bordered with soot. Police later announced that thirteen people, mainly children, had died in the fire.

Despite widespread suspicion that the fire had been intentional, a few days later police announced that the fire had been triggered by 'extreme heat of a transformer' and not any form of criminal activity.[30]

Case closed: end of story.

2015 boat crisis

By early 2015, the situation in Rakhine State remained desperate, especially for the Rohingya. Three years after the violence that swept across the state and led to their displacement, more than 100,000 remained in squalid camps, with little or no access to jobs, healthcare or education. Hundreds of thousands more were in villages dotted around Rakhine that they were unable to leave.

Aware that there were few prospects for their situation to improve, between 2012 and 2015, thousands of Rohingya fled the country, with many boarding decrepit and rickety fishing boats to make a perilous journey to Malaysia or Indonesia.

Their plight captured international headlines in mid-2015, when Thai authorities uncovered the graves of dozens of Rohingya and Bangladeshis on the border with Malaysia at sites used as camps by human traffickers.[31] The embarrassing headlines forced regional authorities to act, by announcing a crackdown on human trafficking, but none of the policies implemented addressed any of the root causes of the issue and in fact created even more difficulties for the trafficking victims, especially those who were onboard boats in the Andaman Sea at the time.

Unable to unload their human cargo, traffickers simply abandoned these boats at sea, leaving hundreds, perhaps thousands, with no food, water or fuel. Many died.

A few years later, I travelled to Kuala Lumpur to attend a conference on democracy in Southeast Asia. While there I got the opportunity to meet many in the Rohingya community, including those who had arrived in the midst of the 2015 boat crisis.

Drinking in a hotel bar one evening after the day's meetings had ended, I got introduced to Mohammed, who was eighteen at the time. While the rest of us were decked out in suit and ties, Mohammed casually strolled in with an easy smile and dressed in a faded T-shirt and jeans. I asked him if he wanted a drink.

'Sure, a limoncello', he said.[32]

Without pause, I responded with a goofy laugh.

'What, man? It's tasty', he responded, laughing.

I ordered him his limoncello, and we chatted at the bar. Over the next few hours, and a follow-up interview the next day, I heard his story.

He'd never set foot in Maungdaw but still regarded it as home. His parents had lived there until they fled among the military's crackdown of the early 1990s, and Hasson and his siblings had been born and grown up in the Nayapara refugee camp, a few miles north of Teknaf at Bangladesh's southern tip.

'I always said to my father that I would go back and see it one day', he told me. 'But now I'm losing hope that I'll ever go back.'

Mohammed's journey to Kuala Lumpur started in late 2014, the day he was kicked out of a school in Bangladesh. He wanted to move abroad and become a doctor but as an unregistered refugee in Bangladesh had been studying for years using a fake ID. Then one day, Mohammed had no idea why, authorities told him they knew his documentation was false.

'They found out I was a refugee and wouldn't let me study anymore', he said with the nonchalant shrug that had followed many of the painful answers he'd given me. 'So I said to myself, "Ok, I have to find a way to go somewhere else." I don't want to just sit around in the camp, wasting my time.'

In early 2015, through the help of a friend, Mohammed found a broker who promised to help him get to Malaysia, and he handed over the required fee. After a painful goodbye with his mother, within a few days he was onboard a boat departing from somewhere along Cox's Bazar 150-kilometre-long beach.

But it was unfortunate timing, and a perilous journey, coming as it did in the middle of the refugee crisis.

Just as the trafficking crackdown was getting underway in Thailand Mohammed's boat, a rickety vessel filled with about 1,000 people was drifting somewhere in the Andaman Sea, slowly making its way towards Malaysia.

Of course, the refugees on the boat had no idea about the developments taking place onshore, and after months at sea, people began to grow desperate; when one man begged to be given water, a trafficker shot him dead.

'After that, we were all very quiet', Mohammed said. 'They told people they would beat them; they said "If you don't give us the money, we will kill you."'

Mohammed was eventually able to contact his mother in Bangladesh, who agreed to pay a ransom of 6,000 Malaysian Ringgit (about US$1,500).

The traffickers fled the boat shortly after, leaving those onboard stranded, until a group of Acehnese fishermen arrived and pulled it towards Indonesia. The fishermen told those onboard that the Indonesia navy would come and take them to shore.

After several hours, the Indonesian navy arrived and gave those onboard food and water and started towing the boat. 'But then they just cut the rope and disappeared', Mohammed said.

In this cruel game of ping-pong, the Malaysian navy then arrived, provided food and water and duly disappeared. The mood turned dark. Fights broke out, and when a hole appeared in the bottom of the vessel, people panicked and jumped into the sea. Mohammed was among them.

'The water was so cold. After a few hours it was dark and I thought I wouldn't see the sun again when it came the next day', he said.

Mohammed estimated that about 700 people on his boat were saved by a flotilla of fishermen who took them to dry land at Aceh, on the northern tip of Indonesia's Sumatra island. He believes that about 300 people on the boat drowned.

'When I got onto that boat [to Aceh], I remember sitting there thinking, "Wow, I have a new life." Man, it was the best day of my life', he said, smiling.

He was eventually able to reach his mother by phone, who was speechless to hear that her son was alive. After about a year in Aceh, Mohammed travelled by boat to Malaysia to find work so that he could send money home.

When we spoke, life was good in Kuala Lumpur, he said.

'I feel proud to say I am a refugee. In Bangladesh I couldn't say where I come from, but I can here', he said.

Back in Myanmar and the situation wasn't improving. Years after the 2012 violence there was little hope for an improvement in relations between the Rohingya and Rakhine, with the communities still heavily divided.

With the Rohingya still being held in camps, or prevented from leaving their villages, across Rakhine there was almost no interaction between the two communities. Before 2012, there had certainly been deep-rooted tensions between the groups going back decades, but they had least been face to face on a daily basis, with Rohingya and Rakhine working together in markets, while children from the two communities would go to school together. Now there was little hope for reconciliation.

Yet there were efforts going on behind the scenes to take some steps to change this. Few of those initiatives were coming from the government, who instead took an 'out of sight out of mind' approach to the Rakhine crisis, and so it was left up to the work of civil society groups to fill the gap and try to mend relations. Given the tension between the communities, many of the organizations conducting this work did so silently, concerned that any publicity would draw negative attention from those strongly opposed to the communities interacting.

In June 2017, I returned to Sittwe with two colleagues. We were there to produce a podcast documentary to mark five years since the 2012 violence and in particular to try and draw attention to the fact more than 100,000 Rohingya were still living in camps they couldn't leave.

Back in Yangon we had applied for permission to enter the internally displaced persons (IDP) camps on the outskirts of Sittwe and immediately after arriving visited the local administrative office where we were told we would still have to wait a few more days. Eager not to waste our trip, we spent the next few days travelling around Sittwe and its outskirts interviewing its

Rakhine residents. The scars of the 2012 violence were still prominent, and most of those we met told us they couldn't imagine a time when the Buddhist and Muslim communities could live side by side again. Many of those we spoke to raised – without prompting – the murder of Thida Htwe at Ramree, the incident that initiated the violence.

But we also met with Aye Lwin, who was running an organization aimed at building trust between Rakhine's Buddhist and Muslim communities. Born in Sittwe, he had spent most of his adult life in Yangon but returned to his hometown a few years after the 2012 violence. Despite the huge challenges, some progress had been made on improving relations, he said.

For Aye Lwin, the key to building trust between the communities was working closely with the youth and gradually bringing people from those communities together.

'Among those we work with, I think we're seeing a change in people's mindsets about understanding the conflict', Aye Lwin told me at his office on the outskirts of Sittwe, a tin hut set back from a main road. 'They've really looked at it and have seen that this conflict only brings negative impacts for their community.'

That's not true of all the people Aye Lwin dealt with of course, and certainly not true of all people across the state, but in his experience those who had started to look critically at what was happening saw that a segregation of communities was not going to help bring any improvement to people's lives in Rakhine.

He added that, in general, the Rakhine felt a strong animosity towards the Rohingya, but that viewpoint was not necessarily shared by many of the state's Muslims.

'Often they [the Rakhine] have been made to think this by the previous generation. So they think bad things about this other religion, but once they learn and improve their knowledge about conflict, peace and dialogue, they start to change their attitude', he said.

I asked him if he thought that the two communities could ever live side by side again.

'It won't be easy, and what happened last year has made it much harder.'

2016 violence

He was referring to an incident that took place near Maungdaw, in the north of Rakhine State, in October 2016.

By pure chance, two of my *Frontier* colleagues, a reporter and a photographer, were in northern Rakhine State when the incident took place, conducting an investigation into the drugs trade.

On October 9, the pair were due to go on a patrol with police officers around Maungdaw, but early that morning received a phone call from a senior police officer telling them to come to a Border Guard Police (BGP) outpost at Kyikanpyin, a twenty-minute drive from Maungdaw town.

The BGP are unique to northern Rakhine. An arm of the Myanmar Police Force, they were established in 2014 and given authority to control the border with Bangladesh. Ostensibly, the BGP was established to replace a much-feared militia force known as Na Sa Kha, which had ruled the border region for decades, often using brutal tactics, but apart from having a different uniform – rather jazzy baby blue fatigues – the BGP is little changed from its predecessors.

For the Rohingya in northern Rakhine, the BGP are the face of the oppression they have endured for decades, including restrictions on movement, marriage and religious practices.[33]

The BGP headquarters are located at Kyikanpyin, and in the early hours of 9 October, a few hundred Rohingya attacked the outpost there, and two others nearby, killing about a dozen security personnel.

I visited Kyikanpyin the following July as part of a government-sponsored trip to northern Rakhine. Around this period, the region had been completely closed off to international journalists, and the only way to visit was through a series of these trips, where authorities strictly controlled where you could go.

It was a tightly controlled affair, and, as expected, we largely only visited areas the government had wanted us to see. This included a guided tour of the areas attacked on 9 October, including the Kyikanpyin outpost, a nearby security base and a weapons-holding facility.

Outside the gates of the outpost, the exact place where the attacks had taken place, a BGP officer gave us a rundown of what had happened in the early hours of 9 October.

He said that about 100 people had marched down the street from opposite directions, chanting 'Rohingya, Rohingya'. The crowd was made up of men, women and children, he said.

'They were marching down the road, chanting, and they had lots of weapons', said the officer. 'They had knives and slingshots . . . and chillis.'

There was a moment of silent confusion among the journalists listening, before one politely asked what the chillis were used for.

The officer – a chubby, mildly buffoonish figure in baggy fatigues – looked taken back at the line of questioning: 'To throw in our eyes, of course!'

I couldn't help but laugh at the officer's explanation, but the group that launched the attacks on the BGP compound was better organized than a few chilli-throwing villagers.

They were initially called Harakah-al Yaqin ('Faith Movement' in Arabic) and announced their arrival on the scene in northern Rakhine with those October attacks.[34] Muslim insurgencies had operated in the area before, notably the mujahadin group around independence, and the Rohingya Solidarity Organization, which operated near the Myanmar-Bangladesh border between the 1980s and late 1990s.[35]

With those attacks, this new outfit looked to be the most serious Rohingya-led operation in decades and would entirely alter the dynamics in the already complex cauldron of Rakhine State. Its leader soon emerged as Ata Ullah, who the government called Hafiz Tohar.[36] His father was from northern Rakhine but soon travelled to Karachi, Pakistan, where Ata Ullah was born, before the family moved to Mecca, Saudi Arabia. Thought to be in his early forties at the time, he disappeared from Saudi Arabia in 2012, shortly after that year's violence in Rakhine State, and is thought to have spent the next few years in the Bangladesh-Myanmar border region helping to establish the group, which is today better known as the Arakan Rohingya Salvation Army (ARSA).

After the Kyikanpyin attacks, fighting continued for several days, before government forces took control through their brutal 'clearance operation' campaign. Almost immediately claims of human rights abuses by security personnel emerged, including those of arbitrary arrest, torture, arson and extrajudicial killing of large swathes of northern Rakhine's Rohingya population.

The military denied that its forces had committed any wrongdoing in its operations and said it was conducting a legitimate campaign to wipe out terrorists.

Over the next several months, reports emerged in state media of sporadic attacks in northern Rakhine, including the laying of small bombs and the kidnapping and killing of suspected government informants. These were consistently blamed on ARSA.

Independent media access to the area was cut off, and it was difficult to verify exactly who was behind the attacks, but it appeared certain that ARSA was growing its presence in the region and would certainly have been responsible for some of the violence. Through scouring news reports in Yangon, however, it was difficult to get a full picture, and the government-organized trip of July 2017 would at least offer some insight on the ground.

We flew first to Sittwe, where we spent the night, before travelling by boat to Buthidaung, twenty kilometres east of Maungdaw. From there, we continued our journey by boat to Maung Hna Ma, a tiny village on the banks of the Mayu River, which winds its way through northern Rakhine.

There I met a Rohingya woman outside her home. Two weeks earlier more than a dozen masked men had entered the family home in the middle of the night and kidnapped her son. She said she believed he had been kidnapped because someone had told 'the terrorists' – she didn't name the group – that he was an informant for the government, which she denied. A few days after the trip ended, state media reported that her son's body had been found in a ravine near the village.[37]

We spent the night in a nearby village, and the next day travelled to the north of Buthidaung Township, to Tin May, a picturesque village a short distance from the Bangladesh border.

When our boats reached the river bank near Tin May, the mood of the security forces, who had been shadowing us, turned serious. BGP soldiers had followed us throughout the trip but had largely taken a back seat. But as we walked through the lush paddy fields to Tin May, the officers filed in closely alongside us and kept a watchful eye on the surrounding area, their guns drawn.

Days earlier, Tin May had witnessed an intense bout of fighting between security forces and what the government said were ARSA fighters.

We were taken to the far reaches of the village, to a surrounding that looked out onto paddy fields. The nearby homes were empty, and in the middle sat a scorched, still-smouldering wreck that had once been a simple bamboo home. Burnt pots and utensils lay on the ground, and ashes from the recent fire were still fluttering in the wind.

It was here, the village chief told us, that security personnel had been conducting a patrol searching for ARSA fighters. When they reached the end of the village, where we were now stood, a group of men hiding in one of the homes had started shooting, and a firefight followed. The village chief said two of the fighters were killed, and another was arrested.

Tin May was a Rohingya-majority village, and it was here that the climate of fear towards security forces was the most obvious. On warm days, like the one we visited, it's common for families to sit outside their homes, and as we walked through the village, closely followed by the BGP officers, countless Rohingya villagers hurried back inside, eyeing the soldiers nervously. It wasn't clear whether the fear was based on something they'd heard or experienced directly, but it was certainly prevalent.

Throughout the trip it had been difficult to assess exactly how organized the insurgent group was. In Maungdaw we met with BGP commander Thura U San Lwin, who told us ARSA had informants in every village of northern Rakhine – something I had heard from an analyst with a strong network of contacts in the area – but when we visited Rohingya villages the following day, residents denied that was the case.

On the final day of the trip, and after some thorough negotiations with the officials escorting us, we were granted permission to deviate from the itinerary and visit Kyar Gaung Taung, a village about a two-hour drive from Maungdaw.

Kyar Gaung Taung had reportedly been the scene of a brutal army crackdown in November 2016, in which dozens of men were arrested, accused of being ARSA members.

Negotiations with the government officials continued at the village entrance, and we were eventually allowed to enter without our government minders. With the guidance of a local villager, we were taken to a far corner of the village that we hoped was away from the eyes of government informants.

We walked through acres of paddy fields and reached a closing at the far end of the village surrounded by large trees. We were introduced to a young lady who said she had witnessed her father being burned alive inside the family home by security forces; the home had since been rebuilt and was covered in tarpaulin. The young lady, her tearful sisters surrounding her, walked us to a nearby field and pointed to a charred area of grass.

'That's where I found my father's burned body', she said.

Word of our presence had obviously spread, and a large crowd had started to gather, including about a dozen women who nervously stepped forward, telling stories about how their sons and husbands had been arrested during the November crackdown.

'My son was working in the field when he was arrested. He did nothing wrong', said one woman.

Our time in Kyar Gaung Taung was limited as our chaperones wanted us back on the road for the long drive back to Sittwe. After a few hours in the village, we squeezed into cars for the five-hour drive along a bumpy track down a thin sliver of land between the Mayu and Naf rivers.

As someone who's vertically challenged, I'm used to being squeezed into the middle of packed cars, and the journey south was no different as I crammed in between a journalist friend from *Reuters* and another from *ABC* in Australia. Along the journey, we talked about the trip, we exchanged podcast and book tips and we slept, only occasionally taking in the scenery around us amid short breaks in the otherwise relentless rain. Little did we know that the villages we passed on that drive would be the scenes of devastating violence within a matter of weeks.

Kofi Annan report and 2017 crackdown

Just over a month after that trip, I was with some friends and colleagues in the bar of a lavish hotel in downtown Yangon, the Sule Shangri-La, better known to many by its old name, Traders.

Our lively contingent was discussing the press conference that had just finished in an adjoining room, that of the Advisory Commission on Rakhine State, which had just submitted its final report to the media. The commission, headed by former UN secretary general Kofi Annan, had been founded a year earlier at the request of Aung San Suu Kyi, tasked with proposing answers to the challenges being faced in Rakhine State.

After the press conference, the general feeling among those who had gathered in the bar was one of relative optimism. Everyone recognized the scale of the task involved in solving the deeply embedded issues in Rakhine, but the consensus was that the best way to go about achieving this was implementing the committee's recommendations, which included providing freedom of movement for all people in Rakhine, unhindered media and access and a review of the 1982 citizenship law.

'We are well aware that our recommendations on citizenship and freedom of movement touch on profound concerns of the Rakhine population', Annan, an incredibly charismatic speaker, said at the press conference. 'Nevertheless, the commission has chosen to square face these sensitive issues because we believe that if they are left to fester, the future of Rakhine State – and indeed Myanmar as a whole – will be irretrievably jeopardised.'

And the government seemed somewhat receptive to the idea. Afterall, the commission had been established by Aung San Suu Kyi, and that morning the state-run *Global New Light of Myanmar* ran on its front page a photo with a smiling Annan handing the report to then president Htin Kyaw.[38] There were not going to be any quick fixes to the issue, but there was a general feeling that after years of inaction by the government, things might be moving bit by bit in the right direction.

The next morning, the sun was just breaking through my bedroom window when the first message came through and was followed immediately after by another. I tried to bury my head in my pillow, but when a third came through straight after, I forced myself to look at my phone.

'You following this?' said one. 'Man, this is bad news', said another.

This being twenty-first-century journalist, I went straight onto Twitter and gathered enough information about what had happened. In early hours of the morning, ARSA fighters attacked numerous security outposts in northern Rakhine, killing about a dozen members of the security forces.

A Twitter account claiming to represent ARSA said the attacks were 'a legitimate step for us to defend the world's persecuted people and liberate the oppressed people from the hands of the oppressors!'.

The stories of brutality, both at the hands of Myanmar security forces and ARSA, were immediate. Reports emerged of ARSA attacking and killing a group of Hindus and Mro – a lesser-known ethnic minority in

Rakhine – and thousands of non-Rohingya were evacuated from villages to displacement camps in major towns. Meanwhile, within days tens of thousands of Rohingya had crossed the border into Bangladesh, with stories emerging of astonishing brutality at the hands of Myanmar security forces.

On its Twitter page, ARSA justified the attacks, accusing the Tatmadaw of increasing its presence in northern Rakhine in the weeks prior, to try and trigger unrest in the wake of the release of the Annan report.

'When their atrocities against the innocent people have reached beyond the point of tolerance and they were about to launch attacks on us, we had to eventually step up to defend the helpless people and ourselves. We will continue our struggles', one of the posts said.

While the start point for the August violence had been the ARSA attacks, the Tatmadaw had been building its presence in northern Rakhine for several weeks, confiscating weapons from the Rohingya that could be used in self-defence, removing fences in Rohingya villages and training and arming non-Muslim groups.[39] Such moves strongly indicate a form of pre-planning ahead of the crackdown.

A few days after the attacks, an interview with a man called Abdullah, who said he was a senior ARSA official, appeared in the regional outlet *Asia Times*.[40]

Abdullah claimed that the attacks launched by ARSA were in fact 'defensive measures' after the military was preparing to strike ARSA bases around northern Rakhine. One of the major triggers, Abdullah said, was a move by the military and armed civilians to seal off a village in Rathedaung township from surrounding hamlets.

'Knowing that Kofi Annan was doing good work, the military had a clear plan to jeopardise it and derail the report', Abdullah said.

This is perhaps true, but it's equally as likely that ARSA's leadership knew exactly what they were doing when they launched those attacks. The group had been gradually building a presence in northern Rakhine for at least a year, and there are several accounts of suspected informants being killed and of young Rohingya men being forced to join the cause.

The ARSA leadership knew that the world was watching when Kofi Annan released his report that night at the Yangon hotel, and their decision to launch the attacks just a few hours later cannot, in my view, be regarded as a coincidence.

The leaders of ARSA encouraged – no doubt, in some cases, forced – desperate young men to launch attacks using crude weapons on a brutal army apparatus that had guns, rocket launchers and helicopters at its disposal. The response by Myanmar's military was always going to be disproportionate –

although I'm not sure anyone could have predicted the utter brutality shown in the Tatmadaw's 2017 crackdown – and it is my view that the ARSA leaders knew that such a move would draw the world's attention to the plight of the Rohingya, perhaps even hoping for direct foreign intervention in the form of UN peacekeepers.

Yet it's also important to remember that ARSA has never represented the broader Rohingya population.

Ata Ullah is thought to have spent significant time, and developed strong contacts, in Saudi Arabia, which likely granted him access to powerful figures and generous resources.[41] He is also regarded among those who have met him as an eloquent speaker, and as a result it is easy to see why a few hundred angry young men, with little hope for the future, supported his cause and took part in the attacks.

But for the million or so Rohingya in camps in Bangladesh, and the hundreds of thousands still living under horrendous conditions inside Myanmar, ARSA does not represent their cause.

'They have only made life worse for us', one Rohingya lady in Bangladesh told me of ARSA, her voice kept low such was the fear she felt of repercussions.

Despite the horrendous conditions the Rohingya continue to face – particularly since 2012, but for decades before that – the vast majority recognize that resorting to violence would do nothing to help their cause; they are well aware that the military needs only the slightest excuse to launch a brutal crackdown on a population they view as subhuman, and the 2017 response is evidence of that.

And despite their best efforts, Myanmar's military did a dreadful job of hiding what they were doing. Within days, thousands of Rohingya had fled over the border into Bangladesh with stories of horrendous abuse. They accused the Myanmar military, often in collaboration with other Buddhist villagers, of committing atrocities that included mass killing, torture, arson and rape.

Despite this overwhelming evidence, of thousands arriving in Bangladesh with similar gruesome stories, the military – supported by Aung San Suu Kyi's government – continuously denied any wrongdoing.

Within days, Aung San Suu Kyi herself said that the situation in Rakhine State was being distorted by a 'huge iceberg of misinformation' with the aim of 'promoting the interest of the terrorists'.[42]

The stories of military-led atrocities kept coming, and as part of an attempt to control the narrative, within a week of the attacks the government invited a group of journalists – a mixture of local and international – to northern Rakhine to see the situation on the ground.

Much like the trip I had been on a few weeks earlier, the visit was tightly controlled by the government. Journalists could only visit areas decided upon by their minders, and security personnel, from the same institution accused of conducting the violence, followed them closely.

At *Frontier*, we were again invited on the trip and chose to send a reporter. While we recognized it wouldn't give a full picture of the situation on the ground, we hoped it would at least provide some insight.

That it did, although not in the way we expected.

The journalists were first taken to a small school on the outskirts of downtown Maungdaw, which was being used as a camp for Hindus displaced by the violence.

People there told the reporters about attacks on their village by ARSA and said they were too scared to return home.

The reporters were then taken to a nearby monastery, where a monk said he had witnessed Muslims setting fire to their own homes. Immediately after the interview, the journalists were handed photos by the government minders apparently showing the acts taking place.

The photos showed men in Muslim-style caps holding machetes as they burned down a thatched roof. In the foreground a group of women – who appeared to have tablecloths over their heads – stood around idly, waving machetes in the air.

It later transpired that at least two of the people in the photos, a man and a woman, had been two of the 'Hindu refugees' they had met at the school earlier in the day.

'Clearly, the photos had been staged', said *Frontier's* reporter.

The government's narrative unravelled even more the following day, when the journalists were returning to Maungdaw town after spending the day conducting interviews near the Myanmar-Bangladesh border.

The convoy passed a village that was on fire and, after negotiations with the authorities, were allowed to stop.

The village was called Gawduthara and had been Muslim majority before the residents fled. *Frontier's* reporter said that, as he was staring at the burning homes, he looked down to the ground and saw religious books, some with Arabic script, strewn across the floor. Also on the floor was an empty plastic jug that smelled of petrol.

Authorities have continuously said that the burning of any homes was carried out by Rohingya, eager to elicit sympathy from the international community. But the reporters on the trip said there were no Muslims nearby.

Standing not so far away though were a group of men, who by their appearance appeared to be Rakhine. They were standing around watching, and some were holding machetes, said *Frontier's* reporter.

He approached one of the men and asked what he had seen. The man said he was from a nearby village and that 'Bengalis' had set fire to their houses at 5 am that morning.

'I checked my watch', the reporter said. 'It was 1.44 pm, almost nine hours after the man said the fires had been lit. It was clear that the fires flickering before us had been set much more recently than that.'

It was another few weeks after that – and almost an entire month since the attacks – that Aung San Suu Kyi spoke publicly about the issue for the first time (the earlier comments had been made in a private meeting, then reported).

On a Tuesday morning, she took to the stage at a convention centre in the capital, Nay Pyi Taw, and addressed the world with a speech in English; it was watched by thousands on a big screen in the heart of Yangon's downtown, where supporters waved images of Aung San Suu Kyi and cheered words of support.

The speech was littered with inaccuracies, and for many observers it was moment of recognition of just how out of touch she was with the realities on the ground.

'We want to find out why this exodus is happening' was one comment that brought raised eyebrows from the group I was watching it with. If Myanmar's government really wanted to understand why more than half a million had fled over the border in the last few weeks, they merely needed to hop on a plane to Bangladesh and speak to the people in the camps. (It wasn't until almost nine months after the violence that a senior official visited the camps for the first time.)

There were other falsehoods in the speech: that the 'fighting' had ended weeks earlier (I was still being sent videos of villages burning), that 'the great majority of Muslims' in Rakhine had not joined the exodus (they had) and that all people in Rakhine receive access to healthcare and education (they didn't and still don't).

Amnesty International hit the nail on the head, when they said after the speech that Aung San Suu Kyi was 'burying her head in the sand'.[43]

Later that night, some friends and I were at dinner unpacking the speech. Across from where we sat were pictures of various celebrities, underneath famous quotes they had made, in a somewhat tacky fashion. Among the group was a picture of Aung San Suu Kyi underneath a quote attributed to her that said: 'Freedom and democracy are dreams you never give up.'

A friend sat next to me took a swig of his beer and nodded in the direction of her picture, then said: 'Will today be remembered as the day The Lady fell?'

It's hard to think of a public figure in recent history whose global reputation has tumbled as quickly as Aung San Suu Kyi's. After the NLD won a resounding victory in the 2015 general election, she was lauded as a global icon for democracy, but less than two years later her standing worldwide had plummeted, whereby she was described 'evil', and there were calls for her to be stripped of the Nobel Peace Prize she was awarded in 1991 (it can't be rescinded).

Has the criticism about her treatment of the Rohingya been fair? I'd argue yes and no.

Firstly, one cannot ignore the point, raised on numerous occasions since the crisis began, that she did not have control over the military and in all reality could have done very little to prevent the military from carrying out its gruesome campaign. But the conversation goes deeper than that.

The dominant global narrative about Myanmar over the last thirty years, of her as the one great hope for democracy in the country, was always overly simplistic. Of course it is true in all countries, no one person can fix all of its problems, but in the Myanmar story there has long been a problematic arc that essentially argued that if Aung San Suu Kyi came to power, and overthrew the men in the green, then the country would have peace, prosperity and democracy.

This was problematic for a few reasons. There's the obvious point that Myanmar is an incredibly complex place, and the legacies of military rule were never going to be sorted overnight. But more than that, for several decades, and long before Aung San Suu Kyi emerged as Myanmar's democracy icon, there have been countless other people in the country who have sacrificed so much for the democratic cause, and could have contributed significantly to the nation-building project, whether in the form of the economy, education, civil rights or a whole host of other issues that needed addressing.

In fairness to Aung San Suu Kyi, she pushed back against the fanciful version of her, saying in 2017 that she was 'just a politician'. 'I am not quite like Margaret Thatcher, no. But on the other hand, I am no Mother Teresa either. I have never said that I was',[44] she told the BBC's Fergal Keane.

But clearly a large part of her believed the hype. She appeared to view her role as the nation's leader – which she became in everything but name after the 2015 election, even creating the state counsellor role for herself – as a dynastic continuation of the work of her father, independence hero General Aung San. Her approach to leadership style was quintessentially micro-management, even authoritarian to some extent, as she rejected any form of criticism and pushed out anyone deemed not loyal enough to her or the NLD. Little meaningful change was achieved during her time in office, and a major factor in this has to be her inability to listen to voices who knew much more about certain topics than she did.

And yet, at the same time, I can fully understand why there has been so much widespread disappointment in her failure to not only take actions but even speak up on behalf of the Rohingya.

There is certainly more she could have done, especially in the immediate aftermath of the August 2017 violence. Despite her reputation taking a huge tumble internationally, inside the country she was, and still is, very much adored, especially by the Bamar majority. The vitriol flying around, both online and in streets, was nauseating, with Myanmar people I considered friends not only accusing Rohingya of lying about what had happened to them but also expressing disbelief about the reported rapes because the Rohingya were 'too dirty'.

As someone held in such high regard with the majority of the population, Aung San Suu Kyi could have used her position to speak up against the hatred that was being spewed and called for calmness from all. It would've gone a long way, I think, in bringing a level of calmness to an ugly situation.

But she remained silent, and in fact, her office shared some dangerous false rumours that international organizations were helping the ARSA fighters, putting many more lives at risk. In those few weeks in particular, she failed to be the unifying force she may have otherwise been.

Of the dreadful situation in Myanmar since the coup, one of the positives has been a recognition from many of those protesting that politics in Myanmar needs to look beyond one person. Aung San Suu Kyi is still held in high regard by many of the people, but as the military's violence has escalated, there has been a drastic shift in many of the calls being made, and they now go beyond just calling for Aung San Suu Kyi's release and instead demand that any future Myanmar must see the military, and all forms of authoritarianism, removed from politics.

In Cox's Bazar

The day after Aung San Suu Kyi's Nay Pyi Taw speech, I travelled with a photographer colleague, Steve, from Yangon to Dhaka, the Bangladeshi capital, en route to the refugee camps in Cox's Bazar at the country's southern tip.

Dhaka is not an easy city to love. Like anywhere, there are likely some endearing elements to it, but you're unlikely to see them during a few hours passing through. It's hot, manic and dusty, and Steve and I tried to get out as quickly as we could.

But, for the most part, the people were remarkably friendly, including the immigration officers. Globally, a journalist visa in your passport does not typically lead to a friendly exchange with the guardians at the gate, but after landing at Dhaka's rundown airport and handing over our passports, we were treated with a level of respect I was not expecting.

'You're here to report on the Rohingya, I assume?' asked the young man who was stamping my passport.

I nodded that I was.

'Good. The world needs to know what's happening', he said as he waved me through.

Learning that we had missed the last flight of the day to Cox's Bazar, we negotiated an extortionate price to take a taxi to the bus station across town. Held up by almost perpetual gridlock, the seven-mile journey took more than two hours, and we just about made the last bus of the night.

Once onboard, I quickly fell asleep and awoke several hours later to find us rolling through the lush greenery of southern Bangladesh.

At 120 kilometres in length, Cox's Bazar is often billed as the longest beach in the world, and it's a point of pride for many Bangladeshis, who often travel there for weekend breaks.

Sadly, it is now better known for the sprawling refugee camps to the south, which are home to about a million refugees, mainly Rohingya, and the majority of which have fled since August 2017.

Arriving in the main town early morning, Steve and I found a hotel, dropped our bags in the room and headed straight down to the camps, about an hour's journey by car.

Along the way, we collected Shamimul Islam who would work as our translator during our week there. Shamimul was a Rohingya refugee who had fled northern Rakhine with his family during the violence of the early 1990s and lived on the camp's outskirts.

As we drove south towards Kutupalong, the largest refugee camp in the area, Shamimul explained how proud he was to work with the media and to help document what was happening to his people.

'We've had it bad for so many years', he said, as we passed crowds of people queuing for food to be distributed. 'But what I've seen these past few weeks is bad as it's ever been. Wait until you see the scale of the suffering.'

Shortly after, we rounded a corner and there ahead of us were the camps. Basic shelters were packed into every available space; high on hills, or in thick forests, were tiny structures made up of nothing more than a piece of tarpaulin held up by bamboo. The only areas where there weren't houses were the huge pools of filthy stagnant water that had filled up as a result of rainy season. In these pools, which were no doubt a hive of diseases, young children played and women washed their hair and utensils.

There were people everywhere. The narrow road that jutted through the camps was packed either side with people, who were marching determinedly in different directions, some carrying materials back to their homes, while others were sat by the side of the road, staring ahead into the distance.

On the first day, we conducted interviews with about a dozen people. Their stories were all gruesome, and difficult to hear, but also remarkably similar.

All were Rohingya and had lived their entire lives in northern Rakhine, although some with brief stints in Bangladesh. All said relations between the Buddhist and Muslim communities in their home villages had been relatively good until the October 2016 attacks. All said soldiers – sometimes alongside Buddhist neighbours – had come to their homes shortly after 25 August to forcefully remove them. Some said they were told to leave before the violence started; others said the violence, which included the burning of home and shooting at people fleeing, started immediately. All had family members killed.

'My husband is dead. Now we have nothing', said one lady who was cradling a child who was only a few months old.

The desperation was confronting too. At one camp, a fight broke out after a man began distributing vouchers for the collection of tarpaulins. The scene quickly grew chaotic; the frustrated man threw the vouchers into the air, prompting a wild scramble.

At another camp there was more order as a small group of men waited patiently for food. Standing at the edge of the crowd I met Rajuma Begum. She was holding her infant child as three other children stood patiently next to her. Her husband had been killed during an attack on their village by security forces and vigilantes, she said.

'I'm not receiving any food', she told me as she stroked the head of one of her young sons. 'All we have is a small amount of rice, but it is not enough. I'm just depending on Allah.'

At the end of an emotional and exhausting day's reporting, we were travelling back towards our hotel at Cox's Bazar. I was drifting asleep in the back of the car when I heard Steve shout for the driver to stop.

He had seen a man lying by the side of the road, looking severely malnourished, and we rushed back to speak with him.

With Shamimul translating through conversations with his wife, we learned that the man's name was Sayed Akbar, and he had arrived in Bangladesh from northern Rakhine State about a week previously following the military's violence.

With his ribs sticking through his skin, and barely with enough strength to lift his head, it was clear the man was dying. His wife said she had taken him to a nearby clinic, which gave him some medicine but said there was nothing more they could do for him.

We tried to figure out how we could help but there was little we could do. We left some water and money for the wife and returned to our hotel.

I thought about Sayed Akbar, lying by that road side, all night, but more death and despair was awaiting us in the camps the next morning. We were travelling through the camps once more, on our way to Teknaf, at Bangladesh's southern tip, when we passed a funeral taking place at the roadside. Through broken interviews with the family, we learned that a man had been run over by a truck the night before while he was walking home from prayers at a nearby mosque – an example of the suffering the Rohingya still faced, even when they made it to the relative safety of Bangladesh.

We continued to Teknaf, from where we took a boat to Shah Porir, an island at Bangladesh's very southern tip. It was here that many Rohingya had arrived by boat. A Bangladeshi soldier patrolling the shore told us that the number of arrivals had slowed in recent days, but that some were still arriving during the night.

We were then taken to a nearby mosque, which was being used as a refuge for those still arriving in Bangladesh. There we meet Jashim Uddin, a Bangladeshi man in his thirties who was managing the site. He told us that about 40,000 people had taken shelter there in the past month before moving onto the mainland.

We also met many of the new arrivals, and their stories were all heartbreaking. There was the young mother, huddled in the corner with her three young daughters, whose husband had been killed in the violence. Or the woman sat alone, staring into the distance. She said she had some family at one of the camps in southern Bangladesh and that she hoped to find them.

One person we met whose story has stayed with me ever since was Nurul Amin, an elderly man who we met sitting on a bench outside the mosque.

He told us he had left his village on the outskirts of Sittwe in late August and travelled to northern Rakhine State to visit relatives living in Rathedaung. The timing of his trip coincided with the ARSA attacks, and Nurul Amin found himself caught up in the crackdown.

'Suddenly the violence started', he told me. 'The military, along with a group of Rakhine, started attacking people and burning villages. I tried to go back home, but it was not possible.'

Nurul Amin, who was sixty-five when I spoke to him, then spent the next three weeks hiding in the villages in northern Rakhine. Eventually, he paid a fee to a broker to take a boat over the Naf River to Bangladesh.

'I have spoken with my family. They know that I am here, that I am safe', he said. 'It's too risky for me to go back. The situation is very difficult, and I cannot move anywhere.'

The next day we travelled several hours east of Cox's Bazar to Naikongchari, a small village, from where we hoped to walk the several hours to the border, to an area where some of the refugee camps were located.

We weren't sure what to expect and Shamimul warned us that there was a good chance we would be turned back at Naikongchari by the Bangladeshi soldiers stationed there.

Sure enough, moments after our car reached the eastern outskirts of the village, a soldier walked into the road and ordered our car to stop. We were beckoned towards a wooden hut, inside which a gruff soldier demanded our passports.

We sat waiting for half an hour as the soldier barked commands into his walkie-talkie.

'Major General will see you', he said, eventually, as if we were waiting for a dental appointment.

We waited patiently once more, a little tentative about what our audience with the major general would involve. As we waited, about half a dozen of his minions cleaned around us and brought out plates of fresh fruit, biscuits and cups of tea. Then the major general emerged, proudly dressed in his finest military uniform.

As we shook hands, he let out a beaming smile. 'Nice to meet you, gentlemen', he said in impeccable, unaccented English.

The major general proudly told us he had spent a few happy summers in the UK and wanted to spend some time speaking with, as he put it, 'some proper English gentlemen' (this didn't go down too well with Steve, an out-and-out Aussie from rural Queensland, but he knew better than to argue).

We sat with the major general for about an hour, talking English literature (he was particularly fond of Byron), cricket and English summers. I smiled, nodded and pretended that my summers of drinking Lambrini under a slide in a Dartford park were similar to his revelries in the Cotswolds.

The conversation eventually turned towards the conflict that had been happening over the border.

'You know, I used to be stationed up at the border with India, and life was very peaceful', the major general said. 'But with these Myanmar . . . it's different.'

He said that in the days following the 25 August attacks, aircraft from Myanmar had entered Bangladeshi airspace, which he believed was a clear provocation.

The major general said that relations had largely calmed down since then, but that there were still occasional flare-ups.

For years after our audience, I stayed in touch with the major general on WhatsApp, and we messaged from time to time. More than a year later, news emerged of Myanmar building up forces near the Bangladeshi border, and I messaged him to ask about it.

'Brother, I have no idea, I'm sorry', came the response. 'I'm with our Indian brothers again, and life is very peaceful.'

After our talk with the major general, we made the two-hour walk to the border, where the refugee camps were located. The major general had phoned ahead, and the Bangladeshi soldiers stationed there were expecting us. After some negotiation, they allowed us to enter the area where the camp was located, which was technically in a 'No Man's Land' between the two countries.

We entered the camps and spoke with the families there. As we were nearing the end of an interview with a family who had arrived in the camps just a few days before, Shamimul picked up snippets of a conversation taking place to the side.

'Ask them about landmines', he whispered in my ear.

One of the men we were interviewing quickly explained that a few days earlier two men had been killed by landmines nearby. The villagers then took us to the area where the incident had taken place.

We were taken to the last house in the village, which stood on a hill at the bottom of which sat a small river. Next to the stream was a single discarded bag of detergent.

'People used to go there to wash, but not anymore', said one of the camp's residents.

Villagers told us that a Rohingya man and three of his buffalo were killed by an initial explosion. A Bangladeshi man who volunteered to go into the heavily forested area to retrieve the body was then killed by a separate detonation – his body was retrieved by the Bangladeshi military, residents said.

'Because people think there are still landmines, the [Rohingya] man's body is still out there', said one of the camp's residents. She said she had heard one of the explosions and had seen the Bangladeshi man's body being carried away.

Several of the camp's residents told us that they had seen Tatmadaw soldiers walking close to the border hours before the explosions and accused them of laying the landmines.

In a separate incident on the same day, at another 'No Man's Land' area about fifty kilometres south, a Rohingya woman lost both her legs after stepping on a mine close to the border fence.

We visited that area the day after travelling to Naikongchari, and residents there told us that they had seen Tatmadaw soldiers near the border fence hours before the explosion happened.

'We could see the military coming down the hill, and then sometimes they would sit down. We could see them sitting down, but couldn't see what they were doing', said Forid Alam. 'After they left, we went to try and find out what was happening and that was when we found the landmines.'

He said that shortly after, camp residents heard an explosion and later learned that the woman had stepped on a landmine. Forid sent me a video showing her being carried across a river, both her legs severed below the knee.

The despair we encountered during a week reporting in Cox's Bazar didn't end there. We also met about half a dozen survivors of Tula Toli, a village in northern Rakhine known in Myanmar as Minn Gyi. Tula Toli was the scene of the one of the biggest massacres against the Rohingya.

Survivors said that when the military arrived, they told people to go to the riverbank where they would be safe. Some villagers believed them and ran to the river, while most of those we spoke to ran in the other direction, towards the forest. Those we spoke to said they had stood on a hilltop as they watched soldiers massacre their friends and family, who had thought they would be safe by running to the riverside. The only Tula Toli resident we interviewed who hadn't fled to the hills was a ten-year-old girl, who said she only survived after jumping into the river after the soldiers had lined the villagers up and told them they would be killed. She witnessed her mothers and sisters burned to death in front of her, she said.

We also met kids as young as three who had seen family members killed in front of them and a man in his mid-twenties who had returned home after visiting a relative to find his children and wife massacred.

'I turned on the light, and there they were. All dead', he said.

Mrauk U crackdown

After the trip to Bangladesh, I left feeling exhausted and shortly after took a month-long break back in the UK seeing friends and family. When I returned to Myanmar in the January, I felt genuinely refreshed, and happy to be back, but after a year that had left me feeling tired and jaded, I tried to take a break from reporting on developments in Rakhine.

It wasn't to be. One balmy Yangon evening in the middle of January, news began to emerge of seven residents in Mrauk U, the ancient town that had once been the capital of the Rakhine kingdom, being shot dead by police during a protest that had heavily escalated. All of the dead were reported to have been not Rohingya but Buddhist Rakhine.

The protest had started after authorities suddenly cancelled a planned protest to commemorate the fall of the Rakhine kingdom, which was annexed by the Burmese Konbaung dynasty in the late eighteenth century.

The day before the anniversary, Aye Maung, a prominent and controversial Rakhine politician, delivered a bombastic speech in nearby Rathedaung. Standing alongside Wai Hun Aung, a prominent Rakhine writer, Aye Maung accused the government of treating the Rakhine people like 'slaves'.

Aye Maung also called for greater sovereignty for the Rakhine people and discussed the need for an armed struggle, an apparent reference to the armed group the Arakan Army, which had been established a few years earlier with the aim of fighting for the Rakhine people and was gradually building its presence in the state.

Angry that the event had been cancelled, a large crowd began marching around Mrauk U, in the direction of the local administrative office. After an argument broke out there, witnesses alleged that police officers guarding the office shot into the crowd, killing seven.

Since the uptick in violence there in 2012, the Rakhine people have often been portrayed as the aggressive villain against the Rohingya, an overly simplistic narrative. As has been mentioned earlier in this chapter, the Rakhine have their own share of grievances. There are certainly some Rakhine I have met whose views towards the Rohingya I found distasteful, but there are also those who are sympathetic towards the struggles their neighbours have faced. However, the overwhelming viewpoint I have heard when speaking with Rakhine people is that they want to live in peace and to be able to provide food and jobs for their family.

For years there has been significant anger towards the government from many in Rakhine, in particular due to the lack of economic development, and the incident in Mrauk U only made that worse.

I visited Mrauk U with a Myanmar colleague a few months after the shootings, and the anger and fear many people felt was very clearly on display. We were told that many of the protestors had left town out of fear of being arrested, and several witnesses refused to speak to us because of concerns for their safety.

Travelling around town with a local tour guide who doubled up as our translator, it took several days to find someone willing to speak, before we were eventually taken to a small house on the edge of town and told that a middle-aged woman would talk to us; her son had been one of those killed.

The lady said that on the evening of the violence, she had assumed her son was at work at a nearby store. Although she had heard the violence, including the gunshots in the distance, she didn't give it much thought until her son's boss arrived at her house asking for his whereabouts.

Unable to locate him, the mother travelled with her son's employer to the local hospital. After some time waiting, and frantic with worry, the woman approached a hospital worker who handed her a phone that had photos of some of the deceased.

'That's when I saw the photo of my son, dead', she said.

The violence at Mrauk U was one of the factors that contributed to the rapid rise of the Arakan Army, which escalated its operations with an attack on security outposts in Rakhine on 4 January 2019, Myanmar's Independence Day.[45] These attacks, which saw about a dozen police officers killed, paved the way for an intense bout of fighting across northern Rakhine, as well as in neighbouring Chin State, throughout 2019 and 2020.

The Arakan Army was founded in Laiza, the headquarters of the Kachin Independence Army, in 2009 mainly by Rakhine youths, particularly migrant workers who had fled their home state to find work in the jade mines around Hpakant.[46] During this period, the group trained and fought alongside the KIA, and the Ta'ang National Liberation Army, in their battles with the Tatmadaw in the country's north.

As it built up its capabilities, including raising funds through the country's multi-billion-dollar drugs trade,[47] the AA began to expand its operations, into Chin State and Rakhine, where it began to launch ambushes against government forces.

Its January 2019 attacks transformed the group 'from a growing nuisance the Tatmadaw could largely contain into a serious security threat',[48] and from there its operations expanded, with tactics including conventional warfare, guerrilla warfare in the form of stealth attacks as well as the punishment of local civilians, including kidnapping of government officials.

The Tatmadaw responded with their own use of violence. Within days of the 4 January attacks, a government spokesperson said that the military had been instructed to 'crush' the AA,[49] and the Tatmadaw deployed additional combat troops to the area. Over the next two years of conflict, the military fired indiscriminately in civilian areas, killing and injuring civilians and damaging homes and other properties.[50]

The violence in Rakhine looked set to escalate further, on course to becoming the deadliest conflict Myanmar had faced in years, but then shortly after the November 2020 election, the two sides announced an informal ceasefire that brought the fighting to an immediate halt.[51]

The truce, which was brokered by Japan's special envoy to Myanmar, was announced as part of efforts for voting to take place in the state, where it had been cancelled ahead of the poll due to security concerns. With the benefit of hindsight, however, at least on the part of the Tatmadaw, it appears more likely to have been a form of pre-planning ahead of a potential coup a few months later, removing its troops from the conflict in Rakhine and deploying them elsewhere in the country.

Since the coup, Rakhine State has been one of the few parts of the country not swept up by large-scale protests and strikes against the junta. In March 2021, the military regime removed the AA from its list of 'terrorist' groups, and through its administrative wing, the United League of Arakan (ULA), the AA has used this relative peace to expand its control across large parts of the state, particularly the north.

'The AA can now be assumed to have control over three-quarters of the entire state', said Rakhine politician Aye Maung.[52]

Elsewhere in the country, amid what appears to be a new-found sympathy for the Rohingya from some in Myanmar, the NUG released a position paper explicitly using the word 'Rohingya' – in contrast to Aung San Suu Kyi and the NLD – and acknowledging the 'violence and gross human rights violations' they were subjected to by the military. The NUG said it would provide 'justice and reparation' for the group.[53]

Meanwhile, the serious restrictions imposed on the Rohingya in Rakhine remain in place, while the camps in Bangladesh witnessed increased insecurity and fear, which sources there blamed on ARSA increasing its presence and violence. In October 2021, Mohib Ullah, a Rohingya prominent leader, was shot dead in his office, which witnesses blamed on ARSA.

The crisis over the last few years in Rakhine State has come about due to a multitude of reasons, including anxieties brought about by the country's opening up, as well as policies introduced by military governments eroding the rights of the Rohingya. One factor that cannot be ignored, however, has been the perilous economic situation for all communities living there, despite the area having significant potential due to its rich natural resources.

It's a scenario that's familiar to communities across much of the country and probably the most effective tool the Tatmadaw has used to maintain its hold on power for decades.

Living off the land

Before dawn on 2 June 2020, hundreds of informal jade miners were already at work at the Wai Khar mine in Hpakant, which straddles the Uyu River in Kachin, sifting through the vast mountainside in search of the slightest glimpse of the precious green mineral.

Myanmar's notorious monsoon season had kicked fully into gear a few weeks prior, creating a temporary lake in the middle of the usually muddy bottom of the jade pit. Above the workers was a giant wall of churned-up mud and waste, leftover from years of excavation at the sight.

The onslaught of rain had been so heavy that, days earlier, authorities had announced the closure of most jade mines in Hpakant, a once-heavily forested area where the landscape has been permanently decimated by years of extraction. But the miners – known as *ye ma say* – were undeterred by the announcement. They are typically poor, travelling from all over the country to come to Hpakant, home to Myanmar's largest collection of jade, in search of that one chance discovery of the shiny emerald that they hope will bring them financial prosperity.

Just before dawn on 2 July, the earth and waste on the mountainside at Wai Khar began to shift, carrying a monumental sea of mud into the valley below, crashing into the temporary lake, and sending a huge wave of water over hundreds of the workers. A local official described it as 'like a tsunami'.[1] At least 172 people were killed, in what was, at least as far we know, the deadliest jade-related landslide in Myanmar's history.

'Within a minute, all the people at the bottom [of the hill] just disappeared', said Maung Khaing, who witnessed the tragedy. 'I feel empty in my heart. I still have goosebumps. . . . There were people stuck in the mud shouting for help but no one could help them.'[2]

Days after the incident, the military announced that two officers in charge of security in the area were fired for having 'failed their responsibilities', by allowing 'trespassing' into a restricted area.[3] But this was nothing more than a short-term measure, aimed at stifling public anger, and did nothing to address the deep-rooted issues of impunity and corruption in Myanmar's jade sector. This has resulted in large-scale mining companies – usually with connections to the military or other armed groups – dumping their mining waste on mountainsides for the *ye ma say* to sift through, often with deadly consequences.

The Wai Khar landslide may have been the deadliest recorded in Hpakant, but it wasn't unique. The area has witnessed at least eighteen deadly incidents since 2015, nearly all the result of mine waste crushing the workers underneath.[4]

As well as being dangerous, jade mining is back-breaking work.

Kyaw Htet, twenty-three, is from Hpakant, and began working as a jade miner when he was fifteen, due to a lack of job prospects in the area. He typically works at night, starting at about 7 pm in the evening, and working through until 4 am, with only a short break in between.

'It is very tiring, and there is a risk of dying if we don't move quickly [if land collapses]', he said.[5]

Although jade deposits are found around the world, Myanmar is the main source, providing about 90 per cent of the world's supply of the mineral, most of it at Hpakant.[6]

Stones found at Hpakant are typically smuggled over the nearby border into China, where they are coveted as a status symbol, or a worthwhile investment. A Chinese saying states that 'you can put a price on gold, but jade is priceless'[7] – a belief fortified by the writings of ancient philosopher Confucius, who described the emerald as a metaphor for the human characteristics of intelligence, truth and loyalty. Today it is believed to possess the power to avert evil and bad luck, while fostering health and good fortune.

That's not the case for miners like Kyaw Htet.

'Our life depends on us finding jade. Last month, I didn't find any jade stones, so I had no money for my livelihood', he said. 'I don't want to mine for jade the rest of my life. I want to start a business, but to do that I need money.'

Informal workers like Kyaw Htet make up only a tiny fraction of Myanmar's jade trade, which has been described as a 'massive organised crime operation' that exploits those at the bottom.[8] In 2015, Global Witness estimated the industry to be worth up to US$31 billion.[9]

The opaque, and highly illicit, nature of the jade trade means that this estimate has been disputed, but whatever the true figure is, Myanmar's jade industry typically makes very little money for people like Kyaw Htet, but major earnings for those who control the mines around Hpakant and elsewhere. These companies are usually closely connected with the Myanmar military, or with other armed group operating in the country's borderlands, including the Arakan Army, Kachin Independence Army and the United Wa State Army.[10]

The KIA, and its administrative wing, the Kachin Independence Organisation, had controlled the Hpakant mines until the early 1990s, when the military wrestled control, leading to a ceasefire signed between the groups, which held until 2011. Since then, the area has seen decades of 'corrupt and destructive resource management'[11] by the military junta, which dished out licences at will, either to its own companies, or those owned by cronies with close connections.

When the National League for Democracy took office in 2016, following its resounding electoral victory a year earlier, it prioritized addressing corruption and mismanagement in the jade sector, by updating related laws, and decentralizing some authority to state and regional governments. Its first move was to suspend the issuing of new jade and gemstone mining licences, although companies would be allowed to continue under existing deals until they expired.

'There are a lot of reasons why we are suspending licence extensions, but the main one is to change the rules and regulations', an official from the state-owned Myanmar Gems Enterprise said at the time.[12]

The NLD's efforts should have struck a blow to the military's economic interests. After all, its companies – through its two major conglomerates Myanmar Economic Holdings Limited (MEHL) and Myanmar Economic Corporation (MEC) – own operations that between them controlled more mining licences than any other entity. By the 2018–19 financial year, when many of the licences granted before 2016 had expired, MEHL alone controlled almost 10 per cent of all jade and gem licences. These conglomerates were also reported to enjoy special privileges, including in the form of preferential access to licences that covered the best plots that were home to the highest quality of jade.[13]

But the NLD's reform efforts ultimately failed, in part because they never properly addressed the major issues at hand, which included holding the numerous 'bad actors' to account, and untangling the many conflicts of interest between private companies and the government's oversight bodies. Their piecemeal reform efforts also created an 'unregulated free-for-all', which military companies and others were able to capitalize upon, colluding with firms linked with other armed groups so that mining continued largely unabated.

'Now both sides are making money and working together', a civil society representative told Global Witness, an environmental NGO that has spent years researching Myanmar's jade sector.[14]

With the military's February 2021 power grab, any hopes of positive change to the sector are extremely unlikely, and in the current context it is all but certain that the military and its affiliated companies will continue colluding with other corrupt actors on the ground, further destroying the environment around places like Hpakant, and bringing more misery to the people living there.

One of those to benefit directly from illicit practices in the jade trade, and other industries, is the family of coup leader Min Aung Hlaing.

Global Witness found evidence linking corrupt practices around the import of explosives into Hpakant – which is used to blast open rocks to find the precious mineral – to the junta chief's eldest son, Aung Pyae Sone. He has also profited from arrangements to mine illegally in Hpakant since the licensing suspension, the group said.

Aung Pyae Sone, a stout fellow in his mid-thirties who was sanctioned by the United States after the February 2021 coup, has emerged as an increasingly powerful figure in the country since his father became commander-in-chief in 2011, having been granted a number of questionable contracts and positions. He heads a company that oversees approvals and customs clearance on behalf of Myanmar's Food and Drug Administration (FDA), despite seemingly having no background in this area,[15] and in 2013 received a cut-price deal for a high-end restaurant in the shadow of Yangon's Shwedagon Pagoda, for which he faced no competition from other companies.[16] This is likely to be just the tip of the iceberg of Aung Pyae Sone's business interests.

Military conglomerates

There's no doubt that Min Aung Hlaing directly benefits from the military's business interests, in particular as the head of MEHL and MEC.[17] Between them, the companies operate more than 100 businesses in industries ranging from banking to tourism, construction, telecommunications, jade, gems and petroleum, and many more in between.

MEHL is the largest of the two conglomerates, established in 1990 by the State Law and Order Restoration Council, which took power following the protests two years earlier, while MEC was founded seven years later. While the military receives billions of dollars per year through the state budget, a significant proportion of its funds are raised through these secretive and sprawling business interests.

Once again, their opaque nature makes it difficult to establish how much the military makes from its economic activities, but it is 'indisputable' that they 'contribute to funding the Tatmadaw's leadership and operations', said the UN's Independent International Fact-Finding Mission on Myanmar, which published a study on the military's business interests in 2019. These operations involve, among other things, the raping, torturing and killing of thousands of innocent civilians, as has been seen both before and after the coup.

Both MEC and MEHL are the brainchild of David Abel, who oversaw the economy as the head of various trade and finance-related ministries during the SLORC era.

I interviewed Abel in early 2016, in his family's consulting office on the edge of Yangon's Kandawgyi Lake. Despite being in his early eighties and clearly struggling from health issues that would contribute to his death three years later, he was a lively figure throughout, often punctuating his speech with passionate laments about the '40 years and 113 days' he spent in the Tatmadaw.

His military service included a stint studying at the Royal Military College, Sandhurst, in the United Kingdom in the 1950s, before returning home where he took part in military campaigns from 'the southernmost tip to the northernmost tip' of the country.

In 1988, he became a senior member of the SLORC administration, regarded as its economic czar, at one point running the ministries of commerce, finance and national planning and economic development simultaneously.

'I was using Singapore as a model. I wanted the private sector to be able to compete', he said of the formation of MEHL and MEC, referring to the state-owned holding company Temasek Holdings, which was created in the 1970s to help bring economic growth to the island state.

He was also inspired by Britain's former Prime Minister Margaret Thatcher, and Abel said he admired her success in privatizing state-owned enterprises (SOEs) and turning 'small- and medium-sized industries into big industries'.

Abel said the strategy was to first create an investment holding company to establish SOEs in a range of sectors, including telecommunications, transportation, energy and resources. These SOEs would then be privatized, in order to expand, improve productivity and competitiveness, create more jobs and ultimately be listed on a stock exchange for the Myanmar public to buy shares.

However, Abel – who as a Catholic was a rare non-Buddhist in the upper echelons of the Tatmadaw – said his ideas for drastic economic reform were blocked, although he refused to say why or by whom.

'I think the [economy] would be much better if I was allowed to implement my ideas then', he said. 'I tried to achieve something, but I didn't succeed. I was successful in terms of forming the MEHL and MEC, but I couldn't bring it forward. It's a big regret.'

Of the senior Tatmadaw figures I met and interviewed during my time in Myanmar, Abel was an exception, in that he was likeable. Like the others, he stubbornly held onto the belief that the army had only ever worked for the good of the country and the people, but he wasn't completely inflexible on this viewpoint, and appeared willing to admit that there were things both he and the institution could have done differently. In the few hours we spent together he struck me as sincere and introspective, and I couldn't help but wonder what might have been had the top brass chosen to listen to people like him, who are thinking about how they can improve the lives of Myanmar's people, rather than protecting their own interests.

The establishment of MEHL in 1990 was part of efforts to reform the country's economy in this period, the dismal performance of which had triggered the anti-government demonstrations that swept the country two years earlier, in particular the demonetizations enacted by Ne Win.

The dictator had already decimated the economy through his disastrous Burmese Way to Socialism. With its vast natural resources, and strategic location between India and China, as well as acting as the bridge connecting South and Southeast Asia, Myanmar has always had significant economic potential. It was something the British colonists were able to capitalize upon, albeit with an unequal system that filled their own pockets, while providing few benefits to the local people.

Economic struggles

During British colonial rule, Burma, as the country was called, was known as Asia's Rice Bowl, exporting millions of tonnes of the product, much of it from the fervent paddy fields of the Ayeyarwady Delta to markets around the world. In part assisted by the opening of the Suez Canal in the late nineteenth century, the colonists were also able to exploit other natural resources including tin, tungsten, jade, rubies and oil.[18]

The myriad armed conflicts that broke out immediately after independence would bring about widespread economic issues, a situation that grew worse following Ne Win's 1962 coup. Private businesses were nationalized, and foreign investment all but disappeared. Wealthy, and economically savvy land owners, many of them of Indian origin, were forced to flee due to Ne Win's xenophobic policies, while few of his administration had the know how to deal with the new highly centralized economic system.[19] Over the next few decades, the country became effectively bankrupt.

Shortly after the 1988 protests were ended through yet another military coup, Abel, in his position as Minister of Trade, announced a new 'open door' policy that would encourage foreign investment and trade. However, due to widespread distrust of the new military regime there were few immediate takers, and the SLORC government embarked on 'a crash programme of selling abroad precious natural resources, including fishery rights, gemstones, timber and oil concessions'.[20] The new government needed to raise revenue and foreign exchange, in particular after the salaries of soldiers and many civil servants had doubled immediately after the coup in order to ensure their continued loyalty.

Some foreign companies soon began to capitalize on the new arrangement, with timber deals struck with businessmen in neighbouring Thailand, while trade with China increased exponentially, based on a deal quietly signed between the two countries in August 1988 in the midst of the anti-government uprisings.[21]

Companies from further afield entered the market too, with new hotels and office buildings sprouting up in Yangon, although most of these deals were struck with military-linked companies, paving the way for their domination of the economy that continues today. The general population survived mainly on a black market that saw food, oil and other essential items brought in from China, India and Thailand.

Among those companies to strike deals with the SLORC regime was Dutch brewer Heineken, at the time the leading foreign brand in the US beer market, who partnered with MEHL to begin work on a sprawling new brewery on the northern outskirts of Yangon. However, just as quickly as they had arrived, they had left again, caving to public pressure and new sanctions introduced in the late 1990s over continued human rights abuses.

'Every billboard in the country will come down. Out is out', Heineken said.

The country's economy largely stagnated for the next decade or so, although business continued with companies based in the region, or those less concerned about the human rights situation. Things began to drastically change, however, when the economic and political reforms began in 2011, including looser restrictions on imports and exports, greater autonomy for the Central Bank and the enactment of new foreign investment laws that were welcoming to international firms.

The impact was immediate, with economic indicators including growth, foreign direct investment and GDP, all showing dramatic rises in a matter of years, with much of the money pouring into Yangon, the commercial capital.

Economic reforms

When I arrived there in early 2012, the changes were taking place everywhere you looked. Along Pyay Road, the main thoroughfare connecting the city's airport with its downtown, dilapidated houses were being replaced with gleaming new high-rises, international brands were announcing their arrivals on a daily basis and there seemed to be a new fancy bar or restaurant opening every night of the week.

On one of my first days in the country I attended the opening ceremony of what was being billed as the country's first international-standard shopping mall, at Junction Square, in the north of the city. An endearing memory stands out in my mind, of two women, perhaps in their mid-forties and in traditional Myanmar dresses, their faces covered in *thanaka*, in fits of laughter as they rode one of the mall's escalators, seemingly the first time they'd ever encountered such a contraption.

But the most obvious cosmetic change in Yangon was the proliferation of cars. Even when I'd arrived, almost a year after the new government had taken office, there were very few cars on the road, and the only ones in existence were almost exclusively clapped-out old bangers, with holes in the floor and the roof, steering wheels attached upside down, and entire windows missing. I remember taking a ride through the city one night in a taxi where the driver's seat was a garden chair strapped down with bungee cords.

Very quickly that changed, with the government first introducing a substitution plan allowing owners to replace their old cars with an import permit for newer models. Import tariffs were also drastically reduced under the new government, leading to new cars flooding the market overnight.

Although this led to seemingly perpetual gridlock on Yangon's streets, it was also an indication of improved investor confidence in the country, and showrooms for major international car brands began appearing in major cities, notably Yangon and Mandalay.

But by far the most drastic change in the country's economic landscape during this period was widespread reforms to the telecommunications sector, which brought almost the entire population online for the first time.

When I arrived, accessing the internet was an infuriating experience, typically spent in a dingy internet café, where emails wouldn't load and it took half an hour to log-in to Facebook. Skype calls with friends or family back home invariably had to be abandoned a few minutes in, as I was unable to hear more than a few words of what the other person was saying (I told myself at the time, not entirely convincingly, this was the reason a girlfriend in Australia had broken up with me).

Eventually I bit the bullet and forked out US$200 for a SIM card from the state-owned Myanmar Posts and Telecommunications, later re-branded as MPT, but this did little to improve my internet access. The price I'd paid had been an improvement on a few years earlier, when SIM cards would cost around US$2,000, and as a result were the exclusive domain of senior military figures.

In 2013, the government introduced a new Telecommunications Law, allowing for a drastic overhaul of the sector, which until then had been entirely dominated by MPT and other military-linked companies, all who offered abysmal services. A year later, the country's first two foreign telco operators – Norway's Telenor and Ooredoo from Qatar – entered the market for the first time, providing fast internet speeds, and more importantly, SIM cards for as little as US$1. Even MPT recognized the need to improve their service, partnering with a Japanese firm, while a few years after Telenor and Ooredoo entered the market, the military established its own telco provider, MyTel, in partnership with the Vietnamese military, a shadier operation than its competitors, which attracted complaints for not abiding by 'sound competition practices'.[22]

Suddenly everyone was online. Everywhere you went, people's faces were lit up with the blue light of a phone screen, while songs from YouTube videos could be heard blaring from houses, shops and buses up and down the country. Facebook came pre-loaded on shop-bought phones, while the company also allowed its app to be used without incurring data charges, resulting in the social media giant effectively becoming the internet in Myanmar.

The down side of Myanmar's internet explosion has been well documented, in particular how it became a platform for hate speech, notably against the Rohingya, but there's no doubt that improved connectivity also brought with it drastic improvements in the lives of many people.

In rural areas, improved access to information meant that farmers knew the fairest price to pay for a product, while a number of health-related apps and platforms emerged, providing advice to people in remote areas that were difficult for doctors to reach.

The tech explosion also enhanced economic opportunities. Before the reforms had begun, most people in Myanmar had few prospects available to them, apart from going abroad in search of work, trading on the black market or taking low-paid jobs in military- or crony-owned businesses.

Now Myanmar had a new generation of entrepreneurs, many who were utilizing the improved connectivity to establish businesses in everything from website design, to human resources, logistics, cartoon publishing and many more in between.

One of these tech entrepreneurs, a Yangonite who had established his own website building company, told me at the time that it felt like he was operating in a 'golden era'.

The knock-on effect could be felt in other sectors too. In tourism, new hotels and restaurants were sprouting up all over the country, including in places away from the well-established destinations of Yangon, Mandalay, Bagan and Inya Lake, capitalizing on the country's new reputation as a 'must see' destination.

In late 2016 I travelled to Kayah, the smallest of Myanmar's fourteen states or regions, located in the east of the country next to the Thai border. Kayah was still only attracting a handful of tourists at the time, but was increasingly appearing on many visitors' radars.

My tour guide for the trip was Min Htoo, a smiling, bespectacled gentleman in his fifties, who had been working in Myanmar's tourism sector for several decades. In 1996, to commemorate the junta's 'Visit Myanmar Year', he was granted his first licence to operate as a tour guide in the state, but could barely use it because there were almost no tourists. That had changed a few years before my visit, after the government allowed visitors to the state after a ceasefire was signed with an ethnic armed group operating there.

'I have tourists every week now. Sometimes every day during the high season', he said.

During the visit, Min Htoo drove me several hours out of Loikaw, the state capital, to Pan Pet, a cluster of villages nestled into the Kayah hills. Pan Pet was home to a large population of Kayan people, sometimes known as Padaung, where the women are commonly referred to as 'long-necked women' due to the distinctive brass coils worn around their necks.

Globally, the Padaung women have come to be known disparagingly as 'giraffe women', and due to the lack of opportunities at home many were forced to travel across the border into Thailand, often working in 'human zoos', where they were made to pose for photographs with tourists.

But Pan Pet was now home to a new community-based programme that aimed to empower women, providing training on how to make and market local crafts. One of the women I met there was a Kayan woman in her sixties who wore the brass rings. She was sat outside her home weaving a scarf, and on the table next to her were a number of crafts she had made, including figurines and jewellery.

'Before, there were no opportunities in this village, so everyone went abroad', she said. 'But now, because the situation in our country is better and this program has created more opportunities, people are returning.'

The reforms that had taken place also led to many Western countries, including the United States, lifting economic sanctions and restoring trade benefits to the country. Although rights groups warned the move may have been too quick, it contributed to further economic growth, particularly in labour-intensive industries such as garments, the export of which rose from less than US$1 billion in 2011 to more than US$6.5 billion in 2019.[23]

Other industries, including the beer market, also attracted new levels of investment, with Heineken and Carlsberg both pumping millions of dollars into state-of-the-art breweries, while Japanese brewer Kirin partnered with MEHL, the market leaders through their flagship Myanmar Beer.

Even David Abel's long-held dream of establishing an exchange came to life, with the Yangon Stock Exchange being established in a striking building in the heart of the city's downtown, although even at its peak the bourse attracted only a handful of companies and witnessed minimal trading.

The bulk of the economic reforms had taken place under Thein Sein's quasi-civilian government, and the NLD administration faced widespread criticism for its economic policies, with Aung San Suu Kyi in particular criticized for lacking the vision to enact further reforms. Investor confidence was also heavily hit by global outrage around the Rohingya crisis in 2016 and 2017.

Despite the widespread changes taking place, the military's domination of the economy was never seriously threatened, and many of their companies capitalized on the situation, partnering with international firms to use their expertise to further entrench their control of key markets.

Meanwhile, even though opportunities typically improved for people living in urban centres, those living in rural areas – which comprise roughly 70 per cent of the population – saw few of the riches during the reform years. Even at this time, most of Myanmar remained a desperately poor place, with entire families living in ramshackle homes, and getting by on little more than a few meals of rice per day. Before the coup, about a quarter of the population lived under the poverty line, a situation that has grown drastically worse since.[24]

Land issues

A major reason for this is the issue of land, which was one of the biggest hindrances to equitable economic growth during the reform years.

Myanmar's great river, the Irrawaddy, which runs directly through its centre, has brought tonnes of alluvial mud down into the country for centuries, resulting in it being home to incredibly fertile land that grows crops such as rice, corn, beans and pulses in great numbers. As a result, Myanmar is a majority agrarian society. If most people were able to own their own land, then it's easy to see how they could become financially stable, and even empowered by this, not only by selling these products in local markets and for export but also living off the land around them.

But in Myanmar, and as a direct result of the military's actions, this is not the case. For decades, land confiscations and forced evictions were a regular feature, with government officials, military personnel and their cronies kicking farmers off their land, and using it for their own enrichment. A large part of the military's revenue is made from agricultural businesses, with trading companies in everything from rice, to rubber, fisheries, tobacco and palm oil, to name a few. Much of this land is also used for large-scale industrial projects that have a devastating impact on the nearby environment, including coal, gold and copper, where villagers have to deal not only with their loss of land to these projects, but also health issues brought about by contamination to their drinking water and land and air quality.

When the reforms began, efforts were made to address the problem, notably through the formation of various committees, and although some land was returned, millions of acres were not.[25] Many were arrested, or even killed, for protesting or working on land that they believed was rightfully theirs.

Just one example where this was the case was at a cluster of villages in Sagaing Region, just across the Chindwin River from Monywa, which before the coup was a pleasant town that was an important trading hub in the centre of the country.

The site today is the home of the Letpadaung Copper Mine, established in 1996 by Canadian company Ivanhoe Mines in partnership with the then-military government's Mining Enterprise No. 1. In 2011, Wanbao Mining Company, a subsidiary of Chinese state-owned arms manufacturer Norinco, formed a partnership with the Myanmar military's MEHL to take over operations under the joint venture Myanmar Wanbao.

In 2019, I travelled to the region with a colleague, to conduct a media training with journalists from a local news outlet, a gritty publication operating in a tiny newsroom in the centre of town. After the training ended, a small group of us took a boat across the Chindwin to the Letpadaung site, a heavily fortified compound. As we conducted interviews in nearby villages, the sound of stones being crushed could be heard in the distance.

One of those we interviewed was a woman in her early 40s, who had lived her whole life in Sete village, and who remembered a time when the area surrounding it was nothing but fields that local residents used to grow an assortment of crops.

'We used those fields for generations', she said. 'We grew sesame, beans, wheat. It depended on the season.'

She said the villagers were kicked off their land for the project, and that they had still not received adequate compensation, and that waste overspill from the mine was destroying the fields and trees that villagers depended on for their livelihoods.

'The [betel] leaves changed to the colour of rust, and the stalks turned red and rotted', said another villager. 'We see particles on the leaves, and have to pour water to clean them before plucking.'

The Wanbao project coincided with political reforms that began in 2011, and local residents used the freer environment to stage large-scale protests, which authorities cracked down heavily upon, declaring them illegal because those organizing them had not received official permission.

In November 2012, police used smoke grenade containing white phosphorus to disperse protestors, causing chemical burns to dozens of people, while two years later a local resident was shot and killed during a demonstration.

The project was suspended after the 2012 protests, and an investigation committee was formed, led by Aung San Suu Kyi, who at the time was opposition leader as the head of the NLD. The committee's report acknowledged that an environmental and social assessment had not been conducted, but advised against cancelling the project because it would hurt the economy as well as relations with China. Work resumed in 2016.

China's influence

The Letpadaung project was one of a few to have attracted anger among much of the population in Myanmar, another being the multi-million-dollar Myitsone Dam project, planned at the start of the Irrawaddy in northerly Kachin State. Both have been met with protests across the country, in part because of the environmental impacts on the local people, but there's also another factor: the influence of China, which has rapidly increased its presence since the 1990s.

Throughout the second half of the twentieth century, the Chinese and Burmese governments had a volatile relationship. Although the newly independent Burma was the first non-Communist country to recognize the People's Republic of China in 1949,[26] it was also the scene of deadly anti-Chinese riots in the 1960s, while its northerly neighbour for many decades financially supported the CPB, one of the Tatmadaw's fiercest rivals until the party's collapse in 1989.

When the SLORC administration made itself open to investment and influence following the 1988 protests, Beijing sensed an opportunity, both to open its poor inland provinces, notably those in its southwest, to trade, as well as gain direct access to the Bay of Bengal and the Indian Ocean.

A few years earlier a former Chinese government official penned an article in the official *Beijing Review* titled 'Open to the southwest: An expert opinion', in which he argued for a network of highways to be constructed connecting Yunnan Province, at that point an impoverished corner of the country's south, with the railways and riverports in Myanmar.[27] The move would, the official argued, provide a new market for Chinese exports, and give landlocked Yunnan 'more than one avenue to the outside world'.

The change in SLORC's policy in the early 1990s, therefore, presented an opportunity for this strategy to be put into place, and over the next few years Beijing cultivated a close relationship with the Myanmar government, defending it at the UN Security Council, as well as becoming a leading supplier of loans, investment and military equipment.[28] Throughout the 1990s, China pumped substantial funds into Myanmar, often through large infrastructure projects that gave few considerations to local people, who had no avenue to complain due to the authoritarian nature of the then-ruling junta.

But for Myanmar's generals, this relationship ultimately became too close for comfort, and a major reason they initiated the reforms in 2011 was a desire to move away from China's sphere of influence, and closer to Western countries such as the United States. This shift was demonstrated most heavily early into Thein Sein's term, when he announced the suspension of the Myitsone Dam following widespread protests against it.

With Myanmar's new leaders cosying up to Western countries – highlighted by the fact that then-US President Barack Obama twice visited the country during Thein Sein's term – China needed a new approach, and its ambassador in the country at the time, Hong Lian, said his country had moved away from its 'government-to-government' approach.

'We want to work with local communities, so we are thinking more about community development and social welfare', he told me in guarded comments in 2016 during a question-and-answer session at his Yangon residence.

The new approach was a successful one. In particular, China had cultivated a close relationship with Aung San Suu Kyi during her time as opposition leader, and when her NLD resoundingly won the 2015 election, Beijing now had a prominent seat at the table. This dynamic was strengthened even further as China shielded Myanmar from international censure amid outrage at its treatment towards the Rohingya in 2016 and 2017.

In early 2020, Chinese President Xi Jinping travelled to Myanmar,[29] holding meetings with Aung San Suu Kyi and Min Aung Hlaing, to put the final touches to the China Myanmar Economic Corridor (CMEC), a key component of the Belt and Road Initiative, which had been drafted years earlier. The deal promised billions of dollars of investments in Myanmar in the form of a high-speed railway from Yunnan to Mandalay, then onwards to the China-backed Kyaukphyu deep-sea port in Rakhine State, as well as a controversial 'New Yangon' city development project on the west of the city's current downtown area. At the time, however, concerns were raised that Myanmar's weak negotiation position caused by the Rohingya crisis risked making the CMEC projects a 'debt-trap'.

Then came the coup. In the immediate aftermath there were widespread rumours in Myanmar that China had been responsible, or at least supportive, of the power grab, particularly after its Foreign Minister, Wang Yi, visited the country weeks before and met with senior officials, including Min Aung Hlaing.[30] Protests were held outside the Chinese Embassy in Yangon, while speculation was heightened after Chinese planes were reported to be flying into Myanmar bringing with them technical personnel. The Embassy responded saying they were regular cargo flights carrying seafood.[31] Chinese-owned factories on the outskirts of Yangon were burned down during protests.

Yet in all reality, it's unlikely that China had any say at all in the coup. First of all, there's the fiercely nationalistic – or xenophobic – nature of the Tatmadaw. As explored in an earlier chapter, the Tatmadaw views itself as the sole saviour and protector of the nation against foreign interference, and one of its major anxieties for decades has been the looming presence of China to the north. There's little chance, therefore it would take instructions from another sovereign state, particularly China.

In the early days of the coup, rumours spread like wild fire on Myanmar social media that the Tatmadaw was being fortified with Chinese troops (the apparent evidence being soldiers in downtown Yangon with lighter skin complexions), but this is highly unlikely, with the Tatmadaw even explicitly saying in a White Paper published in 2015: 'No foreign troops shall be permitted to be deployed in the territory of the Union.'[32]

It's also difficult to see how China really benefits from the coup, due to the billions of dollars of investment it had agreed with the NLD government, not to mention the insecurity the current situation has created at the China-Myanmar border where numerous ethnic armed groups operate, many reliant on China.

But the Chinese government is nothing if not pragmatic, and with the military junta, through its newly established SAC, now overseeing key ministries related to business and foreign investment, Beijing will have had few qualms about working alongside them to push as many of these deals through as possible.

Indeed, although China was careful not to cosy up too closely with the junta in the immediate aftermath of the coup, as time wore on, it strengthened its relationship with the junta. In addition to its shielding role of the junta at the United Nations Security Council, in tandem with Russia, Beijing also invited a junta official, Wunna Maung Lwin, to China for a lavish ceremony, describing him as Myanmar's 'Foreign Minister', something the majority of Myanmar people fiercely reject.

In the meeting, China's foreign minister Wang Yi told Wunna Maung Lwin Beijing would support Myanmar 'no matter how the situation changes' and called on both countries to 'accelerate' the CMEC.

As well as benefitting China, it also works in the junta's favour to ensure the CMEC projects move ahead, raising much-needed funds amid its increased isolation on the international stage, and within a few months of the coup it had announced the re-formation of key committees related to the CMEC, ousting civilian government members and replacing them with their own appointees.[33]

In the current scenario, indications point to a return to the bad practices of the past, with the junta steaming ahead with large-scale projects, in partnership with companies who give few considerations to the impacts they will have on local communities.

Take for example the Kyaukpyu Special Economic Zone and deep-sea port in Rakhine State, which has long been the flagship project of the CMEC. The multi-billion-dollar project aims to create an investment and economic hub at Kyaukphyu, located in southern Rakhine, while also establishing an alternate shipping route for Chinese trade, by linking the Bay of Bengal with Yunnan Province through a high-speed railway.

But the project has been beset by controversy since it was first announced, with concerns about poor transparency, displacement and lack of engagement with those living in the area.[34] Construction of the project will threaten the livelihoods and homes of around 20,000 people in the area, many who depend heavily on the land around it for their livelihoods.

'The projects aren't for the communities. The government and the investors say they are, but they aren't. There is already an existing power plant, but some villagers still don't have power', said a local resident in late 2020.[35]

Beyond the land-grabbing and judicial harassment of those protesting for their land to be returned, there are other ways the military contributed to the dismal situation in many communities across the country, while also making significant sums for itself.

The drugs trade

Myanmar is today one of the world's biggest drugs producers, a scenario that the military's policies over several decades has contributed towards, although it would be overly simplistic to put all of the blame at their door. Many actors are complicit.

The bulk of drug production in Myanmar occurs in the Golden Triangle region in its northeast, a region that also straddles Thailand and Laos. The trade today is worth an estimated US$70 billion dollars per year, largely through the peddling of methamphetamines.[36]

The Golden Triangle first gained notoriety through the explosion of its opium trade in the late twentieth century, first through expansion efforts by colonial powers in the area, notably the British, as well as a unit of the Kuomintang Army who retreated into Burma following defeat in the Chinese Civil War, and rapidly boosted opium production to fund what would be a failed attempt to re-take their homeland from Chairman Mao's Communists.

The Chinese nationalists were followed by a wave of increasingly sophisticated drug lords – many including Lo Hsing-han and Khun Sa, who made their funds through grubby deals with the Myanmar military – who further expanded the trade.

A major shift would again occur in the late 1980s and early 1990s when the CPB, one of the Tatmadaw's fiercest rivals since independence, collapsed in a mutiny. The new SLORC administration in Yangon moved quickly to capitalize on the situation, striking deals with the mutineers, promising widespread development to these impoverished border areas in exchange for their loyalty.

Between the CPB's collapse in 1989 and 1995, the Myanmar government signed more than a dozen agreements that provided armed groups autonomous territories, including the Myanmar National Democratic Alliance Army in Kokang, and the United Wa State Party.

For the most powerful groups, these became largely exclusive areas that the government could only enter after requesting permission, effectively allowing these groups to conduct their activities beyond the reach of the law. In a region where some of the world's largest drugs production was already taking place, it's not hard to guess what lucrative trade they turned to.

Initially it was opium, but around the mid-1990s a shift started to occur, when the controllers of these fiefdoms recognized that methamphetamines were both cheaper to make and easier to transport than opium. Its use was also heavily increasing in the region, notably in Thailand, including by truck drivers and students, both to enhance concentration and as a party drug.[37] The main benefit of the drug, which can be taken in pill form or inhaled, is that it increases energy and confidence, and as one user in Yangon told me 'makes you feel invincible'. However, its over-use can lead to side effects such as hallucinations, severe dehydration, paranoia and extreme depression.

In 1997, about 22 million speed pills were seized in Thailand, rising to 40 million two years later. By 2002, that figure had reached 95.9 million pills.[38]

The trade has grown exponentially since then. Between mid-February and early April 2020 – a period of just a few weeks – Myanmar authorities conducted a series of raids in northern Shan State, seizing 193 million methamphetamine pills (weighing more than 17 tonnes) and 500 kilograms of crystal methamphetamine, the higher-quality drug that is typically exported further afield to places like Australia and Japan. Authorities also seized large quantities of chemicals including ephedrine and pseudoephedrine, which are used in the production of the drugs.[39]

There are a variety of reasons why this explosion in drug use and production has taken place, one being widespread poverty in rural parts of the Golden Triangle, resulting in local residents turning to whatever trade they can to survive. The lack of work opportunities grants the producers with a steady stream both of mules, who are willing to risk arrest for financial gain, and users, who may want to pass the time with mind-altering substances.

'It's something to do', an unemployed drug user in Yangon once told me matter-of-factly.

Corruption is another factor for this exponential growth, with low-paid authorities often either turning a blind eye to convoys passing through their area of control in exchange for handouts, or even taking a cut of the profits for themselves.

But what also can't be discounted is the impact of the deals struck by the military in the 1990s with armed groups operating in the region following the CPB's collapse, who used the impunity granted to their safe havens to rapidly expand methamphetamine production.

Chief among these is the United Wa State Army (UWSA), which, with an estimated fighting force of 20,000 soldiers is the largest and most powerful of the ethnic armed groups in Myanmar. The UWSA was one of the groups to sign a deal with the SLORC regime in the 1990s, which it used to 'build a drug empire that outmatched anything' Myanmar had ever seen.[40]

Today, factories in UWSA-controlled territory are believed to produce the bulk of the drugs coming out of the Golden Triangle, notably methamphetamines, although other groups are involved too, including militias aligned with the military.

For a long time, one of the UWSA's fiercest rivals in this area was the Mong Tai Army – headed by the Sino-Shan rebel leader Khun Sa – which for much of the late twentieth century had dominated the drugs trade between Shan State and Thailand. Wa fighters were influential in overthrowing Khun Sa's army, forcing his surrender to the Rangoon government in 1996, where he was permitted to 'retire' in the then capital in exchange for giving up his drugs empire.[41]

As a reward for helping defeat one of the Tatmadaw's rivals, the UWSA leadership was granted land close to the Myanmar-Thailand border, today known as southern Wa, which, although billed as being part of an anti-drugs programme, granted the group direct access to Thailand, which they used to further expand their own narcotics empire.[42]

One of the epicentres of Golden Triangle's drugs trade is Tachileik, which sits on the Thai-Myanmar border, and which I travelled to in late 2019 to report on the drugs trade with a small group of fellow journalists. After crossing into Myanmar from the northern Thai town of Mae Sai, I checked into my hotel and set out to explore, walking the short distance to a roundabout in the centre of the town. In the middle of the junction sat a red and yellow sign proudly proclaiming Tachileik as the 'City of the Golden Triangle'.

I'd been standing there for a matter of seconds when I was approached by a shifty-looking fellow in a ripped vest, whose vast belly was spilling over his longyi. He was holding what appeared to be a carton of cigarettes in a basket.

'You want girl? You want drugs?' the man said, subtly moving the cigarette boxes aside to reveal a small tube holding five red pills.

'Yabba', he said, referring to the low-quality methamphetamine that is freely available in this corner of the country. 'Very good, very cheap'. He offered me the drugs for the equivalent of US$2.

I politely declined and walked away, in the direction of a restaurant our group had arranged to meet in for dinner that evening when I was approached by another man.

'You want drugs, girls, guns?' said the man. 'Anything you want, I can get you.'

Feeling uncomfortable asking the question, but eager to get a read on exactly where the moral line was in Tachileik, I asked the man what the youngest girl was he could acquire.

'As young as you want, you tell me. I can get it', he said, topping his comment off with a leery wink. I declined and went to dinner.

Tachileik is not an easy place to like. It may be located in one of the most picturesque parts of Southeast Asia, but its entire fabric is built upon the shadowy trades that pass through here – drugs, guns, prostitution, money laundering and many more in between.

On one side of town are the opulent casinos where businessmen of various sketchy stripes wash their ill-gotten gains, while a few hills over is a crumbling graveyard where drug users sit in full-view of local residents, injecting heroin into their arms, or smoking meth through discarded bottles. Back in town, at numerous hotels covered in neon lights, scantily clad women spend the night sat outside the private rooms of the karaoke lounge, fiddling on their phones until they find a customer for the evening.

We spent the next few days travelling around eastern Shan State, as part of a failed attempt to reach a drug-producing factory we had been told existed in a nearby area controlled by the UWSA. We travelled to Mong Hsat, the dusty town that KMT troops had used as their base to drastically build up the region's drugs trade. We also stopped for a few hours at a picturesque village in southern Wa State, and where we'd heard a drug-producing machine may have existed nearby. Local residents denied that was the case.

Despite the disappointment of not completing our stated mission, we did manage to gain some insight into the scale of the drugs trade in the region, and how it had impacted communities there.

As one Tachileik resident told me: 'Everyone here is in on it somehow. Police, army, taxi drivers'.

'Are you?' I asked.

'Of course', he replied, laughing.[43]

The drugs trade is in almost every community in Myanmar, and shortly after flying from Tachileik to Yangon, I interviewed two youths in a suburb in the north of the city. Hidden away in a private room on the top floor of a beer station, the young men said they were regular *yabba* users, and most of their friends were too.

'It's so easy to get, and so cheap, that so many people here use it', said one of the men. 'Most of us don't have jobs, so it's something for us to do. I took it because it made me feel great, but the more I take it the angrier and more paranoid I get.'

As well as ruining the lives of many communities, the drugs trade in Myanmar also brings in substantial funds for a whole range of actors, including Tatmadaw members and militia groups aligned with the military.

Although the messy nature of the drugs trade in Myanmar makes it difficult to estimate the amount, given how important it is as a shadow economy, it's reasonable to assume that vast funds from the narcotics trade are funnelled into the Tatmadaw's operations in parts of the country, including in greasing the palms of the various groups it needs to keep on-side in the myriad conflicts across the country.

As the International Crisis Group said in a report published in 2019, the drugs trade largely functions as normal 'as long as the chain of actors from the Tatmadaw, to larger militia units involved in production, to smaller militias subcontracted to provide localized security, and the armed organisations that levy taxes on the trade all benefit and receive due compensation'.[44]

Illicit economies typically thrive during periods of insecurity, and all indicators point to a surge in methamphetamines flooding other Southeast Asian countries after the coup.

'The best way to make big money fast is the drug trade, and the pieces are in place to scale up', said a UN drugs expert.[45]

While the shadow economy has likely spiked, the legal economy in Myanmar has completely collapsed, with unemployment climbing, and poverty rates expected to double.[46] International investors, many drawn by the liberalizations of the early 2010s, have upped and left, while the once-burgeoning tech sector has ground to a halt.

Within days of the coup, Japanese brewer Kirin announced it was terminating its contract with MEHL, saying it was 'deeply concerned by the recent actions of the military',[47] and Telenor exited in a quick-fire sale after months of restrictions and harassment by authorities, in a move criticized by rights groups, who accused the company of irresponsibly disengaging.

In the domestic economy, the military's business operations have taken a substantial hit since the coup, with citizens expressing their anger by boycotting army-owned goods, a campaign taking place in tandem with the CDM. Restaurants, bars and supermarkets across the country have refused to stock Myanmar Beer, phone users have burned MyTel SIM cards and coffee brands, bus lines, film production companies and other firms with links to the Tatmadaw have been actively avoided.

These actions on the ground are being supported by international efforts, including a campaign by the activist group, Justice for Myanmar, to investigate and publicize the Tatmadaw's business links with international companies. The organization aims to pressure international firms and investors to divest from their operations with the Tatmadaw, as part of efforts to cut off the military's access to funds.

Some governments have also taken steps in this area, including the United States, United Kingdom, Canada and the European Union, who have placed targeted sanctions against figures at the top of the junta, as well as MEHL, MEC and other military-linked departments and companies. These sanctions are different from the past, which came in the form of widespread sanctions across the entire country, and which were criticized for hurting local people, but having little impact on the Tatmadaw's vast funds.

But there are many other areas of the Tatmadaw's wealth that need to be targeted, including oil and gas and timber. Over the last few decades, the military has built up vast funds in almost all aspects of life in Myanmar, many of them secretive, and there have been calls for an international coordinated effort to identify how the military makes its money, and to take whatever steps necessary to cut off this access to funds.

With the prospects of the Tatmadaw giving up power voluntarily all but impossible, the hope is that a campaign that is effective in targeting all of its access to funds would be a crucial step, taking place alongside the many other efforts, to contribute to the Tatmadaw being forced either into some form of negotiation away from power, or something many in Myanmar would like to see, crumbling from within.

8

Epilogue

Myanmar is a country in turmoil

In Tanintharyi Region, in the country's far south, combat between resistance fighters and junta troops has led to thousands being displaced, with soldiers going from village to village, arresting civilians and torching homes. As a result of the travel restrictions put in place by government forces, the previously brisk trade of goods from the nearby Thai border has all but dried up, with food, medicine and other essential items in short supply.

Junta troops have descended on towns and villages in Kayah State, in eastern Myanmar, to try and quell the widespread resistance against it, burning homes and villages, and bombing churches as they go. Shortly before Christmas 2021 in Kayah, almost half of which the population is Christian, junta forces killed dozens of civilians, leaving their charred bodies to be found at the side of the road. Amnesty International also accused the military of committing war crimes by laying landmines 'on a massive scale' in Kayah, including in people's gardens, homes, stairwells and around a church.

Similar stories are being heard out west, in Chin State, another part of the country that has seen widespread resistance to the coup. In September 2021, a thirty-year-old pastor in Chin, a rare Christian-majority area, was shot dead when he went to try and extinguish fires that had been set by junta troops. Those who found his body said the fourth finger on his left hand had been cut off, likely by soldiers stealing the golden wedding ring he had worn there.[1]

These grim stories can be heard elsewhere in the country, in the remote towns of Sagaing Region, in the northwest, as well as in Kachin, Kayin and Shan states in the east and northeast. Major cities like Yangon and Mandalay see almost daily clashes.

Even Nagaland, one of the most remote parts of the country, has not escaped the impacts of the coup and its aftermath, with residents forced to flee over the border into neighbouring India, as food and other supplies have failed to reach towns and villages.

'It feels like history is repeating itself', said a friend, who spent decades in prison during the previous iteration of junta rule.

And yet, amid all of this tragedy and turmoil, the Tatmadaw's coup d'etat of February 2021 remains incomplete, with millions of people across the country refusing to accept the takeover. The junta is unable to control key ministries, entice doctors or teachers back to work or get the economy moving.

In their place, civilian-run structures are continuing to operate, with former government health workers volunteering in underground clinics, and ethnic armed groups offering education services to children whose parents don't want to send them to state-run schools. With junta forces often callously blocking aid, many of these groups are also providing crucial humanitarian assistance to beleaguered communities.

The military coup in Myanmar is not a fait accompli, and to view it this way would be an affront to the millions of people up and down the country who are resisting the junta every day, often at great risk to their lives and liberty.

Their call is clear: for the complete removal of the military from power.

It will not be easy. As explored throughout this book, the Tatmadaw has embedded itself deeply into almost every layer of life in Myanmar, and efforts to eliminate it will be a monumental – although not impossible – task.

For decades, it has used unspeakable cruelty and brutality against the people, seeking to spread widespread fear that allows it to continue to sit at the apex of power. More subtly, it has utilized the education system, to try to force the population to submit to its most oppressive tendencies, while also introducing policies that create disunity between different ethnic groups, to distract from its own inability to create a prosperous state. This tactic was most obviously seen with the treatment of the Rohingya. Finally, and perhaps most importantly, it has exploited the country's vast natural resources to fund both the excesses of its leaders, and violence against the people. As an added insult, the vast majority of the population has remained desperately poor.

But amid the tragedy and suffering of the 2021 coup, one of the few bright spots it has achieved has been to create an awareness among the people of the Tatmadaw's disastrous legacy in almost all aspects of life in Myanmar, and there are now determined campaigns across the country, and abroad, to make the Tatmadaw accountable for its actions, and ultimately remove it from power, or even destroyed and replaced with a new federal army.

As mentioned, it will be a difficult task, and one that will require a range of different levers being pushed and pulled, both domestically and internationally. Taken together, such measures could contribute to the heavily fortified walls the Tatmadaw has built around itself crumbling, either forcing it into some form of negotiation with democratic forces, or its complete demise.

Myanmar's future direction will be driven first and foremost by developments inside the country, but there is a crucial role that the international community can play, in particular foreign governments and certain bodies of the United Nations.

A start point must be addressing the Tatmadaw's deep-rooted culture of impunity. As looked at in several chapters of this book, the Tatmadaw has for decades ruled the country with astounding brutality and terror. Quite simply, it knows no other way.

And whether it was the gunning down of student protestors at Rangoon University in the 1960s, 1970s and 1980s, the rape, beating and murder of villagers in ethnic minority areas during its decades of civil wars or the unspeakable violence it has committed against the people since February 2021, it has never been held to account.

Just a few years ago, the coup leader Min Aung Hlaing was the man responsible for a genocidal campaign against the Rohingya, and yet instead of facing any form of justice for his reprehensible crimes, he has installed himself as head of the junta.

This lack of accountability must change.

Beyond a few bland statements immediately after the coup, the UN Security Council – which, according to its own definition has 'primary responsibility for the maintenance of international peace and security'[2] – has done nothing. This is largely due to the veto held by permanent members Russia and China, but other members of the Council have demonstrated a breathtaking timidity to push for any sort of action. The United Kingdom, as the 'penholder' on Myanmar at the Council, and others have refused to push for resolutions on Myanmar, citing the vetoes held by Russia and China.

As one activist pointed out to me, where's the harm in members of the Security Council – particularly the democratic permanent members, the United States, United Kingdom and France – pursuing a referral on Myanmar to the ICC, for example, forcing China and Russia into a veto and publicly defending a regime responsible for the worst crimes imaginable?

International actors can go further than that, by lending concrete support to the Gambia's genocide case against Myanmar at the International Court of Justice, or by opening their own cases against the Myanmar military under the principle of universal jurisdiction. The latter recognizes that some crimes are so serious that all states have a responsibility to address them, and that is certainly the case with Myanmar, and the recent decision by a German court to convict a former Syrian intelligence officer for crimes against humanity under the principle is proof that such an avenue can provide justice.

The 2021 coup was one built upon the Tatmadaw's deeply entrenched culture of impunity, and if international actors really want to help end the bloodshed and turmoil in Myanmar, then one of the most important things they can do is support measures for international accountability. Without it, the Tatmadaw will only continue acting as it has done for the last few decades, destroying the lives of millions of people across the country.

'Just knowing the world is with us in our struggle is something that gives us so much strength', a Myanmar friend said recently.

With the Tatmadaw routinely using weapons of war against the people, including machine guns, sniper rifles and Uzi replicas,[3] not to mention air strikes against defenceless villagers, there have also been calls for a global arms embargo against the Tatmadaw. A few months after the coup, the UN General Assembly adopted a resolution that 'calls upon all member states to prevent the flow of arms into Myanmar', but it was non-binding.

Once again, no action has been taken in this area by the Security Council, with the vetoes held by China and Russia used as excuses for inaction. Then, what was the point of the General Assembly resolution (which China and Russia abstained on by the way, Belarus was the only country to vote against) if it doesn't pave the way for meaningful action by the Security Council? The three other permanent members of the council – the United States, United Kingdom and France – like to bill themselves as bastions of freedom and democracy. Those are labels that come with global responsibility, and that means showing leadership and acting forcefully in the face of egregious human rights violations, which is currently happening in Myanmar. As a bare minimum, these countries, and others who claim to support democracy and human rights, should work together to draft a legally binding resolution that requires states to halt all arms sales to the junta.

Another important area in the efforts to overthrow the junta in Myanmar is the conflict between the Tatmadaw and the hundreds of People's Defence Forces and ethnic armed groups dotted around the country.

When the National Unity Government announced the formation of PDFs shortly after the coup, questions were raised about the ability of what appeared to be a ragtag cluster of groups to take on an institution like the Tatmadaw, which has hundreds of thousands of troops at its disposal, many experienced in decades of brutal wars in the jungles. It also has superior equipment in the form of fighter jets, tanks, mortars and a whole host of other deadly apparatus.

Over the next several months, however, the PDFs began to make significant advances against the junta's forces across the country, in the form of armed clashes, explosions, ambushes and targeted killings.

The Tatmadaw is now engaged in conflicts in almost every corner of the country, and morale among its rank and file likely the lowest it's ever been. On top of the safety threats they are facing every day, even during the reform years, there was at least some prestige attached to wearing the uniform. Not anymore.

Although currently a long way from overthrowing the Tatmadaw by military means, the PDFs quickly began to improve their capabilities, often teaming up with existing ethnic armed groups for attacks on military positions, all while procuring new arms, taking part in new training, and generally becoming more effective as fighting forces.

The Tatmadaw is stretched like never before, a challenge made worse by the increased number of defections since the coup, with many soldiers expressing disgust at the violent force they have been ordered to use against the general public, the very people they are supposed to protect.

'After I witnessed the killing of civilians, I felt it was my duty to publicly oppose the generals', said Nyi Thuta, a former Tatmadaw captain who defected shortly after the coup.

He's not alone, and believes that the vast majority of Tatmadaw soldiers want to leave the institution.

It's not easy for them to do so, however, with those wishing to defect worried about their safety, or that of their family. Most Tatmadaw soldiers live in heavily fortified military compounds, and their children go to military-run schools. Their social circles are almost exclusively military, and so any moves they make are being closely watched by their superiors and colleagues, whose sensitivity – and anger – towards potential deserters has been heightened in the current climate.

There are also the economic concerns. For most Tatmadaw soldiers, the only adult life they've ever known has been life in the military, which they rely on for monthly salaries. At a few hundred dollars a month, these may be meagre, but in a country with such widespread poverty as Myanmar, are crucial to feeding, clothing and providing for their families. Some also have business interests tied up in the massive military economic machine, which would be immediately lost should they choose to desert.

However, there are organizations working to bridge that gap, and encourage disillusioned soldiers to defect from the Tatmadaw. Typically working online, and operating in areas under the control of resistance forces, these groups either contact soldiers directly or invite those interested to reach out to them. They then vet the soldiers, and if they are deemed legitimate in their desire to defect (and not agents acting on behalf of the military) then they are extracted and provided with food, shelter, security and a stipend. One way international governments and donors could support the efforts to remove the military from power would be to support groups such as these.

The humanitarian catastrophe taking place inside Myanmar, as well as at its borders, can also not be ignored. In June 2022, it was estimated that fourteen million people in Myanmar were in need of humanitarian assistance – a figure that was at one million before the coup. There were also widespread reports of junta forces blocking humanitarian access, and siphoning aid supplies, showing just how important it is that those providing assistance into Myanmar work through trusted groups on the ground, of which there are many, and not the military itself.

Of all the advocacy efforts taking place globally, however, by far the most important is the targeting of the Tatmadaw's finances.

As explored in the 'Abode of Kings' chapter, despite the widespread vilification of the Tatmadaw nationwide, its top generals fiercely believe in its importance as an institution, in particular its role in, as they see it, protecting the nation.

The Tatmadaw doesn't know the meaning of the word compromise. While there may be some inside the institution who want to see reforms take place, and a military brought under civilian control, its deeply hierarchical structure will make this difficult to achieve. As a result, any efforts to weaken the Tatmadaw must ultimately come from the outside.

This means targeting its finances. The Tatmadaw's opaque and corrupt nature makes it difficult to know how much money it has at its disposal, but efforts are underway to chip away at these resources, which directly support the Tatmadaw's military operations.

Inside the country, these funds have been targeted in the form of a boycott campaign against military-owned goods and services, while abroad, pressure has been put on international firms with links to the junta to divest, and targeted sanctions placed by countries including the United States, United Kingdom and Canada against top junta figures, as well as military conglomerates and other entities under their control.

But more needs to be done.

'What we've seen is drip, drip action from the international community', a Myanmar activist told me. 'There needs to be a system put in place to identify which companies and enterprises are owned by the military, and put sanctions on them'.

'We need to cut the money going into the military's pockets, because they care about their money, and they will take international action seriously then'.[4]

The targeted sanctions put in place so far by some countries are far from conclusive in terms of covering all of the junta's business activities. In addition, at the time of writing, Australia, which bills itself as a democratic leader in the Asia-Pacific region, has placed no sanctions against any of the military's business interests, although this may change after a more progressive government was elected in the May 2022 general election.

What's needed is a unified approach by international actors, a specialized body perhaps, that focuses on highlighting all of the revenue channels available to the junta, and ensures that every avenue possible is taken to close off its access to funds, including to foreign currency, preventing it from acquiring new arms. Of course, given how reliant the junta is on illegal channels, not to mention its dealings with China, this is a daunting task, but this merely highlights the importance of democratic-leaning countries pooling together their resources.

Such a task would be made easier with buy-in from countries in Southeast Asia. Although the response of the ten-member ASEAN to the crisis on its doorstep has been deeply disappointing, there have been some members – notably Malaysia and Indonesia – who have shown at least some willingness to intervene in a meaningful way. International actors should work with these more rights-minded governments in the region, and put pressure on the other ASEAN members, and make them see that offering any form of support to the junta is not beneficial in any way to the region.

Since the coup, questions have been raised about what would happen should the Tatmadaw collapse completely in on itself. After all, as explored throughout this book, the Tatmadaw has ingrained itself into almost every facet of Myanmar life, from the government apparatus, to all forms of administration, the economy and many more.

Surely, the argument goes, if the Tatmadaw were to collapse, there would be nothing left.

But that's not necessarily the case, and waiting in the wings is an administration that not only has a popular mandate – by virtue of being formed by MPs-elect in the 2020 election – but also one that has displayed indications that it has the vision to run the country according to the people's wishes. One that is truly democratic and federal.

If it were to come fully to power, the NUG will inevitably face major challenges to implement many of its policies that it has announced so far. In addition, any efforts to rebuild the nation amid the mess left behind by the Tatmadaw would come with a whole host of challenges that would probably fill an entire new book.

But through its federal and democratic charter, its rules of engagement to its soldiers, its commitment to accede to the International Criminal Court and a promise to seek justice for the Rohingya, it has shown at least a willingness to be a much more unifying force than its predecessor, the NLD.

That being said, pressure should be kept on the NUG to ensure it abides by its promises, should it ever fully take power.

Governments should formally engage with the NUG, and begin exploring ways to build up its capacity, with a view towards it one day becoming the government that fully represents the Myanmar people.

Removing the military from power will not be an easy task, nor likely a short one, but through the protests, CDM, armed resistance and a whole host of other avenues, the Myanmar people have said loud and clear what they want. Not a military in power that maims, terrorizes and kills its people, but one that protects them, and remains where any army belongs: in the barracks. The international community should support them in those efforts.

Notes

Chapter 1

1 Myanmar News Agency (MNA), 'Republic of the Union of Myanmar State
   Administration Council Chairman Senior General Min Aung Hlaing Makes
   Speech to Public', 9 February 2021, available at: https://www.gnlm.com
   .mm/republic-of-the-union-of-myanmar-state-administration-council
   -chairman-senior-general-min-aung-hlaing-makes-speech-to-public/?__cf
   _chl_managed_tk__=pmd_oCX4.8TOrIl__.W1soNoKptsiZWd6wWCerVnt
   UxKBIc-1632029079-0-gqNtZGzNA1CjcnBszRVR
2 Asian Network for Free Elections (ANFREL), 'The 2020 Myanmar General
   Elections: Democracy Under Attack', 2021, available at: https://anfrel.org/
   wp-content/uploads/2021/05/ANFREL_Democracy-Under-Attack-F.pdf
3 Australian Broadcasting Corporation (ABC), 'Myanmar's President
   Thein Sein Congratulates Suu Kyi, Promises Smooth Transition of Power',
   13 November 2015, available at: https://www.abc.net.au/news/2015-11-12/
   myanmar-president-thein-sein-congratulates-aung-san-suu-kyi/6936054
4 National League for Democracy (NLD), '2015 Election Manifesto', available
   at: https://www.burmalibrary.org/sites/burmalibrary.org/files/obl/docs21/
   NLD_2015_Election_Manifesto-en.pdf
5 Constitution of the Republic of Myanmar (2008), Article 436(a), available
   at: https://www.wipo.int/edocs/lexdocs/laws/en/mm/mm009en.pdf
6 Ibid., Article 59(f).
7 Tom Lasseter, 'In a Muslim Lawyer's Murder, Myanmar's Shattered
   Dream', *Reuters*, 13 December 2018, available at: https://www.reuters.com/
   investigates/special-report/myanmar-murder-politics/
8 Nyein Nyein, 'Dozens of Myanmar Political Parties Seek Assurances From
   Military Chief Over Election Concerns', *The Irrawaddy*, 15 August 2020,
   available at: https://www.irrawaddy.com/elections/dozens-myanmar
   -political-parties-seek-assurances-military-chief-election-concerns.html
9 San Yamin Aung, 'Myanmar Military Refuses to Rule Out Coup as It Presses
   Claim of Fraud in Nov. Election', *The Irrawaddy*, 26 January 2021, available
   at: https://www.irrawaddy.com/news/burma/myanmar-military-refuses
   -rule-coup-presses-claim-fraud-nov-election.html
10 Poppy McPherson, '"Rude and Insolent": Fraught Talks Preceded
   Myanmar's Army Seizing Power', *Reuters*, 9 February 2021, available at:
   https://www.reuters.com/article/us-myanmar-politics-reconstruction-insig
   -idUSKBN2A9225
11 The Global New Light of Myanmar, 'Only When Every Citizen Has the Will
   to Build a Better Country will the Country Have Prosperity: Senior General',

25 May 2021, available at: https://www.burmalibrary.org/sites/burmalibrary
.org/files/obl/GNLM2021-05-25-red.pdf

12 Simon Lewis, 'Myanmar Army Rulers' Lobbyist in U.S. Ceases Efforts for
Lack of Pay', *Reuters*, 15 July 2021, available at: https://www.reuters.com/
world/asia-pacific/myanmar-army-rulers-lobbyist-us-ceases-efforts-lack
-pay-2021-07-14/

13 Sean Bain, 'Myanmar: with Military Lacking Legitimacy and Control,
Elected Reps Seek Recognition as Government', *Opinion Juris*, 11 May
2021, available at: http://opiniojuris.org/2021/05/11/myanmar-with
-military-lacking-legitimacy-and-control-elected-reps-seek-recognition-as
-government/

14 The Republic of the Union of Myanmar, National Unity Government,
Ministry of Defence, 'Directive to People's Defence Forces (PDFs), Local
Defence Forces (LDFs) and Special Task Forces (STFs)', 7 September 2021,
available at: https://www.burmalibrary.org/sites/burmalibrary.org/files/obl
/2021-09-07-NUG-MOD-Directive-No.3-tu-en.pdf

15 Interview with the author, on 9 October 2021.

16 The World Bank, 'Myanmar Economy Expected to Contract by 18 Percent
in FY2021: Report', 23 July 2021, available at: https://www.worldbank.org/en
/news/press-release/2021/07/23/myanmar-economy-expected-to-contract
-by-18-percent-in-fy2021-report

Chapter 2

1 Clive Parker, 'Naypyidaw: A Dusty Work in Progress', *The Irrawaddy*,
October 2006, available at: https://www2.irrawaddy.com/article.php?art_id
=6427&page=1

2 Dulyapak Preecharushh, *Naypyidaw: The New Capital of Burma* (Bangkok:
White Lotus, 2009), 125.

3 Senate Foreign Relations Committee, 'Opening Statement by Dr
Condoleezza Rice', 18 January 2005, available at: https://web.archive
.org/web/20060325002023/http://foreign.senate.gov/testimony/2005/
RiceTestimony050118.pdf

4 Preecharushh, *Naypyidaw*, 94.

5 Myanmar National Portal, Top Destination, available at: https://myanmar
.gov.mm/en/-/nay-pyi-daw

6 Republic of the Union of Myanmar, 'Defence White Paper, 2015', Naypyitaw.

7 Maung Aung Myoe, *Building the Tatmadaw: Myanmar Armed Forces Since
1948* (Singapore: Institute of Southeast Asian Studies, 2009), 34.

8 Andrew Selth, *Myanmar's Military Mindset: An Exploratory Survey*
(Queensland, Australia: Griffith University, 2021), 14.

9 Interview with the author, on 21 August 2021.

10 Interview with the author, on 22 August 2021.

11 Mary Callahan, *Making Enemies: War and State Building in Burma* (New York: Cornell University Press, 2003), 31.
12 Ibid., 35.
13 Robert Farquharson, *For Your Tomorrow: Canadians and the Burma Campaign 1941–1945* (Toronto: Trafford Publishing, 2007), 24.
14 Callahan, *Making Enemies*, 47.
15 Maung Maung, *To a Soldier Son* (Rangoon: Sarpay Beikman Press, 1974), 17.
16 Donald M. Seekins, *Burma and Japan since 1940: From 'Co-Prosperity' to 'Quiet Dialogue'* (Copenhagen: NIAS Press, 2007).
17 Callahan, *Making Enemies*, 58.
18 Maung, *To a Soldier Son*, 25.
19 Ibid., 34.
20 Callahan, *Making Enemies*, 95–6.
21 Ibid., 108.
22 Ibid., 114–15.
23 Ibid., 159.
24 Myoe, *Building the Tatmadaw*, 138.
25 Sai Zom Hseng, 'Becoming a Member of Burma's "Triumphant Elite"', *The Irrawaddy*, 26 February 2011, available at: https://www2.irrawaddy.com/article.php?art_id=20834
26 Khin Oo Tha, 'Military Cadet Killed During Punishment by Senior', *The Irrawaddy*, 11 October 2016, available at: https://www.irrawaddy.com/news/military-cadet-killed-during-punishment-by-senior.html
27 Callahan, *Making Enemies*, 189.
28 Yoshihiro Nakanishi, *Strong Soldiers, Failed Revolution: The State and Military in Burma, 1962–88* (Singapore: NUS Press, 2013), 218.
29 Ibid., 220.
30 Ibid., 217.
31 Ibid., 220.
32 'The 4 Cuts', *SHAN*, 21 January 2020, available at: https://www.youtube.com/watch?v=AarIjGTJ3w4&has_verified=1&app=desktop&ab_channel=SHAN
33 David Scott Mathieson, 'Myanmar Military's Notorious Foot Soldiers', *The Irrawaddy*, 25 March 2021, available at: https://www.irrawaddy.com/opinion/guest-column/myanmar-militarys-notorious-foot-soldiers.html
34 Nakanishi, *Strong Soldiers*, 180.
35 Ibid., 183.
36 Martin Smith, *Burma: Insurgency and the Politics of Ethnicity* (London: Zed Books, 1991), 78.
37 Martin Smith, 'General Ne Win', *The Guardian*, 6 December, 2002, available at: https://www.theguardian.com/news/2002/dec/06/guardianobituaries
38 Ekkarat Benlang, 'Burmese Spy Activities in Thailand Viewed', *Bangkok Phuchatkan*, 3 March 1998, available at: https://www.burmalibrary.org/reg.burma/archives/199803/msg00046.html

39 Andrew Selth, *Secrets and Power in Myanmar* (Singapore: ISEAS-Yusof Ishak Institute, 2019), 9.
40 Banleng, 'Burmese Spy Activities in Thailand Viewed.'
41 Selth, *Secrets and Power in Myanmar*, 62–3.
42 Selth, *Secrets and Power in Myanmar*, 62.
43 Andrew Selth, *Burma's Armed Forces: Power Without Glory* (EastBridge, 2002), 168.
44 Smith, *Burma*, 361, 362.
45 Nakanishi, *Strong Soldiers*, 282.
46 Images Asia, '"No Childhood at All": A Report about Child Soldiers in Burma', 1997, available at: https://www.burmalibrary.org/sites/burmalibrary.org/files/obl/docs3/NoChildhood-ocr.pdf
47 Ibid.
48 Human Rights Watch, '"My Gun Was as Tall as Me": Child Soldiers in Burma', October 2002, available at: https://www.hrw.org/reports/2002/burma/index.htm#TopOfPage
49 Nay Yan Oo, *A New Tatmadaw with Old Characteristics* (Singapore: Yusof Ishak Institute, 2020).
50 Embassy Rangoon, 'Biography: Shwe Mann, Burma's Dictator-in-Waiting', *Wikileaks*, available at: https://wikileaks.org/plusd/cables/07RANGOON283_a.html
51 Mary Callahan, *The Generals Loosen Their Grip* (John Hopkins University Press, 2012), available at: https://themimu.info/sites/themimu.info/files/documents/Academic_Article_The_Generals_Loosen_Their_Grip_Mary_Callahan_Oct2012.pdf
52 Yan Oo, *A New Tatmadaw With Old Characteristics*.
53 Senior General Min Aung Hlaing, 'Build Standard Army Capable of Fighting Conventional War to Turn Out Tatmadaw with High Defence Power on which State and People Can Rely', 15 February 2020, available at: https://www.seniorgeneralminaunghlaing.com.mm/en/18090/build-standard-army-capable-fighting-conventional-war-turn-tatmadaw-high-defence-power-state-people-can-rely/
54 Griffith Asia Institute, '"Strong, Fully Efficient and Modern": Myanmar's New Look Armed Forces', 2016, available at: https://www.griffith.edu.au/__data/assets/pdf_file/0017/118313/Regional-Outlook-Paper-49-Selth-web.pdf, 7.
55 Stockholm International Peace Research Institute, Arms Transfers Database, 2011–2020, available at: https://www.sipri.org/databases/armstransfers
56 Mrityunjoy Mazumdar, 'Myanmar Navy Showcases Newly Acquired Submarine in Fleet Exercise Bandoola, Janes', 19 October 2020, available at: https://www.janes.com/defence-news/news-detail/myanmar-navy-showcases-newly-acquired-submarine-in-fleet-exercise-bandoola
57 Stockholm International Peace Research Institute.
58 Nanda, 'Min Aung Hlaing Reshuffles Senior Military Ranks Ahead of Election', *Frontier*, 19 May 2020, available at: https://www.frontiermyanmar

.net/en/min-aung-hlaing-reshuffles-senior-military-ranks-ahead-of
-election/
59 ISEAS-Yusof Ishak Institute, 'Min Aung Hlaing and His Generals: Data
on the Military Members of Myanmar's State Administration Council',
Singapore, 23 July 2021, available at: https://www.iseas.edu.sg/wp-content/
uploads/2021/06/ISEAS_Perspective_2021_97.pdf

Chapter 3

1 Luke Harding, 'Outrage in Myanmar after Activist Allegedly Tortured to
Death', *The Guardian*, 15 March 2021, available at: https://www.theguardian
.com/world/2021/mar/15/the-death-of-zaw-myat-lynn-allegations-torture
-used-on-opposition-activist-in-myanmar
2 Jonathan Head, 'Myanmar: The Mysterious Deaths of the NLD Party
Officials', *BBC*, 8 June 2021, available at: https://www.bbc.com/news/world
-asia-57380237
3 Harding, 'Outrage in Myanmar after Activist'.
4 Human Rights Watch, 'Myanmar: Urgently Investigate NLD Official's Death
in Custody', 9 March 2021, available at: https://www.hrw.org/news/2021/03
/09/myanmar-urgently-investigate-nld-officials-death-custody
5 Head, 'Myanmar'.
6 Tom Andrews, 'Special Rapporteur on the Situation of Human Rights in
Myanmar Tells Human Rights Council that the International Community
is Failing the People of Myanmar', 7 July 2021, available at: https://www
.ohchr.org/EN/HRBodies/HRC/Pages/NewsDetail.aspx?NewsID=27284
&LangID=E
7 Robert H. Taylor, *General Ne Win: A Political Biography* (Singapore: ISEAS
Publishing, 2015), 36–7.
8 Ibid., 235.
9 Ibid., 245.
10 Ibid., 256.
11 Ibid.
12 Nick Cheeseman, *Opposing the Rule of Law: How Myanmar's Courts Mae
Law and Order* (Cambridge: University Press, 2015), 79.
13 Taylor, *General Ne Win*, 185.
14 Andrew Selth, *Death of a Hero: U Thant Disturbances in Burma, December
1974* (Queensland: Griffith University, 2018), available at: https://www
.griffith.edu.au/__data/assets/pdf_file/0032/483827/AS-death-of-a-hero-U
-Thant-disturbance-web-final.pdf
15 Interview with the author, on 30 May 2018.
16 Interview with the author, on 19 July 2018.
17 Interview with the author, on 11 June 2016.

18 Bertil Lintner, *Outrage: Burma's Struggle for Democracy* (London: Diane Pub Co. 1990).

19 Aung Zaw, 'Sein Lwin "The Butcher of Rangoon" Dies in Poverty', *The Irrawaddy*, 12 April 2004, available at: https://www2.irrawaddy.com/opinion_story.php?art_id=3825

20 Bertil Lintner, *Burma in Revolt: Opium and Insurgency since 1948* (Bangkok: Silkworm Books, 1999), 276.

21 Interview with the author, on 10 November 2019.

22 Interview with the author, on 4 November 2017.

23 Burma Campaign UK, 'Than Shwe's Daughters Wedding', 17 December 2007, available at: https://www.youtube.com/watch?v=TWj0tDpLAaI

24 Emma Larkin, *No Bad News for the King* (US: Penguin Books, 2011).

25 Alexandra Schwartz, 'Sharing Visual Information Crucial to World Peace', *Yale News*, 23 October 2007, available at: https://yaledailynews.com/blog/2007/10/23/sharing-visual-information-crucial-to-world-peace/

26 Kayleigh Long, 'Miles to Go: Gambira, 7 Years on from Saffron', *Myanmar Times*, 3 November 2014, available at: https://www.mmtimes.com/home-page/in-depth/12183-seven-years-after-saffron-an-activist-s-struggle-continues-2.html

27 Interview with the author, on 2 May 2015.

28 Larkin, *No Bad News for the King.*

29 'Burma: Cronies Launch New Soccer League', *Wikileaks*, 12 June 2009, available at: https://wikileaks.org/plusd/cables/09RANGOON355_a.html

30 Larkin, *No Bad News for the King.*

31 The Public International Law and Policy Group, 'Burmese Constitutional Referendum: Neither Free Nor Fair', May 2008, available at: https://www.burmalibrary.org/docs5/PILPG_Report_Burmese_Constitutional_Referendum_Neither_Free_Nor_Fair-11_May_2008.pdf

32 Barrack Obama, 'Remarks by President Obama at the University of Yangon', 19 November 2021, available at: https://obamawhitehouse.archives.gov/the-press-office/2012/11/19/remarks-president-obama-university-yangon

33 *Journey to Justice*, 17 January 2015, DVB, available at: https://www.youtube.com/watch?v=ENOE8ALLWqM&t=18s

34 'Missing Reporter Killed in Custody of Burma Army: Report', *The Irrawaddy*, 24 October 2014, available at: https://www.irrawaddy.com/news/burma/missing-reporter-killed-custody-burma-army-report.html

35 Interview with the author, on 8 November 2015.

36 Interview with representative from Assistance Association for Political Prisoners Myanmar, 23 June 2018.

37 Htun Htun, 'At Political Forum, State Counselor Urges Break With the Past', *The Irrawaddy*, 11 August 2017, available at: https://www.irrawaddy.com/news/burma/political-forum-state-counselor-urges-break-past.html

38 Koh Ewe, 'Myanmar Coup: Soldiers Flood TikTok with Calls to Violence', *Vice*, 3 March 2021, available at: https://www.vice.com/en/article/jgq34b/myanmar-coup-soldiers-flood-tiktok-with-calls-to-violence

39 United Nations High Commissioner for Human Rights, 'Situation of Human Rights in Myanmar since 1 February 2021', 15 March 2022.
40 Adam Simpson, 'Myanmar's Exile Government Signs up to ICC Prosecutions', *East Asia Forum*, 17 September 2021, available at: https://www.eastasiaforum.org/2021/09/17/myanmars-exile-government-signs-up-to-icc-prosecutions/

Chapter 4

1 Save the Children, 'Myanmar: More than 100 Attacks on Schools in May', 11 June 2021, available at: https://www.savethechildren.net/news/myanmar-more-100-attacks-schools-may
2 John Ebeneezer Marks, *Forty Years in Burma* (London: Hutchinson and Co, 1917).
3 Global Security, 'Diplomacy and Reform under King Mindon, 1853–1878', available at: https://www.globalsecurity.org/military/world/myanmar/history-konbaung-5.htm
4 Zar Ni, 'The Nationalization of Education in Burma: A Radical Response to the Capitalist Development?' 1995, available at: https://files.eric.ed.gov/fulltext/ED385930.pdf
5 John S. Furnivall, *An Introduction to the Political Economy of Burma* (Rangoon: Burma Book Club, 1931).
6 Ni, 'The Nationalization of Education in Burma', 21.
7 Ibid., 20.
8 Ibid., 21–22.
9 Ibid., 23.
10 Yan Pai, 'Ne Win Manipulated Educational Affairs', *The Irrawaddy*, August 2013, available at: https://www.irrawaddy.com/in-person/interview/ne-win-manipulated-educational-affairs.html
11 Interview with the author, 12 January 2021.
12 Interview with the author, 9 January 2021.
13 Interview with the author, 7 June 2020.
14 Wei Yan Aung, 'The Day When Ho Chi Minh Visited Myanmar', *The Irrawaddy*, February 2020, available at: https://www.irrawaddy.com/specials/on-this-day/day-ho-chi-minh-visited-myanmar.html
15 'Burmese Universities Closed As Military Acts to Block Protests', *Reuters*, December 1991, available at: https://www.nytimes.com/1991/12/13/world/burmese-universities-are-closed-as-military-acts-to-block-protests.html
16 Martin Smith, 'Our Heads Are Bloody But Unbowed', December 1992, available at: https://www.refworld.org/pdfid/4754182d0.pdf
17 Ibid.
18 Interview with the author, 7 June 2020.
19 Interview with the author, 5 January 2021.

20 Su Myat Mon, 'Civics Education in Primary Schools is a Lesson in Discrimination', *Frontier Myanmar*, February 2019, available at: https://www.frontiermyanmar.net/en/civics-education-in-primary-schools-is-a-lesson-in-discrimination/

21 Thin Htet Paing, 'Nationalists Oppose NGO's Curriculum for Including National Religion', *The Irrawaddy*, 7 March 2017, available at: https://www.irrawaddy.com/news/burma/nationalists-oppose-ngos-curriculum-including-religious-education.html

22 Interview with the author, 15 January 2021.

23 Thein Sein, 'President U Thein Sein Delivers Inaugural Address to Pyidaungsu Hluttaw', *Nay Pyi Taw*, 30 March 2011, available at: http://www.myanmar-embassy-tokyo.net/news/President-Policy-Speech-English.pdf

24 The Irrawaddy, Letpadan Crackdown, 'A Complete Breakdown of Police Discipline', March 2015, available at: https://www.irrawaddy.com/news/burma/letpadan-crackdown-a-complete-breakdown-of-police-discipline.html

25 Interview with the author, 10 April 2020.

26 Interview with the author, 11 January 2021.

27 Interview with the author, 23 March 2019.

28 Interview with the author, 12 June 2019.

29 Jared Downing, 'Learning to Think', *Frontier Myanmar*, October 2015, available at: https://www.frontiermyanmar.net/en/learning-to-think/

30 Frontier Myanmar, 'Education vs. Revolution: School Reopenings Bring Hard Choices', 17 January 2021, available at: https://www.frontiermyanmar.net/en/education-vs-revolution-school-reopenings-bring-hard-choices/

31 Mary Callahan, 'By the Book: Junta's Education Policy Follows 60 Years of Military Strategy', 9 February 2022, available at: https://www.frontiermyanmar.net/en/by-the-book-juntas-education-policy-follows-60-years-of-military-strategy/

32 Myanmar News Agency, 'MoE Union Minister Tours Universities, Education Degree College in Meiktila', 9 November 2021, available at: https://www.gnlm.com.mm/moe-union-minister-tours-universities-education-degree-college-in-meiktila/

Chapter 5

1 Interview with the author, on 23 March 2016.

2 'The 2014 Myanmar Population and Housing Census', *Department of Population, Ministry of Immigration and Population*, May 2015, available at: https://reliefweb.int/sites/reliefweb.int/files/resources/Census%20Main%20Report%20%28UNION%29%20-%20ENGLISH_1.pdf

3 Persecution of Chin Christians in Burma, Salai Bawi Lian Mang, Chin Human Rights Organization, available at: https://www.chinhumanrights .org/chro-presentation-at-international-conference-on-persecuted -churches/

4 Unsafe State, 'The Women's League of Chinland', March 2007, available at: http://www.peacewomen.org/sites/default/files/vaw_unsafestatesanction edsexualviolencechinwomen_wlc_2007_0.pdf

5 Martin Smith, *Burma: Insurgency and the Politics of Ethnicity* (London: Zed Books, 1991), 40.

6 Ibid., 41.

7 Ibid., 44.

8 Ibid.

9 Ibid., 45.

10 Ibid., 48.

11 Paul Keenan, 'Saw Ba U Gyi', *Karen History and Culture Preservation Society*, March 2008, available at: https://www.burmalibrary.org/docskaren/Karen %20Heritage%20Web/pdf/Voice%20of%20the%20Revolution_1_Saw%20Ba %20U%20Gyi.pdf

12 Smith, *Burma*, 75.

13 Ibid., 79.

14 Interview with the author, on 26 July 2020.

15 Smith, *Burma*, 144.

16 Frederica Bunge, *Burma, A Country Study* (Washington DC: US Government Printing Office, 1983), 68.

17 Transnational Institute, 'Neither War Nor Peace: The Future of the Cease-Fire Agreements in Myanmar', July 2009, available at: https://www.tni.org/ files/download/ceasefire.pdf

18 Burma in Revolt, 288.

19 Transnational Institute.

20 Interview with the author, on 16 February 2019.

21 Kyaw Phyo Tha, 'Daw Aung San Suu Kyi's Jade Necklace at Peace Dinner Raises Questions', 25 May 2017, available at: https://www.irrawaddy.com/ news/burma/daw-aung-san-suu-kyis-jade-necklace-at-peace-dinner-raises -questions.html

22 Jason Tower and Priscilla A. Clapp, 'Myanmar: Casino Cities Run on Blockchain Threaten Nation's Sovereignty', *United States Institute of Peace*, July 2020, available at: https://www.usip.org/publications/2020/07/myanmar -casino-cities-run-blockchain-threaten-nations-sovereignty

23 Smith, *Burma*, 191.

24 Al Jazeera, 'Myanmar Shadow Government Calls for Uprising against Military', 7 September 2021, available at: https://www.aljazeera.com/news /2021/9/7/myanmar-shadow-government-launches-peoples-defensive-war

25 The Irrawaddy, 'Yangon Rocked by Multiple Blasts as Myanmar Junta Chief Visits to Bolster Security Efforts', 11 October 2021, available at: https://

www.irrawaddy.com/news/burma/yangon-rocked-by-multiple-blasts-as
-myanmar-junta-chief-visits-to-bolster-security-efforts.html

26 Khin Maung Soe, 'Rewards for Jets, Helicopters Will Test Loyalty of
Myanmar Military: Former Soldiers', *Radio Free Asia*, 19 April 2022,
available at: https://www.rfa.org/english/news/myanmar/rewards
-04192022213003.html

27 'Federal Democracy Charter Part 1: Declaration of Federal Democracy
Union', 2021, available at: https://crphmyanmar.org/wp-content/uploads
/2021/04/Federal-Democracy-Charter-English.pdf

Chapter 6

1 Interview with the author, on 26 July 2018.

2 F. Wade, *Myanmar's Enemy Within: Buddhist Violence and the Making of a
Muslim 'Other'* (London: Zed Books, 2017), 13.

3 Ibid., 13, 14.

4 Republic of the Union of Myanmar, 'Final Report of Inquiry Commission
on Sectarian Violence in Rakhine State – Appendix C', 2013.

5 International Crisis Group, 'The Dark Side of Transition: Violence Against
Muslims in Myanmar', 2013, 7, available at: https://d2071andvip0wj.cloudfront
.net/the-dark-side-of-transition-violence-against-muslims-in-myanmar.pdf

6 Interview with the author, on 7 July 2016.

7 UNHCR, 'Inside the World's Five Largest Refugee Camps', 1 April 2021,
available at: https://www.unrefugees.org/news/inside-the-world-s-five
-largest-refugee-camps/#:~:text=As%20more%20than%20800%2C000
%20refugees,the%20world's%20largest%20refugee%20camp

8 Wade, *Myanmar's Enemy Within*, 59–61.

9 G. E. Harvey, *History of Burma: From the Earliest Times to 10 March 1824:
The Beginning of the English Conquest* (London: Frank Cass, 1967), 267.

10 N. Win, 'Meeting Held in the Central Meeting Hall, President House,
Ahlone Road', *Rangoon*, 8 October 1982, available at: https://www
.burmalibrary.org/docs6/Ne_Win%27s_speech_Oct-1982-Citizenship
_Law.pdf?__cf_chl_jschl_tk__=pmd_c15e5db696e0dea5fffcb9372ecc65b
052407ba3-1626582615-0-gqNtZGzNAg2jcnBszQqO

11 Working People's Daily, 'Burma Citizenship Law', 16 October 1982, available
at: https://www.burmalibrary.org/sites/burmalibrary.org/files/obl/docs/
Citizenship%20Law.htm

12 *Working People's Daily*. 9 September 1990, a summary of which can be
found at: https://www.burmalibrary.org/docs3/BPS90-09.pdf

13 M. Smith, 'Ethnic Groups in Burma: Development, Democracy and
Human Rights', *Anti-Slavery International*, 1994, available at: https://www
.burmalibrary.org/sites/burmalibrary.org/files/obl/docs3/Ethnic_Groups_in
_Burma-ocr.pdf

14 A. H. Tun, 'Protesters Opposed to Myanmar Census Attack NGO Offices', *Reuters*, 27 March 2014, available at: https://www.reuters.com/article/myanmar-census-idINDEEA2Q0AH20140327

15 Moshe Yegar, 'The Muslims of Burma: A Study of a Minority Group', *Otto Harrassowitz*, 1972, 2, available at: http://www.netipr.org/policy/downloads/19720101-Muslims-Of-Burma-by-Moshe-Yegar.pdf

16 Ibid.

17 Ibid., 32.

18 Ibid., 31.

19 Census of India, 'Burma Part 1 – Report', 1931, available at: https://censusindia.gov.in/DigitalLibrary/data/Census_1931/Publication/Burma/40123_1931_REP.pdf, page 53

20 M. Collis, *Trials in Burma* (London: Faber and Faber, 1938).

21 Yegar, 'The Muslims of Burma', 95.

22 Ibid.

23 Ibid., 99.

24 International Crisis Group, 'Myanmar: The Politics of Rakhine State', 2014, 5, available at: https://d2071andvip0wj.cloudfront.net/myanmar-the-politics-of-rakhine-state.pdf

25 Smith, 'Ethnic Groups in Burma', 241.

26 International Crisis Group, 5.

27 Interview with the author, on 7 July 2016.

28 Republic of the Union of Myanmar, 'Final Report of Inquiry Commission on Sectarian Violence in Rakhine State', 8 July 2013, 15, available at: https://bit.ly/3ipFgQm

29 Interview with the author, on 26 March 2013.

30 A. Shin, 'Mosque Fire was an Accident, Official Investigation Confirms', *Myanmar Times*, 22 April 2013, available at: https://www.mmtimes.com/national-news/6467-mosque-fire-was-an-accident-official-investigation-confirms.html

31 *The Daily Star*, 'Bangladeshi Migrants' Mass Grave in Thailand!', 2 May 2015, available at: https://www.thedailystar.net/country/mass-grave-bangladeshi-myanmar-migrants-found-thailand-80115

32 Interview with the author, on 3 September 2017.

33 Numerous interviews with Rohingya residents in northern Rakhine in 2016 and 2017

34 International Crisis Group, 'Myanmar: A New Muslim Insurgency in Rakhine State', 15 December 2016, 12, available at: https://d2071andvip0wj.cloudfront.net/283-myanmar-a-new-muslim-insurgency-in-rakhine-state.pdf

35 Ibid., 4.

36 Ibid., 13.

37 Global New Light of Myanmar, 'Kidnapped Victim Found Dead in Buthidaung', 17 July 2017, available at: https://www.burmalibrary.org/sites/burmalibrary.org/files/obl/docs23/GNLM2017-07-17-red.pdf

38 Global New Light of Myanmar, 'President Receives Rakhine Advisory
    Commission', (2021), 24 August 2017, available at: https://www
    .burmalibrary.org/sites/burmalibrary.org/files/obl/docs23/GNLM2017-08
    -24.pdf

39 *Fortify Rights*, '"They Gave Them Long Swords": Preparations for Genocide
    and Crimes against Humanity Against Rohingya Muslims in Rakhine State,
    Myanmar', July 2018, available at: https://www.fortifyrights.org/downloads/
    Fortify_Rights_Long_Swords_July_2018.pdf

40 Mike Winchester, 'Rohingya Insurgency Declares 'Open War' in Myanmar',
    Asia Times, 28 August 2017, available at: https://asiatimes.com/2017/08/
    rohingya-insurgency-declares-open-war-myanmar/

41 Adil Sakhawat, 'Who is Ata Ullah – The Man at the Heart of the Myanmar
    Conflict?' *Dhaka Tribune*, 20 October 2017, available at: https://www
    .dhakatribune.com/world/south-asia/2017/10/20/ata-ullah-man-heart
    -myanmar-conflict

42 *BBC News*, 'Rohingya Crisis: Suu Kyi Says 'Fake News Helping Terrorists',
    6 September 2017, available at: https://www.bbc.com/news/world-asia
    -41170570

43 Amnesty International, 'Myanmar: Aung San Suu Kyi "Burying Her
    Head in the Sand" about Rakhine horrors', September 19 2017, available
    at: https://www.amnesty.org/en/latest/press-release/2017/09/myanmar
    -aung-san-suu-kyi-burying-her-head-in-the-sand-about-rakhine
    -horrors/

44 *BBC News*, 'Myanmar: Aung San Suu Kyi Exclusive Interview', 5 April 2017,
    available at: https://www.bbc.com/news/av/world-asia-39510271

45 T. T. Aung, and S. Naing, 'Rakhine Rebels Kill 13 in Independence
    Day Attack on Myanmar Police Posts', *Reuters*, January 2019, available
    at: https://www.reuters.com/article/us-myanmar-rakhine/rakhine
    -buddhist-army-kills-seven-in-independence-day-attack-on-police-posts
    -idUSKCN1OY0N0

46 D. S. Mathieson, 'The Arakan Army in Myanmar: Deadly Conflict Rises in
    Rakhine State', *United States Institute for Peace*, November 2 2020, available
    at: https://www.usip.org/publications/2020/11/arakan-army-myanmar
    -deadly-conflict-rises-rakhine-state, 5.

47 Ibid., 7.

48 Ibid., 9.

49 *Reuters*, 'Myanmar's Civilian, Military Leaders Meet, Vow to "Crush"
    Rakhine Rebels', 7 January 2019, available at: https://www.reuters.com/
    article/myanmar-politics/myanmars-civilian-military-leaders-meet-vow-to
    -crush-rakhine-rebels-idINKCN1P118Q?edition-redirect=in

50 Amnesty International, 'Myanmar: Villages Burned, Civilians Injured and
    Killed as Rakhine State Conflict Escalates', 12 October 2020, available at:
    https://www.amnesty.org/en/latest/press-release/2020/10/myanmar-villages
    -burned-civilians-injured-rakhine-state-conflict/

51 International Crisis Group, 'From Elections to Ceasefire in Myanmar's Rakhine State', 23 December 2020, available at: https://www.crisisgroup.org/asia/south-east-asia/myanmar/b164-elections-ceasefire-myanmars-rakhine-state

52 Myanmar Now, 'As Junta Directs Its Attention Elsewhere, AA Strengthens Its Hold Over Rakhine State', 13 August 2021, available at: https://www.myanmar-now.org/en/news/as-junta-directs-its-attention-elsewhere-aa-strengthens-its-hold-over-rakhine-state

53 A. Choudhury, 'Why the National Unity Government's Statement on Myanmar's Rohingya is Important', *The Diplomat*, 9 June 2021, available at: https://thediplomat.com/2021/06/why-the-national-unity-governments-statement-on-myanmars-rohingya-is-important/

Chapter 7

1 *BBC News*, 'Myanmar jade Mine Landslide Kills 160', 2 July 2020, available at: https://www.bbc.com/news/world-asia-53260834

2 *Reuters*, 'At Least 126 Killed as Myanmar Jade Mine Collapse Buries Workers', 2 July 2020, available at: https://www.reuters.com/article/us-myanmar-mine-idUSKBN2430M0

3 *AFP*, 'Myanmar Army Sacks Officers over Landslide Tragedy', 6 July 2020, available at: https://www.france24.com/en/20200706-myanmar-army-sacks-officers-over-landslide-tragedy

4 Yuning Lin, Park Nina, Wang Edward, Quek Yu, Pin Yu, Jana Lim, Enner Alcantra, Ho Huu Loc, 'The 2020 Hpakant Jade Mine Disaster, Myanmar: A Multi-Sensor Investigation for Slope Failure', *ScienceDirect*, available at: https://www.sciencedirect.com/science/article/pii/S0924271621001489#b0190

5 Interview with the author, 10 August 2021.

6 Natural Resource Governance Institute, 'Myanmar's Jade: From Mine to Market', available at: https://resourcegovernance.org/sites/default/files/documents/jade-info-booklet.pdf

7 The Germological Association of Great Britain, 'Understanding Jade and Its Importance in China', available at: https://gem-a.com/gem-hub/around-the-world/jade-and-its-importance-in-china

8 *AFP*, available at: https://www.france24.com/en/20200706-myanmar-army-sacks-officers-over-landslide-tragedy

9 Global Witness, 'Jade and Conflict: Myanmar's Vicious Circle', June 2021, 52.

10 Ibid., 26.

11 Ibid., 7.

12 Ye Mon and Kyi Kyi Sway, 'Jade Mining Permit Extensions Suspended', available at: https://www.mmtimes.com/business/21593-jade-mining-permit-extensions-suspended.html

13 Global Witness, 'Jade and Conflict', 26, 27.
14 Ibid., 16.
15 Justice for Myanmar, 'Dirty Secrets #2: Sr. Gen. Min Aung Hlaing's Family Selling FDA and Customs Clearance for Profit', 14 August 2020, available at: https://www.justiceformyanmar.org/stories/dirty-secrets-2 -sr-gen-min-aung-hlaings-family-selling-fda-and-customs-clearance-for -profit
16 Chan Thar, 'Military Chief's Son Paid 'Very Low' Rent for His Upscale Restaurant on Government-Owned Land', 18 July 2019, available at: https:// www.myanmar-now.org/en/news/military-chiefs-son-paid-very-low-rent -for-his-upscale-restaurant-on-government-owned-land
17 Independent International Fact-Finding Mission on Myanmar, 'The Economic Interests of the Myanmar Military', 5 August 2019, available at: https://www.ohchr.org/Documents/HRBodies/HRCouncil/FFM-Myanmar/ EconomicInterestsMyanmarMilitary/A_HRC_42_CRP_3.pdf
18 Blair, Eric, Arthur, 'How a Nation Is Exploited – The British Empire in Burma', *Le Progres Civique*, 4 May 1929, available at: https://www .orwellfoundation.com/the-orwell-foundation/orwell/essays-and-other -works/how-a-nation-is-exploited-the-british-empire-in-burma/
19 Martin Smith, *Burma: Insurgency and the Politics of Ethnicity* (Zed Books, 1991), 25.
20 Ibid., 19.
21 Lixin Geng, 'Sino-Myanmar Relations: Analysis and Prospects', *Cultural Mandala: The Bulletin of the Centre for East-West Cultural and Economic Studies*, January 2007. available at: https://cm.scholasticahq.com/article /5874-sino-myanmar-relations-analysis-and-prospects, 6.
22 Yuichi Nitta, 'Vietnam Carrier Stuns Rivals in Myanmar With Half-Price Blitz', available at: https://asia.nikkei.com/Business/Business-trends/ Vietnam-carrier-stuns-rivals-in-Myanmar-with-half-price-blitz
23 Chen Lin and John Geddie, 'Myanmar Crisis Sounds Death Knell for Garment Industry, Jobs and Hope', 8 April 2021, available at: https://www .reuters.com/article/us-myanmar-politics-garments-idUSKBN2BV0MJ
24 Asian Development Bank, 'Poverty Data: Myanmar', available at: https:// www.adb.org/countries/myanmar/poverty
25 Human Rights Watch, '"Nothing for Our Land": Impact of Land Confiscation on Farmers in Myanmar', available at: https://www.hrw.org/report/2018/07 /17/nothing-our-land/impact-land-confiscation-farmers-myanmar#_ftn7
26 Sudha Ramachandran, 'Yangon Still under Beijing's Thumb', *Asia Times*, 11 February 2005, available at: https://web.archive.org/web/20050212014305 /http://www.atimes.com/atimes/Southeast_Asia/GB11Ae01.html
27 Sebastian Strangio, *In the Dragon's Shadow: Southeast Asia in the Chinese Century* (Singapore: Yale, 2020), 150.
28 Ibid., 147.
29 Radio Free Asia, 'Chinese Leader Xi's Visit to Myanmar to Produce New Belt and Road Agreements', 17 January 2020, available at: https://www

.rfa.org/english/news/myanmar/chinese-leader-xis-visit-to-myanmar
-01172020163509.html

30 Ministry of Foreign Affairs of the People's Republic of China, 'Myanmar's President U Win Myint Meets with Wang Yi', 11 January 2020, available at: https://www.fmprc.gov.cn/mfa_eng/zxxx_662805/t1846055.shtml

31 *Reuters*, 'Myanmar Anti-Coup Protesters Rally at Chinese Embassy', 11 February 2021, available at: https://www.reuters.com/article/us-myanmar -politics-china-idUSKBN2AB0HG

32 The Republic of the Union of Myanmar, 'Defence White Paper', Naypyidaw, 2015, 2.

33 *The Irrawaddy*, 'Myanmar Regime Reorganizes Committees to Press Ahead with BRI Projects', 18 May 2021, available at: https://www.irrawaddy.com /news/burma/myanmar-regime-reorganizes-committees-to-press-ahead -with-bri-projects.html

34 Sean Bain, 'Myanmar: It's Time for Transparency Over the Kyaukphyu Special Economic Zone', 12 August 2016, available at: https://www.icj.org/myanmar -its-time-for-transparency-over-the-kyaukphyu-special-economic-zone/

35 Gene Ryack, 'A Hitch in the Belt and Road in Myanmar', 3 December 2020, available at: https://thediplomat.com/2020/12/a-hitch-in-the-belt-and-road -in-myanmar/

36 *UN News*, 'Fighting Drug Trafficking in the Golden Triangle: A UN Resident Coordinator Blog', 20 September 2020, available at: https://news.un .org/en/story/2020/09/1071192

37 Bertil Lintner and Michael Black, *Merchants of Madness: The Methamphetamine Explosion in the Golden Triangle, Merchants of Madness* (Chiang Mai: Silkworm Books, 2009), 13.

38 Ibid., 3.

39 United Nations Office on Drugs and Crime, 'Synthetic Drugs in East and Southeast Asia: Latest Developments and Challenges', 2021, available at: https://www.unodc.org/documents/southeastasiaandpacific/Publications /2021/Synthetic_Drugs_in_East_and_Southeast_Asia_2021.pdf

40 Bertil Lintner, 'The United Wa State Army and Burma's Peace Process', *United States Institute for Peace*, April 2019, available at: https://www.usip .org/sites/default/files/2019-07/pw_147-the_united_wa_state_army_and _burmas_peace_process.pdf

41 International Crisis Group, 'Fire and Ice: Conflict and Drugs in Myanmar's Shan State', 8 January 2019, available at: https://www.crisisgroup.org/asia/south -east-asia/myanmar/299-fire-and-ice-conflict-and-drugs-myanmars-shan -state

42 Lintner, 'The United Wa State Army and Burma's Peace Process'.

43 Interview with author, 16 October 2019.

44 International Crisis Group.

45 Lisa Martin, 'Thailand Faces Meth Trafficking Surge after Myanmar Coup', 26 March 2021, available at: https://sg.news.yahoo.com/thailand-faces-meth -trafficking-surge-041934812.html

46 United Nations Development Programme, 'COVID-19, Coup d'Etat and
    Poverty: Compounding Negative Shocks and Their Impact on Human
    Development in Myanmar', 30 April 2021, available at: https://www.asia
    -pacific.undp.org/content/rbap/en/home/library/democratic_governance/
    covid-19-coup-d-etat-and-poverty-impact-on-myanmar.html
47 Kirin Holdings, 'Statement on the Situation in Myanmar', 5 February 2021,
    available at: https://www.kirinholdings.com/en/newsroom/release/2021
    /0204_01.html

Chapter 8

1 Myanmar Now, 'Junta Soldiers Kill Pastor and Cut Off His Dinger as Houses
    Burn in Chin Town', 20 September 2021, available at: https://www.myanmar
    -now.org/en/news/junta-soldiers-kill-pastor-and-cut-off-his-finger-as
    -houses-burn-in-chin-town
2 United Nations Security Council, 'Peace and Security', available at: https://
    www.un.org/securitycouncil/
3 Amnesty International, 'Myanmar: Vast Arsenal and Notorious Troops
    Deployed During Nationwide "Killing Spree" Protest Crackdown – New
    Research', 11 March 2021, available at: https://www.amnesty.org/en/latest/
    news/2021/03/myanmar-arsenal-troops-deployed-crackdown/
4 Interview with the author, 20 May 2021.

Bibliography

Asian Network for Free Elections (ANFREL). 'The 2020 Myanmar General
Elections: Democracy Under Attack'. 2021. Available at: https://anfrel.org/wp
-content/uploads/2021/05/ANFREL_Democracy-Under-Attack-F.pdf

Blair, Eric Arthur. 'How a Nation Is Exploited – The British Empire in Burma'.
Le Progres Civique, 4 May 1919. Available at: https://www.orwellfoundation
.com/the-orwell-foundation/orwell/essays-and-other-works/how-a-nation-is
-exploited-the-british-empire-in-burma/

Callahan, Mary P. *Making Enemies: War and State Building in Burma*. Ithaca and
London: Cornell University Press, 2003.

Cheeseman, Nick. *Opposing the Rule of Law: How Myanmar's Courts Make Law
and Order*. Cambridge: Cambridge University Press, 2015.

Collis, Maurice. *Trials in Burma*. London: Faber and Faber, 1938.

Furnivall, John Sydenham. *An Introduction to the Political Economy of Burma*.
Rangoon: Burma Book Club, 1931.

Galache, Carlos Sardiña. *The Burmese Labyrinth: A History of the Rohingya
Tragedy*. London and New York: Verso Books, 2020.

Harvey, Godfrey Eric. *History of Burma: From the Earliest Times to 10 March
1825: The Beginning of the English Conquest*. London: Frank Cass, 1967.

Keenan, Paul. 'Saw Ba U Gyi'. *Karen History and Culture Preservation Society*,
March 2008. Available at: https://www.burmalibrary.org/docskaren/Karen
%20Heritage%20Web/pdf/Voice%20of%20the%20Revolution_1_Saw%20Ba
%20U%20Gyi.pdf

Larkin, Emma. *No Bad News for the King: The True Story of Cyclone Nargis and
Its Aftermath in Burma*. United States: Penguin Books, 2011.

Lintner, Bertil. *Burma in Revolt: Opium and Insurgency since 1948*. Bangkok:
Silkworm Books, 1999.

Lintner, Bertil. *The Rise and Fall of the Communist Party of Burma (CPB)*. New
York: Cornell Southeast Asia Programme, 1990.

Lintner, Bertil and Michael Black. *Merchants of Madness: The Methamphetamine
Explosion in the Golden Triangle*. Bangkok: Silkworm Books, 2009.

Marks, John Ebeneezer. *Forty Years in Burma*. London: Hutchison and Co, 1917.

Maung, Maung. *Burma and General Ne Win*. Rangoon: Religious Affairs
Department Press, 1969.

Maung, Maung. *To A Soldier Son*. Rangoon: Sarpay Beikman Press, 1974.

Montesano, Michael J., Terence Chong and Prajak Kongkirati. *Praetorians,
Profiteers or Professionals? Studies on the Militaries of Myanmar and Thailand*.
Singapore: ISEAS Yusof Ishak Institute, 2020.

Myint-U, Thant. *The River of Lost Footsteps: A Personal History of Burma*. Faber,
2008.

Myoe, Maung Aung. *Building the Tatmadaw: Myanmar Armed Forces Since 1948*. Singapore: ISEAS Yusof Ishak Institute, 2009.

Nakanishi, Yoshihiro. *Strong Soldiers, Failed Revolution: The State and Military in Burma, 1962–88*. Singapore: NUS Press, 2013.

Ni, Zar. *The Nationalization of Education in Burma: A Radical Response to the Capitalist Development?*. University of Wisconsin Madison, 1995.

Preecharushh, Dulyapak. *Naypyidaw: The New Capital of Burma*. Bangkok: White Lotus Press, 2009.

Selth, Andrew. *Burma's Armed Forces: Power Without Glory*. Norwalk: EastBridge, 2002.

Selth, Andrew. *Secrets and Power in Myanmar: Intelligence and the Fall of General Khin Nyunt*. Singapore: ISEAS Yusof Ishak Institute, 2019.

Smith, Martin. *Burma: Insurgency and the Politics of Ethnicity*. London and Atlantic Highlands: Zed Books, 1991.

Smith, Martin. 'Our Heads Are Bloody But Unbowed'. December 1992. Available at: https://www.refworld.org/pdfid/4754182d0.pdf

Strangio, Sebastian. *In the Dragon's Shadow: Southeast Asia in the Chinese Century*. Singapore: Yale, 2020.

Taylor, Robert. *General Ne Win: A Political Biography*. Singapore: ISEAS Yusof Ishak Institute, 2015.

Wade, Francis. *Myanmar's Enemy Within: Buddhist Violence and the Making of a Muslim 'Other'*. London: Zed Books, 2017.

Yegar, Moshe. *The Muslims of Burma: A Study of a Minority Group*. Wiesbaden: Otto Harrassowitz, 1972.

Index

www.ingramcontent.com/pod-product-compliance
Lightning Source LLC
Chambersburg PA
CBHW070401270326
41926CB00014B/2648